Casual Shakespeare

Casual Shakespeare is the first full-length study of the thousands of quotations both in and of Shakespeare's works that represent intertextuality outside of what is conventionally appreciated as literary value. Drawing on the insights gained as a result of a major, ongoing Digital Humanities project, this study posits a historical continuum of casual quotation which informs Shakespeare's own works as well as their afterlives. In this groundbreaking, rigorous analysis, Regula Hohl Trillini offers readers a new approach and understanding of the use and impact that quotes like the infamous 'To be or not to be' have had throughout literary history.

Regula Hohl Trillini is a Lecturer in English Literature at the University of Basel.

Routledge Studies in Shakespeare

For a full list of titles in this series, please visit www.routledge.com.

21 **Shakespeare and Complexity Theory**
   Claire Hansen

22 **Women and Mobility on Shakespeare's Stage**
   Migrant Mothers and Broken Homes
   Elizabeth Mazzola

23 **Renaissance Ecopolitics from Shakespeare to Bacon**
   Rethinking Cosmopolis
   Elizabeth Gruber

24 **Shakespeare's Lost Playhouse**
   Eleven Days at Newington Butts
   Laurie Johnson

25 **Shakespeare's *Hamlet* in an Era of Textual Exhaustion**
   Edited by Sonya Freeman Loftis, Allison Kellar, and Lisa Ulevich

26 **Shakespeare's Suicides**
   Dead Bodies That Matter
   Marlena Tronicke

27 **The Fictional Lives of Shakespeare**
   Kevin Gilvary

28 **Jonson, Shakespeare, and Aristotle on Comedy**
   Jonathan Goossen

29 **Shakespeare and the Cultivation of Difference**
   Race and Conduct in the Early Modern World
   Patricia Akhimie

30 **Casual Shakespeare**
   Three Centuries of Verbal Echoes
   Regula Hohl Trillini

Casual Shakespeare
Three Centuries of Verbal Echoes

Regula Hohl Trillini

LONDON AND NEW YORK

First published 2018 by Routledge

2 Park Square, Milton Park, Abingdon, Oxfordshire OX14 4RN

52 Vanderbilt Avenue, New York, NY 10017

Routledge is an imprint of the Taylor & Francis Group, an informa business

First issued in paperback 2020

Copyright © 2018 Taylor & Francis

The right of Regula Hohl Trillini to be identified as author of this work has been asserted by her in accordance with sections 77 and 78 of the Copyright, Designs and Patents Act 1988.

All rights reserved. No part of this book may be reprinted or reproduced or utilised in any form or by any electronic, mechanical, or other means, now known or hereafter invented, including photocopying and recording, or in any information storage or retrieval system, without permission in writing from the publishers.

Notice:
Product or corporate names may be trademarks or registered trademarks, and are used only for identification and explanation without intent to infringe.

Library of Congress Cataloging-in-Publication Data
CIP data has been applied for.

ISBN: 978-1-138-71014-6 (hbk)
ISBN: 978-0-367-59301-8 (pbk)

Typeset in Sabon
by codeMantra

I turne and tosse over bookes, but do not studie them; what of them remaines in me, is a thing which I no longer acknowledge to be any bodies else. Onely by that hath my judgement profited: and the discourses and imaginations, wherewith it is instructed and trained vp. The Authours, the place, the words, and other circumstances, I sodainely forget.
MICHEL DE MONTAIGNE (1580)

Not a period in Socrates' oration, which closed with a shorter word than transmigration or annihilation – or a worse thought in the middle of it than to be – or not to be, – the entering upon a new and untried state of things, –, or, upon a long, a profound and peaceful sleep, without dreams, without disturbance; – that we and our children were born to die; but neither of us born to be slaves – No – there I mistake; that was part of Eleazer's oration, as recorded by Josephus (de Bell. Judaic) – Eleazer owns he had it from the philosophers of India; in all likelihood Alexander the Great, in his irruption into India, after he had over-run Persia, amongst the many things he stole, – stole that sentiment also; by which means it was carried, if not all the way by himself (for we all know he died at Babylon), at least by some of his maroders, into Greece, – from Greece it got to Rome, – from Rome to France, – and from France to England: – So things come round.
LAWRENCE STERNE (1761)

Thus all is derived; all is unoriginal.
RICHARD HURD (1751)

Contents

List of Figures and Table		ix
Acknowledgements		xi
Notes on the Text		xiii
	Introduction: A 'New Object'	1
1	To Quote or Not to Quote	16
2	'He should be stop'd': Too-Casual Shakespeare	35
3	'Honey-tongued Shakespeare' and the Classics	53
4	'Shakespeares fine filed phrase'	76
5	'The old parody': A Post-Shakespeare Genre	99
6	Peak Casual: Romantic Routine	118
7	Jane Austen: 'I must keep to my own style'	142
	Conclusion: The Lightness of Quotation	154
	Appendix I: The HyperHamlet *database*	159
	Appendix II: A Marston-Shakespeare concordance	163
	Bibliography	173
	Index	193

List of Figures and Table

Figures

6.1 Defining Romantic Routine. Marking of Shakespeare quotations in percent of all quotations in the *RR Corpus:* the eighteenth and nineteenth centuries by decade. Author's own — 120

6.2 The onset of Romantic Routine. Marking of Shakespeare quotations in percent of all quotations in the *RR Corpus:* the 1770s by year. Author's own — 122

6.3 The end of Romantic Routine. Marking of Shakespeare quotations in percent of all quotations in the *RR Corpus:* the 1830s and 1840s by year. Author's own — 123

6.4 The voices of Romantic Routine. Marking of Shakespeare quotations 1776 to 1837 by genre and voice. Author's own — 132

Table

3.1 The 'pillow cluster'. Author's own — 67

Acknowledgements

Like Hamlet, I feel 'poor in thanks' when I consider the riches of friendship, intellectual exchange and financial support that this book is indebted to; unlike Hamlet, I am sincerely happy 'to thank' all the friends who have been so very unlike Rosencrantz and Guildenstern.

This book grew out of 'Passages We Live By', a four-year research project that was generously funded by the Swiss National Science Foundation to build the *HyperHamlet* database. My most fundamental thanks is owed to Balz Engler of the University of Basel for conceiving the idea of investigating Shakespeare quotation through a hypertext database and for letting the *HyperHamlet* team foster this idea. Being part of this team was a truly memorable experience. The discussions with Sixta Quaßdorf which established the analytical categories of the database were essential eye-openers. Writing articles and presenting conference papers with Balz, Sixta and Andreas Langlotz was intellectually stimulating and a lot of fun. Annelies Häcki Buhofer's suggestion to think about taxonomy cleared the way to a major conceptual breakthrough. Christian Gebhard and other student assistants shared four years of quotations, valuable insight and invaluable laughter. All of us were endlessly amazed by the creativity and programming skills of Lukas Rosenthaler and Tobias Roth, who transformed literary epiphanies, analytical hunches and concepts-in-progress into a working database.

My second great debt is to the friends who commented on draft versions of chapters. The generosity and acuity of Delia Da Sousa Correa, Ina Habermann, Ladina Bezzola Lambert, Carol Leininger, Barbara Sträuli and Susan Barton Young has been a great joy. This book would simply not exist without them. Delia's editing skills and elegant writing have been a treasured lifeline to British academic culture. Barbara's erudition prevented many howlers, and her article on Shakespearean image clusters was an essential inspiration, as were Ladina's eloquence and Carol's relentless focus on reader-friendliness and positive rhetoric. Susan, who taught me how to cut-and-paste work-in-progress 25 years ago, came back to monitor my topic sentences. Ina Habermann saw the book's potential and pushed its theoretical underpinnings into the twenty-first century. Péter Dávidházi and Brian Vickers shared inspiring drafts of their own. The most incisive comments came from the anonymous readers for Routledge, who appreciated the manuscript even before their suggestions had taken effect; any passages that remain 'excessively convoluted' are my responsibility.

I presented work-in-progress at several conferences and seminars, and the comments of colleagues and students have significantly improved my understanding of what I am on about. Thank you Ridvan Askin, Heike Behrens, Werner Brönnimann, Martin Danneck, Marcel Dräger, Nicola Glaubitz, Gustavo Grandi De Souza, Sonja-Irène Grieder, Julika Griem, Andreas Hägler, Elizabeth Kaspar-Aldrich, Danièle Klapproth, Ian Mackenzie, Markus Marti-Cimitro, Lucia Michalcak, Wolfgang Mieder, Christoph Ribbat, Johanna Schüpbach, Philipp Schweighauser, Kathrin Steyer, Kirsten Stirling, Judith Wieser and Claude Ziltener.

I am indebted to Rainer Ostermann for the layout of the figures, to Derek Gottlieb for the index and to Alessandro Lattanzi for checking my little Latin and less Greek. Nick and Di Clay, Sarah and Ruedi Ebner-Walton and Doris Eckstein were generous hosts in Brittany and the Bernese Oberland. Doris Kunz reminded me of my self-confidence. Sibylle Wyss-Hug, one-time teacher, long-time friend and current boss, and Thomas Henzi, more recently my boss, continue to appreciate my teaching and give me space, perhaps the most precious gift of all. The Department of English of the University of Basel generously funded the index and the long-service leave granted to the employees of the canton of Solothurn enabled me to complete the manuscript on time.

Basel, 27 November 2017, Regula Hohl Trillini

The substance of Chapters 1 and 5 was first published in two articles. I am grateful to the publishers for the reproduction rights on 'Hamlet and Textual Re-Production 1550–1650' in *Swiss Papers in English Language and Literature (SPELL) 22 The Construction of Textual Identity in Medieval and Early Modern Literature* (2009): 163–176 and 'Hamlet's Soliloquy: An Eighteenth-Century Genre' in *Borrowers and Lenders* 7:1 (Spring/Summer 2012).

Notes on the Text

This book defines 'quotation' simply as a verbal, semantic or structural overlap between two texts, ranging in length from a single word to a paragraph or a short block of verse lines. Such **overlaps** are highlighted by bold **type** throughout. This typographical device should not compromise readers' understanding of the ways in which Shakespearean phrases are marked by those who quote them: none of my sources employ bold type to signal quotations. Instead, they use quotation marks, indentation and italics, which can all be recognized through bold type. Verbal markers for quotation, such as names or phrases like 'as the poet says', are highlighted by underlining, another typographical device that is not found in the primary texts.

Unless otherwise indicated, Shakespeare's plays and poems are quoted from www.folgerdigitaltexts.org (with the spelling adapted to UK conventions), giving act, scene and line numbers. The Bible is quoted from www.biblegateway.com, giving chapter and verse numbers.

The full texts and bibliographical references for primary sources that are mentioned only *passim* can be found at www.hyperhamlet.unibas.ch.

Introduction: A 'New Object'

William Shakespeare's works are quoted far more than they are read or watched; Shakespeare himself borrowed countless phrases and most of his plots from his wide and varied reading. These are two facts universally acknowledged, and they are generally considered to indicate Shakespeare's stature and versatility. Two related facts have been almost as universally ignored: Shakespeare often quotes without acknowledging his sources or establishing in-depth relationships with them, and most quotations from his works do not establish any significant relationship with the Shakespearean contexts. Shakespeare and most of the writers who use his words rarely quote to engage with or honour their sources. They may quote to show off; mostly they quote simply because they can. This book draws on thousands of tokens to make the following claims about such casual quotations from the mid-sixteenth to the mid-nineteenth century:

> Casual quotations are casual about *what* is quoted but highly sensitive to *how* the borrowed bits of language are fitted into the new text and serve its requirements.
> Casual quotations foreground the act of quotation itself at the expense of intertextual meaning.
> Casual quotations often obscure the identity of the quoted text and reduce its impact by modifications of the original wording and by cross-quoting other sources in the immediate vicinity.

These three claims use the word 'quotation' to mean a lexical, semantic or structural overlap between two texts which may extend in length from a single word to a paragraph or a short block of verse lines. Nothing else. This study does not privilege any of these overlaps over any others for aptness, exact repetition, correct reference or symbolic value, and therefore needs a shorthand term that is neutral and does not imply any *a priori* assumptions. The word 'quotation' was chosen for this because its many meanings are easier to set aside than the more specific connotations of terms like 'allusion', 'reference' or 'citation', which have more specific connotations. In this book, 'quotation' simply means a verbal trace.

2   Introduction: A 'New Object'

Let me start with a few examples. The following extracts are taken from Daniel Defoe's 1706 'Hymn to Peace', from a letter written by the Earl of Chesterfield in 1758, from an anonymous romance published in 1799 and from two articles by Karl Marx from the 1840s.

> Attempts to square th' Extent of Souls,
> As Men mark Lands, by Butts and Bounds,
> Wou'd **the Great *Be*, and *not to Be*** Divide,
> And all the Doubts of *Entity* decide (Defoe *Hymn* 10).

> Take care of your health as much as you can; for, **To BE, or NOT To BE, is a question** of much less importance, in my mind, than **to be or not to be well** (Chesterfield *Letters* 555).

> 'If the Colonel should take it in his head to make me an offer, how shall I answer?' thought Sophia [...]. She debated [...] yet she could not resolve what line of conduct she should pursue. **To be, or not to be, that was the question**, and **a question** which Sophia could not answer (Anon. *Sylph* 233).[1]

> Wenn wir also [...] die *Philosophie* kritisieren, so steht unsere Kritik mitten unter den Fragen, von denen die Gegenwart sagt: **That is the question** (Marx 'Hegels Rechtsphilosophie' 383).[2]

> Souveränität des Monarchen **oder** des Volkes, **das ist die question** (Marx 'Hegels Staatsrecht' 230).[3]

None of these passages use inverted commas or mention Shakespeare, and yet in each of them, something is recognizable as a quotation, even to readers who are ignorant of *Hamlet* or do not understand German. This recognition is made possible by various subtle markers (not including the **bold** type that highlights quoted words throughout this book) which signal the presence of an inset phrase. In Defoe, the odd syntax of 'the great Be' is such a marker, while Chesterfield uses block capitals and Marx a language switch. All these anomalies indicate 'quotedness', as does the *non sequitur* in *The Sylph*: why should Sophia ponder whether 'to be or not to be' when choosing a husband, if not because she is quoting *Hamlet*? In Marx's *Critique of Hegel's Constitutional Law*, the single, alien word 'question' is enough to tell us that an English text is being quoted and that the quoted phrase must be extremely famous, because this most casual of hints is enough.

While there is no doubt that these quotations feature what I call MARKING FOR QUOTATION, they do not evince the slightest interest in the context of what is quoted: the play, the prince's predicament or the famous soliloquy. Marx, an avid Shakespeare reader, was of course perfectly capable of investing *Hamlet* quotations with complex meaning,[4] but he did not always choose to do so. Instead he often played around with favourite tags like 'that is the question' or 'out-heroding Herod', for which he coined the German expression 'den Tyrannen übertyrannisieren'.[5] In 1782, the German aphorist Georg Friedrich Lichtenberg mimicked a sheep's bleat with **'To bäh or not to bäh, that is the Question'** ('Vossens Verteidigung' 139) in order to ridicule misguided ideas about the pronunciation of classical Hebrew. Like Marx, the passionate Anglophile and theatregoer Lichtenberg most assuredly knew what he was quoting – he was just not out to be profound. In England, such casual use of Shakespearean phrases was a widespread routine from the mid-1770s onwards. Lichtenberg's article and *The Sylph* both represent this period: they adapt a popular phrasal template to their own use, just as we do when we say that 'information **is the new** fat' or speak of '**the mother of all** cat videos'. Completely detached from its original context and looking as if it had never had one, the *Hamlet* phrase becomes a kind of verbalized Boolean function, an elaborate synonym for 'either-or'. Writers who use 'to be or not to be' in this way mostly know what they are doing and give their readers a chance to identify the tag, but they do not make Shakespeare and his play contribute anything to the text that they are writing. Casual quotations are quotations because they contain an identifiable intertextual element, and they are casual because they do not generate significant intertextual meaning.

Casual quotations and mobile lexias

Casual Shakespeare quotations are not 'references' in the sense of Latin 're-ferre', 'to carry back'; they do not take the reader back to a Shakespearean context that would give them meaning. They are 'quotations', though, insofar as they undoubtedly repeat Shakespeare's words. Like poems according to Archibald McLeish, who famously maintained that 'A poem should not mean but be' ('Ars Poetica' 462), casual quotations may not *mean* much yet they indisputably *are*. This incongruity between factual presence and absent significance is irritating to literary scholars. We want to think that Shakespeare meant something by the verbal scraps that he imported into his texts and that his words in turn carry some kind of Shakespearean meaning into their new contexts. There is a 'gentleman's agreement to take the parts of a work for the whole', and if a quotation has no such synecdochic interest in its original 'whole', it runs the risk of being ignored as 'a hermeneutical dead end' (Price *Anthology* 2). Shakespeare scholars do not like to consider 'evidence of the absence of Shakespeare, where one might expect his presence' (Taylor 'Shrinking Bard' 198). Marjorie Garber, for example, calls Shakespeare '[b]oth "of an age" and "for all time"' because he is 'the most cited and quoted author of every era' (Garber 3) but then qualifies the value of being quoted by remarking that it would 'not be especially useful' to chronicle 'the disappearance of confident and knowledgeable Shakespeare quotation'

(Garber 35). However, 'knowledgeable' use of Shakespeare's language alone would not have made him the most quoted author ever. Casual quotations have been an essential part of Shakespeare's impact in 'every era', including his lifetime and those periods when most English-speaking writers were quite 'confident and knowledgeable' about his works. They did just not invest this knowledge every time they used one of his phrases, as is made clear by the sheer number of their borrowings. While this is an unsatisfactory state of affairs for literary hermeneutics, there are some excellent theoretical precedents for taking an interest anyway.

It has become almost compulsory to open a study of sources, quotations or influences with a nod to Julia Kristeva's 1969 seminal essay 'Word, Dialogue and the Novel', which introduced the term 'intertextuality' to the world. What follows such an introductory gesture, though, often obscures the radical potential of Kristeva's article. Hannibal Hamlin's recent *The Bible in Shakespeare*, for example, mentions 'Word, Dialogue and the Novel' on the first page, only to claim a few sentences later that Shakespeare's Biblical allusions are all 'deliberate and significant' (1). Such casual quotation of Kristeva, as it were, glosses over her radicality. She introduces the neologism 'intertextuality' to distance her project from the conventional literary study of sources and influences and to reduce the interest in the 'deliberate' decisions of authorial subjects. The study of 'intersubjectivity' is to be 'replace[d]' by 'the notion of intertextuality' (37); the focus should be on language, on the dialogue between words and phrases and 'several writings' (36), rather than on the meanings that authors may have intended such words to carry. This book, with its focus on verbal detail, takes the radical programme of 'Word, Dialogue and the Novel' as an encouragement to study the undeniable presence of Shakespeare's language in thousands of texts which gloss over his identity and ignore the context of his plays and poems.

The casual intertextuality that circulates around Shakespeare's works also exemplifies a second poststructuralist idea that could do with reviving in Shakespeare studies: the Death of the Author. Like 'intertextuality', the demise of the individual subject who generates retrievable meanings is an often-quoted theoretical staple, but the rich halo of Shakespeare, English genius and global icon, has tended to blind us to the implications of this axiom. Shakespeare the author just won't die (which is why an early draft of this book was called *Kill Will*). We perform literary postmortems on texts that we expect to yield symbolic or political signification; perhaps we should start to read 'post mortem', literally 'after [the author's] death', as Shakespeare's words continue to flourish in casual use. We should dare to start reading both his texts and quotations from his texts 'without the guarantee of [their] father' (Barthes 'Work to Text' 161) and at least consider ignoring the 'myth of filiation' (160). The insistence on what could be called textual patriarchy obscures the casual patterns of usage that are evident in so many borrowings from Shakespeare which do not reflect 'paternity but continuity' (Corti 127, my translation[6]). We will understand better how such borrowings work if we put aside family metaphors. They distract unduly from the continued life of quoted phrases that 'have left the book' (Engler *Poetry and Community* 55) to prosper outside it.

What can we say about Shakespearean intertextuality if we take the Death of the Author as a working hypothesis and refrain from talking about his intentions and those of the writers that quote him? To show that a radical post-author concept of intertextuality need not 'explode' the 'practice' of literary studies, Roland Barthes himself suggested some 'operational procedures' for literary analysis ('Valdemar' 172 and 173). Focused on short verbal units, these procedures are supremely applicable to the phenomenon of quotation. As a first step, Barthes defines a 'unit of reading' which he calls the *lexia* (plural *lexias*). Like quotations, lexias range in length from a single word to 'a group of three or four sentences' ('Valdemar' 172). Their precise extent is not determined by the author; it is the reader who sometimes absorbs one word after another, sometimes goes phrase by phrase and sometimes takes in a longer chunk. Every individual reading process progresses by a different sequence of such units, generating a 'mobile structuration' of the text that is 'displaced from reader to reader throughout history' ('Valdemar' 172). When an active reader divides the text into lexias and then turns into a writer who quotes them, this 'mobile structuration' is extended even further. When we quote, our writing is 'reading [...] that has become productive' (Kristeva 'Sémiologie des paragrammes' 120, my translation[7]). This productivity can be observed at work in the uses of 'to be or not to be' that I have discussed: Each writer selects a lexia of different length from Hamlet's soliloquy, displaces this string of words into the new text, adapts it to the requirements of the new surroundings and subtly marks its presence in these surroundings. These processes are the subject of this book.

The second step of Barthes' reader-determined text analysis concerns meaning and is just as applicable to quotation as the concept of the lexia. Having defined the lexia as the basic unit of comprehension, Barthes proposes to 'observe the meanings to which that lexia gives rise' ('Valdemar' 173). The plural 'meanings' is important: the analysis is not concerned with retrieving a lexia's one true significance, and even 'forgetting meanings is in some sense part of reading'. In quotation, the loss of earlier meanings of a borrowed phrase is the most frequent kind of forgetting. Active reading, which may lead to quotation, thrives on 'departures of meaning, not arrivals' ('Valdemar' 174). It is less important to decode meaning than to observe words and phrases that are in 'departure' from their home texts. A famous passage in Michel Foucault's essay 'What is an Author?' celebrates the liberation that would ensue if quotations could be enjoyed without reference to 'original' meanings. We could dispense with 'tiresome repetitions' of questions such as 'Who is the real author?' 'Have we proof of his authenticity and originality?' 'What has he revealed of his more profound self in his language?' Instead, there would be space for more interesting enquiries, such as 'What are the modes of existence of this discourse? [...] how is it circulated; who controls it?' (138).

'Surface reading' quotations

There are some more recent approaches to cultural appropriation that also step away from 'authors' and 'originals', schools of thought which accept that cultural artefacts may grow up and leave home, as it were. Stephen Greenblatt developed Roland Barthes' concepts of 'circulation' and 'mobility' with great success in *Shakespearean Negotiations* (1989) and more recently in *Cultural Mobility* (2009), and Franco Moretti's 'Distant reading' likewise abandons the intentions of the individual author as the guiding principle for the data-based kind of approach that is shared by this study. Neither Moretti nor Greenblatt, however, pays detailed attention to short verbal items. Greenblatt's list of cultural units that are 'disentangle[d]' from earlier contexts in order to become 'mobile' (82) includes 'peoples, objects, images, texts, and ideas' (250) but not words and phrases, and Moretti's quantitative historiography does not include the analysis of individual tokens. In contrast, this book maintains that a data-based approach does not need to 'spell the end of close reading' (Compagnon 279); it is based on the detailed analysis of textual details such as MARKING FOR QUOTATION. The recent model that has the most affinity with this approach is the concept of 'surface reading' as proposed by Stephen Best and Sharon Marcus. The traditional literary approach, which Best and Marcus call 'symptomatic reading', 'describes textual surfaces as superfluous, and seeks to unmask hidden meanings'. In significant contrast, surface reading

> broadens the scope of critique to include the kinds of interpretive activity that seek to understand the complexity of literary surfaces – surfaces that have been rendered invisible by symptomatic reading (Best and Marcus 1).

In a similar way, the study of casual quotation complements 'symptomatic' studies of literary reference by paying attention to what has been 'rendered invisible': the tens and hundreds of thousands of Shakespearean phrases which are used in texts that take no interest in Shakespeare's works and merely 'ripple' the surfaces of their host texts. To investigate the phenomenon of casual quotations with such close attention is still in many ways a 'new object' which is looking for its 'place in the field' (Barthes 'Work to Text' 155).

An enquiry into 'the modes of existence' of quotations along the lines suggested by Foucault would include some of the following questions about the way in which they are 'circulated': What do quotations repeat? How do they modify what they repeat? and What is the effect of juxtaposed quotations from different sources? The most important questions for this book concern MARKING: How do quotations draw attention to the fact that something is repeated? and What information do texts provide about what is repeated? The most familiar kinds of MARKING FOR QUOTATION are TYPOGRAPHICAL, such as quotation marks, capital letters, indentation or italics, and the most conspicuous are METALINGUISTIC tags like 'in the poet's words' or 'as Ophelia says'. The marking in my introductory examples mostly consists of a third kind, linguistic ANOMALIES. These include archaisms, unusual syntax, an iambic pentameter in the middle of a prose passage or a language switch. Finally, MARKING for QUOTATION may or may not include MARKING FOR DERIVATION, that is, information on the quoted author and work. A passage in italics or a 'methinks' in a *Guardian* article may be complemented by a mention of 'Shakespeare' or 'Hamlet', by epithets like Coleridge's 'our great dramatic poet' ('Logic' 13:247) or by phrases that seem themselves to be witty mini-quotations, like Joyce's 'beardless undergraduate from Wittenberg' (*Ulysses* 170). MARKING FOR DERIVATION is an extremely directive signal: the information that a phrase is taken from *Hamlet* severely limits the 'reader's autonomy' of interpretation. Michael Riffaterre has claimed that such limitation is essential to the 'monumentality' of a text (36) and that a text which does not fully reference its quotations loses 'its identity' (35). This may be true for many books but as a description of Shakespeare's works, it is patently absurd. Nobody could dispute the 'monumentality' and 'identity' of the Shakespearean canon and yet his works have proved endlessly inviting to casual as well as intensely creative responses.

From the start, Shakespeare's works have activated their audiences and readers to become (re-) writers and to participate in the generation of meaning. The result has been an extraordinary amount of criticism, interpretation, adaptation, parody and quotation. In the terminology of Roland Barthes, Shakespeare's works are 'writerly' texts to the highest degree. The way in which Shakespeare's phrases are (not) marked in quotation demonstrates the independence of their users: only 5% of the tokens which this book is based are accompanied by the word 'Shakespeare', the title of a play or the name of a character.[8] Moreover, even MARKING FOR DERIVATION is no guarantee of an in-depth engagement, as Roland Barthes' description of his own casual quotation practice indicates: 'He pays his visits, i.e. his respects, to vocabularies, he invokes *notions*, he rehearses them under a name; he makes use of this name as of an emblem'. This name – MARKING FOR DERIVATION – then 'dispenses the reader from following to its conclusions the system of which it is the signifier' (*Roland Barthes* 74). In other words, a writer who uses 'to be or not to be' and points out that it is from *Hamlet* or by Shakespeare is not necessarily more concerned with Shakespeare's tragedy than a writer who does not name names. In fact, a quotation with overt MARKING FOR DERIVATION may be more casual than others. A name or title that seems to point to the quoted work and direct the reader's interpretation can *replace* the original context and its possible meanings. There is no interpretation to achieve: *Hamlet* mentioned, job done. Casual quotation is a gesture which means itself and nothing else; that is why it most frequently employs MARKING FOR QUOTATION ONLY. When Karl Marx writes 'das ist die **question**', the single, ungrammatical English word 'question' does point to *Hamlet*, Shakespeare or English literature. Its main effect, however, is to mark the immense quotability of the phrase. The weird sentence 'Das ist die **question**' acknowledges how difficult it is to say 'das ist die Frage' or 'that is the question' without feeling that one is echoing *Hamlet*. Marx's switch to English is a symptom of *déjà lu*, of the recognition of a familiar string of words that is '[a]lways anterior, never original' (Barthes 'Death of the Author' 170). It will be forever second-hand, although it has long ago become innocent of a genuine association with *Hamlet*, and this association may be tenuous even if the play, the hero or their author is mentioned next to the quotation.

The tenuous relationship between a casual quotation and its source that is typically signalled by MARKING FOR QUOTATION ONLY is often further diluted by intertextuality that does not refer back to one main source but sideways to other texts. A text that quotes a particular line may point to or betray an awareness of roughly contemporary texts that refer to the same passage, or it may contain additional quotations from a different Shakespeare play or from different works altogether. Such cross-quotation, as I call it, is one of the most telling characteristics of casual intertextuality because the juxtaposition of several quotations weakens the impact of every individual text that is quoted. Cross-quotation is beautifully described in Roland Barthes' most personal metaphor for intertextuality, the echo chamber. Speaking of his own reading and quoting activity in the third person, Barthes says:

> In relation to the systems which surround him, what is he? Say an echo chamber: he reproduces the thoughts badly, he follows the words (*Roland Barthes* 74).

This image catches two of the most important characteristics of casual quotation. First, the echo chamber describes quotation as a physically triggered repetition of signifiers, which is not concerned with the (original) signified and cannot be expected to have meaning. Second, the echo chamber is not a single wall (read: single consciousness) which clearly reflects an utterance after a short interval; it is a place in which multiple echoes intersect and overlap, repeat each other and make it hard to discern what was first said. The original version of an echoing phrase – if there ever was one – is lost even as it continues to reverberate. This is why I prefer to speak of MARKING FOR DERIVATION rather than marking for 'origin': the words 'origin' and 'original' would raise expectations that the echo chamber of casual quotation does not meet. Rather than focus on an often irretrievable origin, this book investigates the multiple verbal traces of Shakespeare's language by focusing on what the quoting texts themselves tell us about this intertextuality. This is done by quantitative analysis, using an online database of several thousand Shakespeare quotations and their 'surface' markings for 'distant reading'. The number of quotations that have made Shakespeare 'most cited and quoted' several centuries cannot be usefully managed without an electronic research medium. Ultimately, though, all statistical findings are validated and refined by the close reading of selected tokens, the classic and still indispensable technique of literary studies.

Digital quotation research: The *HyperHamlet* database

The material basis of this book is the *HyperHamlet* database, an open-access corpus of 11,000 quotations from *Hamlet* that can be searched and browsed at www.hyperhamlet.unibas.ch. This resource has made it possible to carry out a data-based study of formal features of quotation, particularly MARKING. It is laid out as a hypertext of *Hamlet*, whose every line offers access to extracts from other texts which quote that line or are quoted in Shakespeare's play. 'Vertical' browsing allows users to focus on a single phrase and to follow, for example, the fortunes of 'sea of troubles' from Aeschylos to *Hamlet* and from William Bradford's *Of Plymouth Plantation* (1647) to Twitter. 'Horizontal' searches, on the other hand, can filter out sets of tokens from a given period or genre. Such a data set could consist, for example, of *Hamlet* quotations in 1790s English journalism which are marked by inverted commas but go without a mention of the name 'Shakespeare'. These extracts, MARKED FOR QUOTATION ONLY, could be compared to other newspaper passages from the same period that do name Shakespeare, or to extracts from Gothic fiction with the same marking characteristics or to quotations in journalism of a different period or language. The search options of *HyperHamlet* allow researchers to move, like a Barthesian reader, 'through a web or network of texts and continually shift the center – and hence the focus or organizing principle – of [their] investigation' (Landow 556). From the focus on the extraordinary work of a singularly gifted individual, scholars can widen their enquiry to investigate a world of mobile phrases, and so perform Roland Barthes' suggested move 'From Work to Text' in a twenty-first century way. This kind of research enables us to identify and 'study widely attested patterns' of use (Lavagnino 15) and so reveal 'a new literary landscape' (Moretti 180).

Data-based quotation research needs computer support because casual quotations surpass any other post-Shakespeare manifestation in quantity, generic range and cultural diversity. Unlike adaptations, they are not limited to a specific literary temperament: while it seems 'unlikely' that Jane Austen 'would have elected to rewrite *Hamlet*' (Thompson and Taylor *Hamlet 1603 and 1623* 126), she certainly quoted it – and so did thousands of journalists, pamphleteers, politicians, diarists, bloggers, screenwriters, copywriters and Twitter users. One can cope with such masses of material only with the help of computers, which can 'find features that texts have in common in ways that our brains alone cannot' (Best and Marcus 17). The possibility to manage large numbers of items allows an important widening of the horizon research in intertextuality: scholars can move beyond single-author studies of the 'Shakespeare quotations in Defoe' and 'Shakespeare's quotations from Spenser' type. A concentrated comparison of *Hamlet* and *The Faerie Queene*, for example, will certainly bring to light a lot of fascinating material and with it a certain danger of overstating thematic connections because editors and source historians naturally tend 'to find connections between Shakespeare's plays and the works which they themselves kn[o]w best' (Burrow 21). Any enquiry into his use of a single source should be put into perspective by a consideration of other texts which may be reverberating in any passage of Shakespeare's works. Casual quotations *from* Shakespeare, too, should be read in the context of each other as much as in the context of the play they are taken from. 'Shakespeare quotations in the novels of Samuel Richardson' is a very different research project from 'Shakespeare quotations in the work of Samuel Richardson and *Tom Jones*', from a comparison of quotations in mid-eighteenth-century epistolary novels or from an enquiry into how Richardson's favourite Shakespeare lines were used before and after him. Without a broad database, it is easy to overlook the sheer possibility of certain contexts; with a database, we can discuss intertextuality as 'enacted and staged through writing practices and not simply by mode of theoretical assertion' (Allen 209).

While the concept of a database of quotations such as *HyperHamlet* implements twentieth-century concepts of intertextuality in a twenty-first-century electronic research tool, the contents of the database are owed in roughly equal parts to Digital Humanities and an older academic tradition. About half the *HyperHamlet* entries come from the harvest of nineteenth- and twentieth-century scholarship that is stored in large scholarly tomes, in indexes, concordances, footnotes and tiny *Notes and Queries* articles. *HyperHamlet* owes a great debt to the achievement of these scholars, on which modern Shakespeare research 'sometimes builds but mostly rests' (Burrow, preface, n.p.); thousands

Introduction: A 'New Object'   11

of elusive references that are opaque to computer analysis because of paraphrase and historical spelling could only have been spotted by readers who know their Shakespeare, their Bible and their Ovid. What the *HyperHamlet* research team did was to upload and edit these bits of information so that they can be searched and studied together with other entries that had been newly identified. The new entries were spotted by running hundreds of *Hamlet* phrases through full-text databases of English writing, including literary works from several centuries (*LION*), eighteenth-century texts from all genres (*ECCO*) and an extensive body of Romantic novels, letters, memoirs, diaries, journalism and non-fiction (*The Romantic Era Redefined*). The corpus as it now stands has come about thanks to traditional learning and digital data generation, and the searchable, open-access format in turn serves different scholarly communities by bringing their findings to life in new contexts. Once uploaded on the database, a seventeenth-century *Hamlet* quotation which a computer would never have recognized may now appear in search results together with source materials that were never discussed before they were harvested electronically. Based on painstaking archival and electronic research, *HyperHamlet* allows students to revel in the abundance of infinite, jumbled echoes. A researcher who traces the use of a phrase to its earliest known use or compares its use to others from the same period or genre can appreciate in philological detail how 'any text' that crosses paths with one of Shakespeare's is 'a mosaic of quotations' and 'the absorption and transformation of another' (Kristeva 'Word, Dialogue' 37).

Busying oneself with data, with practical evidence, would have spelled treason to the poststructuralist pioneers of radical intertextuality in the late 1960s and early 1970s: a return to patriarchal philology, the worship of master texts, the very establishment that was being rebelled against. This rebellious attitude reflects the fact that these print-bound decades knew no research tools that would have done justice to the complexity of their vision. Attempting to map the ways in which texts such as Shakespeare's intersect with others would have meant being swamped in unmanageable masses of material like Edward Casaubon in *Middlemarch*, who fails so dismally at putting together a 'Key to All Mythologies'. A 'Key to All Quotations' (cf. Hohl Trillini and Quaßdorf) in the spirit of radical intertextuality must needs be based on large numbers of texts that overlap, repeat and echo fragments from each other, and this is only possible with digital tools to which the pioneers of radical intertextuality had no access. Only decades later have words like 'web' and 'network', which were pure metaphors in the 1960s, become (virtual) reality. Thanks to computers, we can explore radical visions of intertextuality in ways that approximate its complexity. At the same time, computers can cope with the quantity and detail of information that traditional philology offers. The combination of digital research and re-contextualized philological scholarship has enabled *HyperHamlet* to map a small corner of that universe of circulating bits of text which poststructuralist thinkers could only present as a mental model. Marrying these two aspects of intellectual endeavour is the great potential of Digital Humanities and the basis of this book.

Overview

HyperHamlet has one obvious limitation: it is not what we could call *HyperWill*. At the time of writing, a database of quotations from the entire Shakespeare canon exists only as the draft of a research grant proposal; the pilot database had to be based on a single play. In addition to the fantastic prestige and popularity of *Hamlet*, which promised the widest possible range of references, the play fortunately represents several of the most interesting facets of Shakespeare quotation. The philosophical, generalizing nature of many scenes, which makes the play 'almost one continu'd *Moral*' (Shaftesbury 117), has allowed a high number of individual lines to become casually proverbial. Moreover, *Hamlet* is much-quoting as well as much-quoted: it contains more borrowings than any other Shakespeare play except the famously derivative *Love's Labour's Lost*. *Hamlet* perfectly exemplifies the two meanings of 'Casual Shakespeare': our thoughtless use of four-hundred-year-old phrases and the magpie Will Shakespeare, who steals all 'his' best phrases in *Shakespeare in Love* and other bio-fiction. He quotes casually and we quote casually what he quotes. Just as we remember Shakespeare's stolen plots as his (*Romeo and Juliet* rather than Bandello, *Hamlet* rather than *Gesta Danorum*), we use many Shakespeare quotations that are actually Shakespeare's quotations. 'Hamlet' was a cliché for over a decade before *Hamlet*; the pompous style parodied in the speeches of Claudius and the First Player was a byword of unoriginality already in 1589, when Thomas Nashe wrote:

> English seneca read by candle light yeeldes manie good sentences [...] if you intreate [Seneca] faire in a frostie morning, he will affoord you whole **Hamlets**, I should say handfulls of tragical speaches' (Nashe *Menaphon* 10).

Always already quoted and including many 'handfulls' of lines and speeches that are supremely quotable to this day, *Hamlet* is the perfect embodiment of the great poststructuralist metaphor of the text as an 'intersection [...] where at least one other word (text) can be read' (Kristeva 'Word, Dialogue' 66). Such readings and re-readings proliferate also within the play, which is obsessed with second-hand words, with echoes, rewritings, reports, puns, hearsay, proverbs and classical literature. Finally, and paradoxically, *Hamlet* is a good representative of Shakespearean intertextuality because it has so often been read as Shakespeare's most personal work. Despite its dependence on pre-texts, *Hamlet* has not so far been outed as a collaborative work in the way of *Macbeth* or *Timon of Athens*. If we consider that Shakespeare's most intertextual play is quintessentially Shakespeare's and Shakespeare's alone, 11,000 quotations in and from this text can be considered a solid basis for investigating 'Casual Shakespeare' in general.

The following presents casual quotation in six roughly chronological chapters preceded by a sample overview. Each chapter explores the casual intertextuality surrounding Shakespeare's works with a different focus and draws on digital and traditional research in different ways to complement the narratives of intentional, complex allusion that studies in Shakespeare reception have favoured. Chapters 1, 5 and 6 are based exclusively on the *HyperHamlet* corpus, including substantial amounts of material that are not mentioned in previously published research. Chapters 2, 3, 4 and 7 extend the analytical categories of *HyperHamlet* to other Shakespeare texts.

Chapter 1 outlines the life cycle of one Shakespeare quotation and the following chapters explore selected moments from this historical process, covering casual quotation from the mid-sixteenth to the mid-nineteenth centuries, the three centuries mentioned in the subtitle (I consider the editions of the Bible and the classics that were available to Shakespeare as 'sixteenth-century' texts). 'To be or not to be' has been identified with several potential sources. It was memorably presented by Shakespeare, increasingly associated with him over the course of the seventeenth century and established as a famous quotation in the eighteenth. After 1770, it was used with the characteristically casual routine of the Romantic decades and then became tedious. Like hundreds of other lines, it finally detached itself from the famous author and so regained at least part of its earlier potential as an anonymous formula. Chapter 2, 'He should be stop'd', discusses Shakespeare's quotations of folk materials and the Bible and Chapter 3, 'Honey-Tongued Shakespeare', investigates his casual uses of the classical heritage. These two sections owe a substantial debt to the nineteenth- and twentieth-century scholars who identified thousands of unacknowledged quotations in the Shakespeare canon and who unearthed and re-published the early comments on Shakespeare which support my argument throughout. Critical ('he should be stop'd') or admiring ('Honey-tongued'), the remarks of his contemporaries reflect their perception of Shakespeare's casual intertextual practice. One especially perceptive remark, which praises 'Shakespeares fine filed phrase', anticipates future Shakespeare quotation with the claim that the Muses themselves would be happy to use his phrases 'if they spoke English'. Such English phrases are investigated in Chapter 4, which discusses Shakespeare's own borrowings and those of his early quoters with a special focus on John Marston.

14   Introduction: A 'New Object'

Chapters 5 to 7 continue the history of Shakespeare quotation into the 1830s with a more obviously quantitative approach. The analyses of seventy parodies of the 'to be or not to be' soliloquy ('The old parody') and more than three thousand *Hamlet* quotations from texts of all genres ('Peak Casual') confirm that casual Shakespeare is not a twentieth- or twenty-first-century phenomenon. In fact, a conspicuous peak of 'routine' uses of his language is evident in the decades around 1800. In the middlebrow verse parodies discussed in Chapter 5, the original context of the Shakespearean set piece is regularly eclipsed by references to a generic framework of similar 'imitations' and famous soliloquies, by topical allusions and by cross-quotation from other texts. The same features can be observed in the massed quotations of 'Romantic Routine', which starts in the 1770s and pervades every written genre until the 1830s. Novelists, playwrights, essayists and poets embraced Shakespeare quotation and all of them, from the most derivative, forgotten hacks to the greatest and most independent minds like Byron, Shelley and Scott, quoted casually. The only exception has the final Chapter 7 to herself: Jane Austen kept her novels as well as her private correspondence completely free of routine intertextuality. The critique of a fashionable practice which Austen's abstinence implies is complemented with explicit ironical hints and the same kind of 'characterization by marking for quotation' that Shakespeare used, and so offers a final, different perspective on Romantic Routine.

This volume concludes with an investigation of Romantic Routine because this is how far a data-based, genre-inclusive enquiry into English Shakespeare quotation can meaningfully go at present. To complement the quotations already identified in canonical texts with instances from 'minor' writers and genres, extensive electronic searches were indispensable. Together with *Literature Online*, the full-text collections *Eighteenth-Century Collections Online* and *The Romantic Era Redefined* offered a rich and solid basis for a broad study of Shakespeare quotation up to and including the early nineteenth century.[9] To research and document a representative range of materials for the Victorian period and the twentieth century with their proliferating print culture (let alone the Internet Age) would have required resources beyond the scope of the *HyperHamlet* project. In the near future, work in Digital Humanities may discover other ways to mine the diverse media of these decades and become able to extend the data-based exploration of intertextuality in ways that we can only posit theoretically at the moment.

Notes

1 The title of this novel, which was serialized in the *Weekly Entertainer*, is itself a casual quotation, possibly intended to capitalize on the success of the eponymous novel by Georgiana Cavendish, Duchess of Devonshire (1778).

2 My translation: 'If we criticize [...] philosophy, our critique is one of those questions of which our present time says: That is the question'.
3 My translation: 'Sovereignty of the monarch or of the people, that is the question'.
4 Most famously in 'Eighteenth Brumaire', cf. Harries 'Homo Alludens' and Stallybrass 'Well grubbed'.
5 Another example: 'nachdem [Brandenburg] mit seinem rohen, widerlichen Unteroffiziersdialekt die Kammer empört hat, läßt er den "Tyrann übertyrannisieren" und pariert Ordre der Nationalversammlung' (Marx 'Kontrerevolution' 10–11).
6 The original Italian runs: 'non paternità, ma continuità'.
7 The original French runs: '"[É]crire" serait le "lire" devenu production'.
8 The significance of this percentage is reinforced if we consider that quotations which are marked with 'Shakespeare' or 'Hamlet' have a much higher chance of being recognized and recorded in the first place.
9 *ECCO* digitalizes a catalogue of all books and pamphlets printed in Britain between 1701 and 1800, and *Romantic Era* adds letters, diaries, memoirs, journalism and political and philosophical non-fiction.

1 To Quote or Not to Quote

> *'To be or not to be! that is the question'*
> *Says Shakespeare, who just now is much in fashion.*
> LORD BYRON (1823)

To say that 'to be or not to be' is the most frequent literary quotation ever is trite. To investigate how it came to be so famous is interesting because the success story of these Anglo-Saxon monosyllables involves significant aspects of Shakespeare's intertextual creativity and the creativity that he stimulated in others. 'To be or not to be' is typical because it is in transit: It came from somewhere and went everywhere after Shakespeare had used it. Long before Shakespeare conceived of *Hamlet*, the phrase existed in many shapes and discursive contexts, and it continued to be used independently of the play for decades after the first performance. Shakespeare's use of these words, however, proved so memorable that 'to be or not to be' was increasingly perceived as his. He detached 'to be or not to be' from its possible sources and made it so much his own that it could not but develop into a quotation over the course of the seventeenth century. Eighteenth-century bardolatry boosted this process to the tipping point where the line became unbearably banal. Today, it has the ambiguous status that is characteristic of Shakespeare quotations in the twentieth and twenty-first century. For many, it is and will remain always already quoted so that they can use it only self-consciously; for others, it is an anonymous ready-made formula; and yet other people, who know it as Hamlet's, use the phrase with studied or genuine indifference to the original context. Sayre Greenfield, who has studied the phrase's fortunes in the seventeenth century with a focus on the topics of texts that quote it, finds that 'many of the "borrowings" are not explicit or even implied references to *Hamlet*' ('Early Seventeenth' 512). 'To be or not to be' is unobtrusive. Unencumbered by rare words or tell-tale archaisms that would give away a line like 'get thee to a nunnery', it can blend smoothly into English surroundings from any century; it only stands out from its surroundings if a writer goes to the trouble of adding quotation marks or other signals to the reader. This means that 'to be or not to be' can illustrate a wider range of quotation modes than is available to more salient lines; its rise to fame is more significant because we can observe it starting from and returning to complete obscurity. For this phrase, the somewhat embarrassing title of this chapter is a real question: we can never take for granted whether the aim was to quote or not to quote.

An available structure: To verb or not to verb

The pre- and outside-*Hamlet* life of 'To be or not to be' did not start with a phrase. It started with a phrase *structure:* 'to verb or not to verb'. This construction was frequently used for talking about decisions, for foregrounding, postponing and questioning binary choices in the simplest possible way: not even as 'one or zero', just as 'one or not one'. Long before *Hamlet*, its contexts ranged from existential to trivial. In 1582, a school primer used it to set out the spelling issue of 'where **to write or not to write** the qualifying, e, in the end of simple words' (Mulcaster sig. T4^{recto} [150]). More dramatically, a Euphuistic romance insisted on an unhappy lover's responsibility for his own death in 1583:

AURELIA: But hath not he free choice, **to loue or not to loue?**
PHILOTIMUS: He hath.
AURELIA: Then he killes himself that loues (Melbancke sig. G2^{recto} [50]).

The psychological complications in this passage are typical. Successfully achieved decisions are rarely expressed with 'to verb or not to verb', which is most effective for dilemma, indecision and struggle. A young woman may lose the will '**to doe, or not to doe** any thing whatsoeuer' (Brome sig. G1^{recto}, 1632) because of love melancholy, while other girls have their choice taken away by a father who '*hath power of his own will* **to give or not to give** his child in marriage, as he shall see occasion' (Perkins *God's Free Grace* 728, 1616). In both instances, true choice is denied. In the anonymous play *Tom o'Lincoln*, Angellica reflects on her lot as the captive of a powerful king: 'well then inforcte I yeld, though not inforcte / for tis in me **to yeld or not to yeld**' (Anon. *Tom o'Lincoln* 5). This beleaguered heroine has no outward choice; instead, she takes comfort in the residual agency of deciding whether to yield *deliberately.*

The concept of deliberate choice in temptation, which we have just seen deployed in fiction, also interested Protestant theologians, who frequently use 'to verb or not to verb' for moral decisions. Richard Hooker explains in *Ecclesiastical Politie* that Joseph's choice '**to yield or not to yield** to the impotent desire of his lewd mistress' (1:171, 1594), Potiphar's wife in Genesis 39) is a question of 'absolutely good or evil'. In smaller matters, Christians are free and may choose, for instance, '**to follow, or not to follow** a certaine text of Scripture' in writing sermons or '**to come or not to come**' to a prayer gathering (Perkins *Exposition* 141, 1616).

'Christ having purchased [our] liberty in all those things indifferent', every Christian is free '**to do or not to do, to use or not to use** them' and Catholics betray this freedom 'through superstitious feares and want of faith' (Downame *Christian Warfare* 38, 1634). Such unnecessary additional regulations range from fasting in Lent to more fundamental theological questions such as the value of praying for the dead or transubstantiation. Belief in the latter should not be asked of the faithful, given that Christians had been 'free **to believe or not to believe**' in it for 'at the least eight hundred years after Christ' (Bradford 250, 1555). Apparently trivial decisions, such as '**to use or not to use** the means whereby **to attend or not to attend** to reading, **to pray or not to pray**', may test obedience just as well, and a Christian must not consider it 'a matter indifferent either **to yield or not to yield** obedience' (Hooker 1:171 and 1:239). To yield obedience is a form of Christian behaviour that can be actively chosen, and this is made quite clear by the use of the double *to*-infinitive.

If Christian obedience is to be worth anything, it must be yielded by subjects who can exercise free will. Enforced obedience is of no interest, as John Milton put it in *Paradise Lost*: 'Not free [...] what praise could they receive?'[1] Conversely, 'no man is to be punished for his sins' without the 'free-will **to sin or not to sin**' (Perkins *Reformed Catholic* 561, 1611). Many sixteenth- and seventeenth-century uses of 'to verb or not to verb' focus on the far-reaching consequences of human free will. The most frequently cited examples are Adam, Judas and Christ. Adam, who would have 'had power **to keepe or not to keepe** the commandement' (Perkins *Exposition* 160, 1616) freely chose to be disobedient. Judas' betrayal was, similarly, not preordained since 'in him it was / **To do, or not to do** that damn'd dispight' (Davies *Yehovah* sig. 11[recto], 1607); in contrast, Christ used his 'power **to die or not to die**' (Perkins *Exposition* 215, 1616) for the good of all mankind. Even those theologians who regard faith rather than works as decisive for salvation think in terms of binary choice, assuming that 'there is given unto men a free will either **to believe or not to believe**' (Perkins *Christian Treatise* 624, 1617).[2] This phrasing turns faith itself into an act of obedience that we can choose to perform or not, highlighting the ever-present risk of disobedience, of making the wrong binary choice. Consequently, many believers ask to be protected from their own fallible faculty of will in pious variations on the Lord's Prayer's 'Thy will be done'[3] and say things like: 'giue me no pow'r **to will or not to will** / But as thou wilt' (Davies *Muses' Sacrifice* 25, 1612). The phrase 'to will or not to will' perfectly sums up Christian submission because it represents the possibility of handing one's will back to God volition both grammatically (*to*-infinitive) and lexically ('will'). George Wither's poem 'Wither's Motto' takes this abdication of human will to its logical conclusion:

> I have not of my selfe the power or grace,
> **To be, or not to be**; one minute-space. [...]

Or thinke out halfe a thought, before my death,
But by the leaue of him that gave me breath (367, 1621).

In this frame of mind, the human inability 'to will' what is right equals the impossibility of existing independently of God. For pious Christians, 'to will' is not desirable without God and 'to be' without Him is impossible. This does sound '*Hamlet*-like in its sense of uncertainty, but [...] the real subject [is] religious' (Greenfield 'Early Seventeenth' 527): as choice is rendered up for Christian certainty, Hamlet's doubts become irrelevant.

While devout believers offer up their will and existence to God, secular-minded seventeenth-century heroes in drama focus, more energetically than Hamlet, on the capacities and limits of the purely human will. Their frame of reference is the involuntary, mathematically determined motion of clocks and stars. 'It is not in the power and possibility of the sun **to move or not to move**' (Hooker 2:39) and the tragic protagonists assert or refute free will in contrast or in alignment with this rigidity. The 'heroicke' pirate captain John Ward, a convert to Islam, completely denies free will in Robert Daborne's *Christian Turned Turk* (1612):

JOHN WARD: [...] we haue no will **to act,
Or not to act** more, then those orbes we see,
And planetary bodies (sig. B4^{verso}).

Another non-Christian, Eleazar in William Heminges' *The Jews' Tragedy* (1662), is similarly pessimistic:

ELEAZER: We know the weakness of our State to be
Vnable to resist, yet know not how
**To yeeld, or not
to yeeld**, or what to do (13).

There are characters, though, who do use 'to verb or not to verb' to affirm that the human will is governed by reason *in contrast* to heavenly bodies. George Chapman's Byron says in 1608:

BYRON: I haue a will, and faculties of choise,
To do, or not to do: and reason why
I doe, or not doe this; the starres haue none (315).

God is nowhere, the sky is filled with mechanically orbiting stars and human will stands alone. This situation is more in line with Arthur Hugh Clough's Victorian vision of a manly, decisive Elizabethan age, whose individuals stand 'as on the mount of vision', considering 'all the possible varieties of which were delivered into [their] power, **"to be or not to be"**' (Clough 340). The most insistent celebration of the human option 'to do or not to do' came in *An Essay Concerning Human*

Understanding in 1689). In his chapter on 'Power', John Locke uses the 'or not to' structure at least fourteen times to define 'Human liberty' as 'a power **to act or not to act** according as the Mind directs' (1:367 (2.21.73)). The ability to face a dilemma defines freedom and humanity: 'as far as a Man has a power **to think, or not to think: to move, or not to move**, according to the preference or direction of his own mind, so far is a man *free*' (1:315 (2.21.8)). Locke's argument culminates with '**to will or not to will**'; while devotional contexts use this phrase to represent the subordination of human desires to God, Locke turns it to stark paradox: 'This then is evident, That a Man is not at liberty **to will, or not to will**' because 'he has not a power to forbear willing'. 'To will or not to will' is the only choice that is denied to a creature with free will, and so the phrase is an oxymoron for Locke: the phrase structure expresses choice, the infinitive expresses intention and both are make little sense with this particular verb.

Only one double infinitive is even stranger than 'to will or not to will' as a choice between two courses of action: 'to be or not to be'. Indeed, this version was never used before *Hamlet* to express moral or psychological alternatives; it was reserved exclusively for logical statements, as in a treatise on logic from 1584 and a convoluted passage from *The Testament of Love* in an edition from the 1540s:

> An Axiome or sentence is that ordering of one reason with another, whereby a thing is saide **to bee or not to be** (Fenner sig. C1^(recto)).
>
> wherfore whā I sey yt god toforne wot any thyng, thorow necessitie is thilke thyng to be cōmyng, al is one if I sey if it shalbe: but this necessitie neither cōstrayneth ne defēdeth any thing **to be or not to be** Therfore sothly yf loue is put **to be**, it is said of necessitie **to be**, or els for it is put **not to be** it is affirmed **not to be** of necessite: not for ye necessite cōstraineth or defēdeth loue **to be or not to be** (Usk n. p.).

In this kind of context, 'to be or not to be' remains unaffected by *Hamlet* because it does not describe decision-making. A theological treatise argued in 1631 that past actions cannot be 'said to be possible **to be or not to be**' because not even God is able to 'make that the works of men and Angels should not be possible **to be or not to be**' (Twisse 290).[4] In 1678, Ralph Cudworth writes in his *True Intellectual System of the Universe* that things 'Caused by Something else' are 'Contingently Possible **to Be or not to be**', whereas God exists '*Absolutely*' and without any *Ifs* and *Ands*'. He is a 'Perfect Being', which is not' Contingent **to Be or not to Be**; but that it Certainly Is, and Cannot but **Be**; or that it is Impossible it should **not Be**' (723). Unless we want to read Cudworth's preference for 'be' without 'to' as a sign of studied avoidance, the formal logic in these passaged carries no hint of *Hamlet*, even at a time when writers in other genres were beginning to show an awareness of this possible context. In John Norris' *An Idea of Happiness* of 1683, 'the phrase comes close to the philosophical meaning it has in the soliloquy' (Greenfield 'Early Seventeenth' 526):

> For if the Good and the Evil be equal-balanc'd, it must needs be indifferent to that man either **to be or not to be**, there being not the least *Grain* of good to determine his Choice (sig. A2^{verso}).

This is indeed quite Hamletian, especially as Norris concludes after further deliberation: 'I am very well satisfied, that 'tis **better not to be than to be**' (A3^{recto}).

A quotable phrase: To be or not to be

Before turning to the first texts that can definitely be said to present 'to be or not to be' as a quotation, I want to consider what made this phrase so useful to Shakespeare and how he made it quotable in a way that earlier and contemporary texts could not hope to match. The structure of the formula, its history and the way in which it is framed in *Hamlet* all contributed to this success. To begin with, 'To be or not to be' has excellent formal prerequisites. Its Anglo-Saxon monosyllables are natural to native speakers and understandable to anybody with the most basic knowledge of English. Its effortless iambics fit into colloquial prose or T-shirt slogans just as well as into verse, and the charm of alliteration[5] further adds to its appeal. Moreover, the phrase is extremely economical: the question is not 'to live or to kill yourself', 'to be or to stop being' but 'to be or not to be'. Choice is dramatized with an almost algebraic simplicity, which makes the phrase memorable and self-contained and encourages repetition out of context. The second formal advantage are 'to'-particles, which underline the element of active choice. 'To be' is a more archetypally verbal form than 'being'; unlike the noun-like gerund 'being', the infinitive 'to be' implies intention and planned action. The infinitive looks forward, the gerund is static. The difference is beautifully obvious in Coleridge's description of Hamlet as a person who is 'continually resolving *to do*, yet *doing* nothing but resolve' ('Shakespeare and Milton' 390, emphasis mine). Intriguingly, Coleridge substitutes 'do' for Shakespeare's 'be'. Familiarity has made it easy to overlook just how oddly the drive of the 'to'-infinitive sits with the meaning 'exist', how strange it is for a man to decide 'to be' rather than 'to act, to do, to perform', as the First Gravedigger says (*Hamlet* 5.1.12). Hamlet himself longs to *do*: 'I do not know / Why yet I live to say "This thing's to do"' (4.4.46–47). His tragic paralysis is underscored by his failure to uses any of these verbs in the soliloquy (cf. Bruster *To Be Or Not To Be* 50). Infinitives like 'to die', 'to sleep' and 'to be' embody Hamlet's deplorable loss of 'the name of action'; they conserve just the shadow of action in the little word 'to'. The subjectless construction of 'to be or not to be', which shifts agency away from the speaker, further underscores this paralysis. To use the double infinitive 'to be or not to be' for an urgent yet impossible personal choice: that is Shakespeare's oxymoronic stroke of genius. He makes Hamlet communicate his indecision with the axiomatic stringency of formal logic, which makes his situation so vividly memorable although it is not clear what the problem is. Is he worried about the advisability of suicide, the probability of an afterlife or something completely different? 'General to the point of emptiness' (Hohl Trillini and Langlotz 157), 'to be or not to be' preserves the secret of Hamlet's problem while communicating its urgency. This is one more reason for its success.

The semantic openness of 'to be or not to be', which is so effective on stage, makes it hard to decide which earlier version Shakespeare may have had in mind, a question to which we will return again and again. The most securely established candidate is a passage in Cicero's *Tusculanae Quæstiones*,[6] which recounts Plato's description of the death of Socrates and focuses on the idea of death as sleep. Plato's account was often quoted and paraphrased[7] and Cicero's version itself was available to Shakespeare in three versions: the original, John Dolman's translation and Thomas Bedingfield's *Cardan's Comfort*. All three versions contain phrases that may have inspired the soliloquy's wording, such as the following:

> B7[verso] istuc ipsum, **non esse, cum fueris,** miserrimum puto (Cicero *Tusculanae* 1:12) [n]ot to be when you **have bene**, I thinke is the greatest misery (Dolman *Five Questions* sig.
>
> B7[verso]) quicquid isto modo pronunties, id **aut esse aut non esse** (Cicero *Tusculanae*, 1:14) 'lwhatsoeuer you do so pronounce must not either **be or not be** (Dolman *Fyve Questions* sig.

The second Latin phrase has the doubling of two words ('esse'/'aut'), which makes Shakespeare's double *to*-infinitive so effective but this feature is missing in the translation so maybe Shakespeare took his inspiration from Cicero here. Maybe he was 'attempting to render [Cicero's] original ideas' independently of Dolman. Or maybe he never saw this 'expression of the preferableness of death to life' in a Latin context (Baldwin *Small Latine* 2:604). Thomas Baldwin was certain that the phrase 'that is the question' pointed to Dolman's Cicero translation, whose full title runs: *Those fyve* **Questions,** *which Marke Tullye Cicero disputed in his Manor of Tusculanum*. The word 'question' would remind every theatregoer who had been to grammar school of *Tusculanae* and prompt them to recognize the soliloquy as a 'grammar school exercise on the original passage'. The author of this particular 'exercise' may have been 'Shakespeare himself; it may have been someone else, whom he is following' (2:605). On the other hand, the expression 'that is the question' also appeared 'consistently amid theological and legal disputations' (Greenfield 'Early Seventeenth' 528), as, for example, in John Whitgift's *Admonition to the Parliament*: 'you should rather haue proued, that women may not in time of necessitie administer baptisme, for **that is the question** and not the other' (sig. CC2^{recto}, 1573). Both parts of the opening line of Hamlet's soliloquy can be related to multiple earlier texts, which may have echoed in the minds of Elizabethan *Hamlet* audiences as they did for William Shakespeare.

The third USP of 'to be or not to be', in addition to an adaptable structure and familiar antecedents, is the way in which it is framed in *Hamlet*. The phrase 'that is the question' is more than just a marker for derivation pointing to Cicero's *Quaestiones*; it is a metatextual phrase which takes up 'to be or not to be' with the pronoun 'that'. This turns 'to be or not to be' into a single item, into a noun phrase that functions as the grammatical subject of a sentence (What is the question? To or not to be is the question). This syntactic device is called nominalization. It can foreground any phrase as a distinct item which stands out from its context; we could say that nominalization puts invisible quotation marks around the nominalized item. In fact, nominalization is considered 'the "classic" anomalous feature of quotations' (Quaßdorf 91), and is an extremely useful feature for identifying casual quotations in documents where punctuation is not standardized or unreliably transmitted by printers. Shakespeare's wording in the second half of Hamlet's famous line makes it clear, independently of any typographical efforts, that the first half is spoken in invisible quotation marks, singled out as a memorable saying that will bear repetition. With 'that is the question', Hamlet's utterance turns itself into a quotable *sententia*. The move was so effective that even the second half, the marking for quotation, became quotable, as can be seen from the Karl Marx' passage mentioned in the introduction: 'Souveränität des Monarchen **oder** des Volkes, **das ist die question**' ('Staatsrechts' 230). The metatextual effect is reinforced by the French layer of the English vocabulary which the word 'question' adds to the Anglo-Saxon monosyllables, a feature which recurs in other early versions of the line. The *First Quarto* has 'To be, or not to be – I, there's the point' (sig. D4^{verso}) and in the first adaptation of the soliloquy the line runs: '**To be, or not to be, I there's the doubt**' (Heminge *Jews' Tragedy* 37).

To compound the self-framing of 'to be or not to be', the complete soliloquy is made conspicuous on stage. Heralded by Polonius, who announces Hamlet's entrance to Claudius, this speech is Hamlet's first utterance after his ominous decision to 'catch the conscience of the king' (2.2.634).

POLONIUS: I heare him coming: withdraw, my lord.
[They withdraw. Enter Hamlet.]
HAMLET: To be, or not to be: that is the question (3.1.63–64).

Claudius, Polonius and Ophelia, who have just withdrawn when Hamlet starts to speak, remain within earshot so that

> the most famous of all soliloquies is not, strictly speaking, a soliloquy at all: three other characters are present although Hamlet speaks as if he is alone (Thompson and Taylor *Hamlet 1603 and 1623* 284, note to line 54).

These witnesses on stage, who complement the theatre audience, lend additional weight to Hamlet's words. Moreover, at least in the First Quarto, he enters 'poring vppon a booke' (*First Quarto* sig. D4[verso]), a marker of quotation which may indicate that the soliloquy is read from a printed page. All in all, the quotability of 'to be or not to be' is overdetermined. Later versions, which still use one or more of its salient features, can afford to be more diffuse because of the association with the forceful original. Although its bland components are completely inconspicuous, the form and internal tension of 'to be or not to be' make it visible as a pre-existing, imported item in most texts – even in *Hamlet* itself.

A quotation?

The semantic and structural characteristics of 'to be or not to be', combined with Shakespeare's presentation in *Hamlet*, enabled this simple string of words to emerge from the general phrase stock of English as a recognizable quotation. The process was more gradual than with other lines – 'A horse, a horse, my kingdom for a horse' was a joke by 1598 (cf. pp. 90–91) – and therefore interesting to observe. Long before tags like 'as Hamlet says' accompanied it by default, we can trace a slowly growing awareness of a noteworthy linguistic item. The first signs that the phrase might be quoted (rather than simply used) are subtle and often equivocal: any suspicion of a *Hamlet* echo must be supported by further evidence such as the more general intertextual habits of certain writers. John Davies of Hereford, for one, produced a vast and stylistically varied *œuvre* that evinces a distinct imitative capacity. The number of verbal overlaps between his writings and *A Lover's Complaint* even led Brian Vickers to re-attribute the latter to Davies rather than to Shakespeare (cf. Vickers *Shakespeare and John Davies*). Whatever the validity of this controversial claim, Davies' propensity for borrowing does make it more probable that certain verb patterns in his poems are *Hamlet* echoes.[8] The following passage was published in 1602, and so could have come on the heels of a *Hamlet* performance.

> And which of both (thinkst thou) would Reason choose?
> **To be** made capable of endlesse blisse,

With possibility the same to loose,
And winne a Hell, where all is quite amisse;
Or not **to Bee** at all, both those to misse:
Sure, Reaz'n the first would choose,
because the last is lowest hell, where highest horror is;
For in **Not-beeings** bottome, being fast,
Ought would to worse then nought, vnworen wast (Davies *Mirum* sig. L1^{recto}).

'To be' and 'not to be' are here treated as separate units and nominalized separately. The two new nouns are framed by an introductory 'which of both' and the verb 'choose'. Davies repeats the syntactic oddity three lines further on, giving the noun 'being' a negative prefix and a genitive ending: 'Not-beeings bottome'. This may be a random gag or the trace of an exciting afternoon at the theatre; the latter hypothesis is supported by the topic of death, which is developed from life-versus-death to eternal-existence-versus-annihilation. Any claim that Davies was thinking of *Hamlet* – which he could not yet have read in print when he was writing – can be supported only by the co-occurrence of these weak markers of intertextuality; Davies is not out to signal a quotation; his writing gives readers a chance to distinguish something that could be one.

Davies' experience as a professional letter writer may account additional intertextual echo in Davies' poem may be inspired by his. The sequence 'or not to be at all' is a cliché from literary love letters, part of the recurring formula 'Wholly yours, or not to be at all' which was recommended by samples in anthologies like the following:

[I] pray you to haue pitie on him, who (attending the rest and final sentence of his death or life) doth humbly kisse your white and delicate hands, beseeching god to giue to you like ioy as his is, who desireth **to be**, Wholy yours, **or not to be** at all. Philiberto of Uirle (Painter sig. ZZZ2^{verso}).

[M]y good desyres [...] greatly couet **to be** accoumpted. Wholy yours, **or not to be** at all. Finis (Chettle *Forest of Fancy* sig. R^{verso} [lines 3681–3689]).

Such courtly, ardent contexts add a cruel, mocking twist to the choice that John Caryll's villainous Richard III offers to Princess Elizabeth: 'Prepare for marriage, or a Funeral / **To be** my Wife, **or not to be at all**' (*English Princess* 26). In Dryden and Lee's *Duke of Guise*, there may be a *Hamlet* hint when Charles IX of France attempts to rouse himself with this phrase: "Tis time to push my slack'nd vengeance home, / **To be a King, or not to be at all**' (287).

Over the seventeenth century, more distinct if still not unequivocal markers for quotation appear. Thomas Heywood's 1635 emblem book *Hierarchy of the Blessed Angels* makes the possible *Hamlet* phrase more conspicuous in an address to an 'Atheist':

> Tell me, (ô thou of Mankind most accurst)
> Whether **to be, or not to be**, was first?
> Whether **to vnderstand, or not to know**?
> **To reason, or not reason**? (well bee't so,
> I make that proposition:) all agree,
> That our our **Not-being**, was before **To be**
> For we that **are now, were not** in Times past:
> Our parents too, ev'n when our moulds were cast,
> Had their progenitors: **their fathers, theirs**:
> So to the first. By which it plaine appeares,
> And by this demonstration 't is most cleare,
> That all of vs **were not**, before **we were** (sig. A6^{recto} [11]).

Again 'to be or not to be' is turned into a noun and spelled with a capital initial. Even if Heywood's topic is different from Hamlet's, this subtle foregrounding can be taken as evidence that Heywood is conscious of using an established phrase. The repetition and the playful modifications – 'not being' rather than 'not to be', 'to do or not to do' – confirm this. Finally, there may even be an echo of Claudius' bathetic consolation to Hamlet: 'you must know, your father lost a father; / **That father lost, lost his**' (1.2.93–94), completing a group of markers that is more salient than that in Davies' poems. A similar number of weak signals can be found in Abraham Cowley's powerful 'Life and Fame':

> Oh Life, thou Nothings younger Brother!
> So like, that one might take One for the other!
> What's Some Body, or No Body?
> In all the Cobwebs of the Schoolmens trade,
> We no <u>such nice Distinction</u> woven see,
> <u>As 'tis</u> **To be, or not to Be.**
> **Dream of a Shadow**! a Reflection made
> From the false glories of the gay reflected Bow,
> Is a more solid thing then Thou (*Works* 2:201–202).

Like Heywood, Cowley nominalizes 'to be or not to be' and emphasizes this by capital letters. The phrase 'dream of a shadow' may echo Hamlet's 'A dream itself is but a shadow' (2.2.279). Individually, nominalization, capitalization, variation, typography and positioning may mean nothing more than the 'scare quotes' or 'shudder quotes' that have come to indicate emphasis or ironical distance from a string of words. When they occur all together and are supported by a nihilistic mood similar to Hamlet's, these devices provide quite credible evidence of quotation.

Quite a few of the passages discussed so far modify 'to be or not to be' in ways that sound not so much like quotations as like the kind of wordplay we like to make on common phrases. Is there such a big difference between a *Guardian* headline that runs '**To beard** or not to beard' and one that introduces flatbread recipes with '**Flat's** the Way to Do It'? Technically, the two puns are distinguishable only by the derivation of the phrase that is played with. Both 'To be or not to be' and 'That's the way to do it' have a form which is implicitly recognized as basic and which is distorted in punning; in both cases, the comic effect lies in the difference between the 'original' and the modified form. Whether the author of the 'original' is non-existent (in the case of idioms) and merely irrelevant (in the case of casual quotations), playful modifications confirm that we are thinking of a pre-existing unit with an original form (cf. Langlotz *Idiomatic Creativity*). Modification can even be used to identify casual quotations, as in Philip Ayres' poem 'Love's New Philosophy' from 1687, which could be read as playing around with a recognizable item:

> Whilst in this Torment I remain,
> <u>It is no Mystery</u> **To be, and not to be;**
> I dye to Joy, and live to Pain.
> So that, my Fair, I may be justly sed,
> **to be, and not to be,** Alive and Dead (Ayres 66, emphasis mine).

If this is a quotation, it modifies *Hamlet* in new ways. The two halves of the dilemma are forced together by substituting 'and' for 'or' in the second line; the last line extends the stark infinitives 'to be' and 'not to be' into the more bathetic 'to be alive' and 'to be dead'; and '*Alive and Dead*' paraphrases 'to be or not to be' with the new 'and'. These somewhat heavy-handed games may indicate that something familiar is being handled. However, there is no *Hamlet* context; the lines' position in the penultimate stanza of a 70-line poem may also evoke the standardized closing formula for love letters that I mentioned before. Twelve years later, John Mason's 'Dives and Lazarus' treated 'to be or not to be' more lightly, just with a telling nominalization:

> Nothing's a Barren Womb. If that could breed,
> **To be** and **not to be** were well agreed (Mason 16).

Mason turns Hamlet's dilemma into two nouns that might be reunited ('agreed'); this split refers to Hamlet's difficulty of choosing between the components of a single noun phrase. Both poems support the conclusion that something 'like a general recognition of the unsurpassable quotableness of Shakespeare's lines' (Bentley 75) had been established by the 1690s.

A quotation!

As Shakespeare's quotability established itself in in the early eighteenth century, a new kind of evidence for quotations being meant as quotations becomes available: the habits of individual writers who are particularly apt to quote Shakespeare. If a writer's work contains several undoubted references, quotation can be more plausibly assumed in more ambiguous passages. Daniel Defoe, for example, quotes Shakespeare at least 30 times, although he only started after 1700, at the age of 40 (cf. Moore 72). These quotations include the striking couplet that is mentioned in the Introduction: 'Would **the Great Be, and *not to Be*** Divide, / And all the Doubts of *Entity* decide' (*Hymn* 10). Nominalization indicates that this is a quotation and 'Doubts of Entity' may allude to Hamlet's indecision. Other less certain versions include the following:

> Might end by death all human misery, / Might have it in our choice, **to be, or not to be** (*Political History* 38).
> [He] left her at liberty either **to tell him or not to tell him** (*Moll Flanders* 49).
> [I]t was necessary that we should resolve either **to go, or not to go** (*Robinson Crusoe* 154).
> [I]was impossible for her to resolve what wou'd be fit **to do, or not to do**, till she was there (*Roxana* 215).

The topic of suicide in the first of these passages, together with the supporting evidence of 'The Great Be' and the fact of Defoe's other Shakespeare references may lead readers to decide that some or all of the following passages are quotations.

By the mid-eighteenth century, Shakespeare quotation had become a done thing and quotations were more frequently marked in less equivocal ways, often including marking for derivation. This development is accompanied by shifts in the use of typographical markers. Before 1700, markers for emphasis and quotation could be confused with each other; in the eighteenth century, the two were 'becoming distinct' (King 41). Inverted commas, which were closed after the last word of the inserted phrase, established themselves as the accepted standard for literary quotation (King

53), although markers such as spacing, parentheses and italics could also still be found (cf. King 52). A passage from 1736 uses small caps for Hamlet's line: '*Charles I* declared, that *Parliaments* themselves were, by the Constitution, to BE or NOT TO BE, at his Pleasure' (Osborne 798) and in 1758, the Earl of Chesterfield capitalized it as follows: '**To BE, or NOT To BE**, is a question of much less importance, in my mind, than **to be or not to be** well' (*Letters* 555). The first French edition of Chesterfield's letters reflects the fame that the line had acquired by 1777: the line is given in English and set in italics.

> Ayez soin de votre santé autant que vous pourrez, car *to be or not to be* **est une question** de bien moin d'importance, selon moi, que *to be or not to be well* (*Lettres* 4:177).

The striking English insert also includes Chesterfield's jokey, bathetic extension 'to be well'. This kind of addition to Hamlet's phrase, which removes the extraordinary existential quality of the double *to*-infinitive, had been introduced in 1687 in Philip Ayres' 'to be, and not to be, / Alive and Dead' (66). In the later eighteenth century, it became a popular comic effect, as in Isaac Bickerstaff's comic opera *The Padlock* (1768):

> DIEGO: Thoughts to council – Let me see –
>   Hum – **to be, or not to be,**
>   A husband **is the question** (1).

Fumbling for something to say, Diego is relieved to remember the *Hamlet* catchphrase, whose banal use is clearly meant to show him up as half-educated; the presentation of the complete line, even though interrupted by 'a husband', leaves no doubt that this is a quotation.

The overt, clearly signalled quotation in direct speech in *The Padlock* is typical of mid-eighteenth-century literature, where it becomes widely used, 'sophisticated tool for characterization' (Rumbold *Eighteenth-Century* 8). Quoting Shakespeare can be admirable or ridiculous or anything in between. Samuel Richardson, for example, makes both a maidservant and a young upper-class gentleman quote *Hamlet* to very different effects. Here is the foppish aristocrat pleased to have found a conversational cue for a Shakespeare quotation:

> Lord *Jackey*, in the Language of some Character in a Play, cry'd out, **A palpable Hit,** by Jupiter, and laughed egregiously, running about from one to another, repeating the same Words (*Pamela* 3:205).

The maidservant Pamela, who describes this scene in a letter, does not seem to identify the quotation although she (mis-)quotes 'Angels and ministers of grace' as something she 'had read in a book a night or two before' (1:37). Richardson is clearly at pains to establish 'that his lowborn [Pamela] is capable of reading *Hamlet*, even if she then misquotes the text' (Keymer 123 and 124). Some of Richardson's ambivalence may stem from insecurity; research indicates that many of his 'pedestrian, didactic and artless' quotations (Connaughton 194) may be taken from popular anthologies. Richardson's contemporary and rival Henry Fielding, with no reason to be self-conscious about education, treated Shakespeare quotation in a more relaxed manner. The narrative of the erudite 'Author' figure in *Tom Jones* is studded with all manner of quotations, also in Latin, but takes a careful distance from the habit of overt Shakespeare quotation that may already have felt too fashionable to Fielding. Claudius' line 'When sorrows come, they come not single spies, / But in battalions' (*Hamlet* 4.5.83-84) expresses a commonsensical platitude in a military metaphor. Fielding's 'Author' gives it back its commonplace, proverbial form but adds a rather mystifying introduction: 'It hath been observed <u>by some Man of much greater Reputation for Wisdom than myself</u>, that **Misfortunes** seldom **come single**' (131). This phrasing, superficially a vague kind of marking for derivation, does not so much *mark* as practically *mask* the quotation, as if The 'Author', in line with Fielding's friendly scorn for so many fashionable (ab-) uses, was indulging the trend for explicitly marked Shakespeare only in a politely mocking, distant manner.

By the late 1770s, the elaborate marking of Fielding, Richardson and their peers was on the wane and more lightly framed forms of casual quotation became the norm. Writers continued to mark a substantial part of their borrowings but now assumed a familiarity that could dispense with detailed information. In this climate, almost any tag of the 'to verb or not to verb' kind could be read as *Hamlet* lite, as a careless, well-mannered homage to a 'celebrated line', as in this magazine article from 1773:

> The Thought is Comprised <u>in this celebrated line</u>: '**To be, or not to be? that is the question.**' but <u>a question of this kind</u> can have no foundation in the nature of things, [...]. **To be, or not to be? is not the question** with an enlighten'd and discerning mind [...]. But happyness, or misery hereafter, Which, as we now persue, we shall acquire, Which of them we shall then possess? **that is The high important question** which concerns us (Anon. 'Correction' 283).

The irredeemable tedium of such 'banal Shakespeare' (cf. Rumbold 'Common-Hackneyed') is not even relieved when 'to be or not to be' attracts quite creditable additional *Hamlet* echoes:

> What is it all but *Fooling*?
> If men will think, if men will see,
> <u>That all this</u> *To, – or not to be*,
> Is as we're hot, or cooling
> To-day on Expectation's wing,
> To-morrow off, *'tis not the thing*,
> ***What is the thing?*** – why Fooling (Stevens 246–247).

The possible echo of 'the play's the thing' (*Hamlet* 2.2.633) does not do much for profundity here; quoting *Hamlet* is unavoidably and disappointingly banal. This perception carried over into literary dialogue, where characters that practice overt marking sound inevitably faddish or pretentious. In John Minshull's comedy *He Stoops to Conquer*, whose title is itself a comic quotation, we find (in 1804) a maidservant who seems to have been to the theatre: 'O my good Signora, now is the time of trial <u>as the man says in the play</u>, **To be, or not to be**' (Minshull 24). In fact, a *LION* search for the phrase 'as the man says in the play' yields a dozen hits in plays and novels before 1830, introducing, among others, three *Hamlet* quotations and one from *Macbeth*. Even the apparently genuine memory of a performance cannot make such quotations sound impressive. Although Hannah Cowley's Sir Marvel Mushroom has picked up Hamlet's line in the theatre rather from a quotation dictionary, the way in which he conflates the role with the star actor confirms the lack of sophistication implicit in his name:

> [Please] introduce me to Lady Beauville [because] **not to be** at her route, would be **to be and not to be** – <u>as Kemble says</u>. Pray Ma'am have you seen Kemble? (Cowley *More Ways* 90).

As Shakespeare turns into Hamlet and Hamlet into a star of the stage, quotation becomes just a brief flash in the cant of celebrity-watching.

Around the turn of the nineteenth century, Hamlet's question had a brief period of specialization on the weighty subject of marriage. One such passage has been quoted in the Introduction: '**To be, or not to be, that was the question,** and **a question** which Sophia could not answer'; here are two more which both use 'to be or not to be' as shorthand for 'dilemma'.

> WHITTLE: Your daughter –
> SIR PATRICK: Your wife that is **to be**. Go on –
> WHITTLE: My wife that is **not to be** – Zounds! will you hear me?
> SIR PATRICK: **To be, or not to be, is that the question?** I can swear too, if it wants a little of that (Garrick *Irish Widow* 33–34).
> WIDOW GREEN: What! – Master Waller, and contemplative!

32   To Quote or Not to Quote

> Presumptive proof of love! Of me he thinks!
> Re[s]olves <u>the point</u> 'to be or not to be!'
> 'To be!' by all the triumphs of my sex! (Knowles *Love-Chase* 51–52).

The expansion into 'be married', 'be a husband' or similar was understandably popular, too: 'A Widow knows the Good, and Bad, of Life / And, has it in her Choice, **to be, or not to be,** a Wife!' (Philips *Humphrey* 88). Finally there were, of course, 'to marry or not to marry' (the title of at least one poem, one novel and one comedy) and, perfectly iambic, 'to wed or not to wed'. The latter became the most perfect opening for at least twenty topical parodies of Hamlet's soliloquy that are discussed in Chapter 5. These uses of Shakespeare really push the boundaries of banality, most symptomatic of the Romantic epidemic of Shakespeare quotation (cf. Chapter 6). Small wonder that Maria Edgeworth concluded in 1826 that '"**To be or not to be**" – **is a question** we can no longer bear' (Edgeworth 'Bores' 325). But of course the line had to be borne for two more centuries.

'To be or not to be' continued to be quoted until it was the epitome of intertextual paralysis, just as an early version of *Hamlet* was for Thomas Nashe (cf. Introduction). In 1901, it is described as ripe for a mercy killing in *Longman's Magazine*: the journalist uses 'to be or not to be' to exemplify the sad fate of 'shreds of literature' in need of a 'happy despatch'. This sad situation comes at the end of a complete life story of a 'poor quotation', which intriguingly develops the family metaphor that is implicit in Barthes' terms 'paternity' and 'filiation'. Even the humble quotation mark is given a position in the family saga:

> [B]egotten of some noble father, no sooner has [a quotation] passed the pains of birth than it is torn by some alien from the nourishing bosom of its mother context, and wrapt in the swaddling clothes of inverted commas: interest or brief affection move one putative father after another to undertake its maintenance; the swaddling clothes are taken off by one of them, but another, ignorant of the adolescent's years, swathes it up again, until at last, in books, its maturity is recognised, and thenceforth it is left severely alone; but there remains for it a dishonoured and mutilated old age on the lips of common men (Fowler 'Longman's Magazine' 67).

With predictable gendering, a quotation's origins are assigned to the womb-like original context and a male author, its 'onlie begetter'. To be quoted is to be painfully detached from the mother text, to be born into a confusing, unsafe textual world where paternity is uncertain and can be faked. The literary sin of casual quotation is likened to a sexual scandal – it would require a paternity suit to decide whether 'to be or not to be' is quoted appropriately.

Beyond quotation

In a pleasing parallel with the lightening of Victorian morality in the twentieth century, casual quotations have become more frequent and less scandalous. A few years after the sexual revolution had broken, Roland Barthes decreed that texts and presumably quotations could 'be read without the guarantee of [a] father' ('Work to Text' 161). Their 'dishonoured' old age forgotten, phrases like 'to be or not to be' have come back to life as adaptable phrasal templates. 'Snowclones', in twenty-first-century terminology, are fixed expressions with blank slots such as 'in space, no-one can verb', 'have something, will travel' or 'keep calm and carry on verb-ing'. Three years after the term had been coined in 2003, 'to be or not to be' headed a list of snowclones in the *New Scientist*:

> Snowclones spring from a rich diversity of sources, from Shakespeare ('To X or not to X?') to *Star Trek* ('It's X, but not as we know it.') and movie titles ('Dude, where's my X?') – if the source is known at all. Who, for instance, knows the origin of the snowclone 'X is my middle name'? (Anon. 'Snowclone' 80).

Most people who use a snowclone do know or even wonder about its origin, and this is the state in which Shakespeare's phrase structure can now go on in countless reincarnations and with countless new verbs. Thanks to the force of the particle 'to' and the elasticity of English grammar, the 'verb' in 'to verb or not to verb' does not even need to be a verb. Linguists have wondered whether **'to Grice or not to Grice'** in the *Journal of Pragmatics* (cf. Mey 911), and questions like **'to bikini or not to bikini'** or 'to bidet or not to bidet' yield dozens of Google hits. The 'verb' does not even need to be a word: the online *Urban Dictionary* has a separate entry for **'2b or not 2b'**. Shakespearean snowclones are quotations that have died and come back to haunt us as friendly ghosts; as oblivious to their origins as any idiom or everyday pun, they have no need to wail 'Remember me!' For a rough idea of just how much these words are cut off from the text that made them famous, I did several Google searches for <"to be or not to be"> and for <"to be or not to be" -Hamlet -Shakespeare>. Every time, the number of hits for the second search, i.e. the number of completely unmarked quotations, amounted to at least 90% of the number of hits for the first, more general search. In German, Spanish, Portuguese, French, Russian and Italian, the figures ranged between 84% and 98%. It seems safe to say, even allowing for search engine vagaries, we that in the twenty-first century, 'to be or not to be' is most frequently encountered in contexts that do *not* contain the words 'Hamlet' or 'Shakespeare'. Having passed through *Hamlet*, 'to be or not to be' has re-entered the English language with more options than it had before 1600. It can be used as a fully paid-up literary quotation; it can function as an anonymous structural blueprint; its Shakespearean 'origin' may be remembered or not, and if it is remembered, this memory may be significant or not. The following chapters investigate these varieties of casual Shakespeare quotation in their historical development up to the Romantic Age, beginning with the three main kinds of Shakespeare's own casual borrowings in Chapters 2–4: folk materials and Scripture, the Latin classics and English texts.

Notes

1 Milton *Paradise Lost* 59 (Book II, lines 103–106). Interestingly, *Paradise Lost*, Milton's panegyric to free will, does not contain a single instance of 'to verb or not to verb', not even in Satan's most Marlovian speeches.
2 The phrase evidently had a powerful appeal, cf. two other passages: 'power of our understanding **to believe, or not to believe**' (Ainsworth 5) and 'a mans free will **to believe, or not to believe**, to obey or disobey the Gospel of truth preached' (Cartwright 360).
3 An example from 1575: 'Thy will be my will, and my will be always to folow thy will. Let there be ever in me one will and one desire with thee, and let me never desire **to will or not to will** but as thou wilt' (Bull 182).
4 Twisse uses the formula 'to be or not to be' six more times in the same paragraph.
5 In other languages, the phrase is less elegant and versatile. Danish 'At vaere eller ikke vaere' or Italian 'essere o non essere' are unwieldily polysyllabic, while Spanish 'ser o no ser' lacks the metrical relief of unaccented syllables and French 'être ou ne pas être' is clumsy. The striking German word 'Nichtsein' (nonbeing) that features in the canonical Schlegel-Tieck translation has had very little life independent of *Hamlet*. The exception are philosophical treatises, where 'Nichtsein' was used already before Christoph Wieland's pioneering German translation of *Hamlet* in the 1760s.
6 My initial exploration of this topic was greatly advanced by an unpublished manuscript which Brian Vickers generously shared.
7 Other possible sources include passages in Stobaeus and Eusebius, Plutarch's *Consolatio ad Apollonium,* Xenophon's *Cyropaideia*, Montaigne's *Essais* and Philippe de Mornay's *Discourse of Life and Death* as translated by the Countess of Pembroke (cf. Baldwin *Small Latine* 2:604 and 2:605 and Anders 275).
8 Charles O. Fox lists echoes like '(all-)devouring time' between the Sonnets and some complimentary verses by Davies which preface John Guillim's *A Display of Heraldrie* of 1610 (370).

2 'He should be stop'd': Too-Casual Shakespeare

All that he doth write
Is pure his own.
LEONARD DIGGES (1640)

In Shakespeare's time, quotability was easier to achieve than in any other period before electronic copy-pasting. Renaissance education was 'based largely on the collection and use of commonplaces' (Knowles 'Shorthand' 153) and quotation, the decontextualized re-use of small portions of texts, was taken for granted. In Elizabethan grammar schools, the 'reading and translating of classical texts [...] was intended ultimately to enable them not to display mastery in reading a dead language but to write' (Burrow 39). Erasmus recommended having 'the greatest number of [quotations] on hand and in ready money as it were' (*On Copia* 87). Anthony Scoloker wrote in his dedication to *Daiphantus*: 'If [an author] haue caught vp half a Line of any others, / It was out of his Memorie, not of any ignorance' (sig. A2^{verso}). As Roland Barthes would have put it, inherited and reconfigured 'lexias' were exceptionally mobile, 'displaced from reader to reader' (Barthes 'Valdemar' 172) and indeed from writer to writer with unprecedented ease in a dense verbal traffic (cf. Clare *Shakespeare's Stage Traffic*) in which every textual component was 'susceptible to recombination' (Taylor 'Middleton' 32). Shakespeare was thriving in this climate, as the *Hamlet* sample confirms. At least five hundred phrases and images from the 3000 lines of the play (this count excludes expressions like 'I will, my lord') are on record in the *HyperHamlet* database as having been identified in older texts. The actual number of passages that replicate proverbs or *sententiae*, Scriptural tags, phrases from the classics or from recent English books may be considerably higher, but even at the most conservative count, about every sixth line of the play can be related to an identifiable earlier text. A remarkable number of comments and anecdotes confirm that using other people's words was early on perceived as intrinsic to Shakespeare's 'distinctly reactive' creativity (Lynch 188). The attitudes range from an almost moral indignation at irreverence and literary theft through patronizing remarks on an undisciplined imagination to admiration for abundant and elegant quotations. Chapter 3 discusses contemporary praise for the classical references used by 'honey-tongued Shakespeare' while this chapter starts from the critical comments that deplore Shakespeare's irreverent puns and allusive folksiness.

Shakespeare's puns and 'such like, which were ridiculous'

The difference between puns and casual quotations is smaller than one might think and was even smaller in the sixteenth century, when the word 'allusion' could still mean 'pun'. Puns are fundamentally intertextual because they echo verbal surfaces and because the memory of the original, incongruous 'meanings' (Hollander 63) of these surface verbal elements is what makes puns funny. The share a basically intertextual structure with quotations, the repetition of a short verbal element in a new context. Shakespeare was doing these all the time. In a mid-seventeenth-century anecdote, he and Ben Jonson were one day playfully composing rhyming epitaphs for themselves. Jonson had written: 'Here lies Ben Jonson – who was once one'. Shakespeare 'took the pen from him' and topped the wordplay: 'Here lies Benjamin, with short hair upon his chin, / Who while he lived was a slow thing, and now he's buried is no thing' ('Plume Manuscript' quoted in Munro 2:68). This is stand-up comedy mode, taking up and taking advantage of a conversational cue or a heckler's comment. It is also a pun when Hamlet quips: 'The King is a thing [...] of nothing' (4.2.28–30). We may never learn whether the compiler of the 'Plume Manuscript' took his cue from *Hamlet* in reconstructing or making up a biographical episode, whether Shakespeare quoted his own play or whether he remembered that exchange with Jonson when penning *Hamlet*. Both the *Hamlet* passage and the conversational joke may be echoing Psalm 144:4 'Man is like a thing of nought' or Isaiah 41:12 'the men that war against thee [shall be] as a thing of nought'. Endlessly repeated and shifted from reader to reader, this lexia has become a commonplace, and given the spectacular ease with which Shakespeare picked up phrases, it is pointless to enquire whether it is 'quoted'.

Several contemporaries proffered advisory comments on Shakespeare's cavalier handling of his sources. Ben Jonson, who probably knew him best, could be quite unsentimental about his friend's endless jokes. He disliked all 'promoters of other mens iests' that habitually stuff their texts with other people's materials 'as if their inuention liu'd wholy vpon another mans trencher' ('Cynthia's Revels' 184). The most annoying instance for Jonson was an inappropriately humorous use of Julius Caesar's name:

> Many times [Shakespeare] fell into those things, could not escape laughter; as when he said in the person of Caesar, one speaking to

him, 'Caesar, thou dost me wrong; he replied, 'Caesar did never wrong, but with just cause'; and such like, which were ridiculous ('Discoveries' 539–540).

One may wonder what exactly Jonson found so 'ridiculous'. Perhaps he disapproved of the too-casual reference to a great historical figure, or he thought of it as a pun, which would have been appropriate only in 'comedy and other non-serious usage' (Silk 19). Disapproval of puns would link Jonson to the eighteenth-century scorn for puns as the 'fatal Cleopatra', 'the golden apple' for which Shakespeare would 'always [...] stoop from his elevation' (Johnson 'Preface to Shakespeare' 2398).[1] In 1657, the antiquarian Thomas Plume aligned the anecdote with one of Shakespeare's geographical howlers: 'He – said – Caesar never punishes any but for a just Cause & another time [Shakespeare] makes Athyns in Bohemia' (quoted in Chambers *Facts and Problems* 2:247). In the eighteenth century, critics unwilling to find fault with Shakespeare attempted to shift the blame for the embarrassing item. One of them explained the quip as 'some blunder of an actor' (Furness 137) that is preserved in Jonson's anecdote; others assumed that Jonson did not report Shakespeare's utterance correctly, either because his memory was failing or because the 'surly Laureate' was intent on 'wounding the memory of a poet' (Furness 137). If nothing else, 'the heat of composition' (Furness 138) apparent in an early draft could excuse Shakespeare. Colin Burrow, in 2013, shows more equanimity: he calls this 'magnificent' line 'either an oxymoron or a tautology, or perhaps a miraculous fusion of the two' and explains it as a failed early 'attempt to evoke absolute moral authority' which was then revised out of *Julius Caesar* (217). In fact, suggestions have been made as to where the sentence could fit into that play, for example in act 3, scene 2, where it could come 'very humorously [from] the mouth of a Plebeian' (Furness 136), but it has never been accepted as plainly and intentionally part of Shakespeare's definitive work: too silly, too funny, too casual.

Maybe the Julius Caesar who 'did never wrong' seemed inappropriately 'ridiculous' to Ben Jonson because he was too folksy. Shakespeare's characters mention the Roman general more than twenty times as a stock figure of popular legend. These rather simple uses of a familiar type form an intriguing contrast to the complex characterization of both Caesar and Brutus in Shakespeare's own play. Julius Caesar is just one of many Biblical, historical or mythical personages who recur with fixed, folkloric attributes in Shakespeare's plays. He is the murdered general who said 'veni vidi vici', just as Cain is the first murderer, Jephthah the unhappy father and Socrates the comic downtrodden husband in Petruchio's claim that he' would marry any woman 'rich enough' even if she were 'as foul [...] As Socrates' Xanthippe, or a worse' (*Taming* 1.2.68–72). Such a figure is Shakespeare's Julius Caesar outside the cosmos of the Roman plays. Sometimes he is simply comic, inspiring uneasy jokes about mortality (Hamlet reminds Horatio that 'Imperious Caesar, dead and turn'd to clay, / Might stop a hole to keep the wind away' (5.1.220–221)) or serving to mock the absurdly named Pompey Bum in *Measure for Measure*: 'How now, noble Pompey! What, at the wheels of Caesar? art thou led in triumph?' (3.2.44–45). Alternately, phrases like 'a disaster of war that **Caesar himself could not have prevented**' (*All's Well* 3.6.52–54) or 'a soldier fit to stand by **Caesar** / And give direction' (*Othello* 2.3.26–27)[2] make him the epitome of military glory; the highest praise for a soldier is '**Caesar's Caesar**' (*Richard III* 4.4.350), a folksy doubling like 'out-heroding Herod'.

Macbeth makes a subtler reference to Julius Caesar when he feels condemned by the virtue of Banquo, by which his 'Genius is rebuked; as, it is said, / **Mark Antony's was by Caesar**' (*Macbeth* 3.1.61–62). The detail about Mark Antony may come from Plutarch's *Life of Caesar*, which Shakespeare studied in the late 1590s in preparation for writing *Julius Caesar* (cf. Wechsler and Sträuli 41), but the tag 'it is said' frames the anecdote as a piece of folklore. Once again, Shakespeare marks one kind of source as another and makes popular memory and classical historiography indistinguishable. The reverse swap can be observed in *Richard III*, where Prince Edward, soon to be put to death in '**Julius Caesar's ill-erected tower**' (*Richard II* 5.1.2), quizzes Buckingham about the Tower of London with a touching schoolboy curiosity:

> PRINCE EDWARD: I do not like the Tower, of any place.
> **Did Julius Caesar build that place**, my lord? [...]
> PRINCE EDWARD: Is it upon record, or else reported
> Successively from age to age, he built it?
> BUCKINGHAM: Upon record, my gracious lord.
> PRINCE EDWARD: But say, my lord, it were not regist'red,
>   Methinks the truth should live from age to age,
>   As 'twere retail'd to all posterity,
>   Even to the general all-ending day [...]
>   **That Julius Caesar was a famous man** (*Richard III* 3.1.69–85).

This is a sweet and clever child developing what he has learnt at school; the conversation turns the legend that Julius Caesar built the Tower of London into a historical 'record'. A similarly careful explanation of school syllabus details looks less good on the elderly councillor Polonius. He prides himself on having been 'accounted a good actor' for playing the Roman dictator in a student performance and then spoils the effect of his anecdote somewhat by adding: 'I was killed i'th'Capitol. Brutus killed me.' This spells out the single most popular, proverbial fact about Caesar, which everybody in contemporary audiences knew from school primers, from reading a Roman historian or from attending a play such as the anonymous 1595 *Caesar and Pompey* or indeed Shakespeare's own *Julius Caesar*. This is embarrassing, and Hamlet reacts with a double pun that is every bit as embarrassing, as if to emphasize Polonius' comic pedantry: 'It was a brute part of him to kill so capital a calf there' (3.2.109–112). TMI.

The popular *Julius Caesar* has just one feature that could be called a quotation: the phrase 'veni, vidi, vici'. Shakespeare uses it five times, always to comic effect; even the one Latin version does not really denote a historical context. The language switch is given centre stage only briefly:

> BOYET: [...] Zenelophon [...] might rightly say, **Veni, vidi, vici;** which to annothanize in the vulgar – O base and obscure vulgar! – videlicet, **He came, saw, and overcame:** he came, one; saw two; overcame, three. Who came? the king (4.1.74–79).

This elaborate marking, which includes a translation and a comment, enables audience members who do not understand Latin to appreciate Boyet's baroque ramblings and to feel superior and smart *with* him at the very moment when he is slighting their own language. The publican in *The Merry Wives of Windsor*, talking to Falstaff, blends the phrase and the name of its author: 'Thou'rt an emperor – **Caesar, Keiser,** and **Pheazar**' (1.7.9–10). This almost Joycean creativity is reminiscent of Leopold Bloom falling asleep at the end of *Ulysses*:

> He rests. He has travelled. With? Sinbad the Sailor and Tinbad the Tailor and Jinbad the Jailer and Whinbad the Whaler and Ninbad the Nailer and Finbad the Failer and [...] Linbad the Yailer and Xinbad the Phthailer (Joyce 606–607).

The other instances of Caesar's famous phrase are in English, and they all deprecate it or its author. Falstaff applies it to himself, boasting about a brawl: 'he saw me, and yielded; that I may justly say, with the hook-nosed fellow of Rome, "There, cousin, I came, saw, and overcame"' (*2 Henry IV* 4.3.40–42). Two more mentions are made by women, who both nominalize the phrase. Nominalization may express a certain respect, as when Daniel Defoe speaks of 'the Great Be, and not to Be' (Defoe *Hymn* 10); it can also belittle the quoted expression. This happens in *Cymbeline*, where the Queen mocks Caesar's inability to conquer Britain, which has worsted 'his brag / Of "came", and "saw", and "overcame"' (3.1.26–27). In contrast, Rosalind in *As You Like It* has no patriotic issues with Caesar, and uses this understated marking device with wonderful lightness; her marking for derivation doubles as throwaway mockery of both Caesar and masculine pretence in general.

> ROSALIND: O, I know where you are: nay, 'tis true: there was never any thing so sudden but the fight of two rams and Caesar's

thrasonical brag of 'I came, saw, and overcame:' for your brother and my sister no sooner met but they looked, no sooner looked but they loved (5.2.33–35).

This is very cheeky. With an adjective that is itself a classical allusion (to the legendary, boastful Indo-Greek ruler Thraso), Rosalind hitches the greatest of Roman names to two unreasoning male animals, with an extraordinary confidence *vis-à-vis* the overwhelmingly masculine Latin canon. The impressive swiftness of Caesar's military campaign in Gaul is made a ridiculous analogy for people who fall overhastily in love. Rosalind's marking for derivation does not express respect for or interest in the names she drops; Caesar's sole function is to underline the charm of a witty girl.

Rosalind's happy fluency – 'When I think, I must speak' (*As You Like It* 3.2.253) – sounds like a beautifully elaborate and crafted version of the looser and coarser spontaneous wit that is evident in certain 'Shakespeareana'. All of the anecdotes and tidbits that describe William Shakespeare's conversation include improvised puns and quotations, and there is some reason to believe that also 'Caesar did never wrong' was not so much a cul-de-sac in the composition history of *Julius Caesar* as a typically casual bit of everyday banter. When Jonson says that '[m]any times he fell into those things', he seems to report a token incident, one of too many 'such like' to mention, one of those jokes that one just had to expect from Will. No less than four of Jonson's verb forms suggest a spoken rather than written phrase: 'said', 'replied', 'with one speaking to him' and, especially 'speaking in the person of Caesar'. The 'Virgil' in Jonson's *Poetaster* that has been identified as Shakespeare tends to 'repeat part of his workes, / As fit for any conference he can vse' (293). 'Conference' can be a bit of dialogue in a play as well as a real-life conversation that plays around with remembered lines. Jonson similarly links written and spoken quotation when he criticizes both 'the stale *apothegmes*, or olde books' which quoters 'can heare of (in print, or otherwise)' and the wit they find in 'euerie laundresse, or hackney-man' ('Cynthia's Revels' 184). To 'hear of' things 'in print' expresses the contiguity of writing and reading, stage speech, play script and everyday chit-chat that is central to Shakespeare's linguistic playfulness. One indeed 'fancies' that Shakespeare 'received as much from the spoken word as he did from the printed page' (Davenport 371). For Shakespeare, 'mind and hand went together' (Preface to the *First Folio* quoted in Chambers *Sources* 44) and we may add, so did his mouth. In all the media in which we 'hear' Shakespeare, in authored print, in reminiscence, reported speech and in theatrical banter, puns and quotations are at their intertextual game. As the godfather to one of Jonson's children, he promised 'a douzen good Lattin Spoones' which the more formally learned Jonson should 'translate'; the word 'latten' designates a cheap metal and is on record in the OED as having first been used 'with a pun on Latin' in 1607 in 'Congealing English Tynne, Græcian Gold, Romaine Latine all in a lumpe' (Tomkis *Lingua* sig. F2^{verso}). Since Ben Jonson married in 1594 and had children baptized between 1596 and 1610, Shakespeare perhaps did originate this pun. Perhaps he, too, was quoting something, suiting his purpose by recycling a recent or familiar joke. In any case, the result is, again, slightly embarrassing, and not as polished as the lines that did make it into his plays.

The most embarrassing Shakespeare anecdote of all perfectly fits the pattern of undisciplined intertextuality that I have described, and was provided with the same kind of scholarly excuses that followed Caesar doing wrong 'with just cause'. In a famous diary entry of 1602, the lawyer John Manningham recounts how an enthusiastic theatregoer invited Richard Burbage to her home after his exciting performance as Richard III. Shakespeare got there first,

> was entertained, and at his game ere Burbidge came. Then message being brought that Rich. the 3.d was at the door, Shakespeare caused return to be made that William the was before Rich the 3 (quoted in Munro 1:98).

Ouch. What is worse here: the vulgarity or the punning? E. K. Chambers defuses the story by noting that it is 'an adaptation of an old motive, traceable in late Greek and in French and Italian literature, long before Manningham's day' (Chambers *Sources* 50). This explanation turns Manningham's report into a fabrication and absolves Shakespeare from creating yet another 'ridiculous' quip (and possibly from fornication). Of course, it could also have been Shakespeare who was casually quoting an old chestnut so that Manningham could have been truthful when he reported that 'William the Conqueror' was able to indulge in allusive wordplay even when 'entertaining'. The two-edged account of Shakespeare's conversation in a famous passage in Ben Jonson's reminiscences confirms at least the readiness in repartee:

> Hee was (indeed) honest, and of an open, and free nature: had an excellent Phantasie; brave notions, and gentle expressions: wherein hee flow'd with that facility, that sometime it was necessary he should be stop'd: Sufflaminandus erat; as Augustus said of Haterius. His wit was in his own power; would the rule of it had beene so too ('Discoveries' 539).

This acknowledges a fertile imagination ('phantasie') full of noble concepts ('brave notions') and abundant in smoothly flowing phrases ('gentle expressions'). Whether these phrases were his own or not seems irrelevant; inspiration and imitation become indistinguishable in an indiscriminately voluble flow of verbal echo and verbal improvisation. It is extremely characteristic that Jonson underscores his critique of this flow in a fully referenced Latin quotation, which provides an added reproof of a facility that could be perceived as thoughtlessness, as a lack of the appropriately meaningful reference to an original context. Later in the seventeenth century, Jonson's disapproval solidified into a reputation for sloppiness: Shakespeare's work is called 'a fine Garden, but it wanted weeding' (quoted in Munro 1:lii) and Edward Phillips speaks of 'unfiled expressions' and 'rambling and undigested Fancys' (quoted in Munro 1:lii). In the *First Folio* of Beaumont and Fletcher's complete works of 1647, Jonson's 'flow' metaphor, which contains some admiration for the abundance of Shakespeare's imagination, becomes definitely patronizing: 'Brave Shakespear flow'd, yet had his Ebbings too, Often above Himselfe, sometimes below' (Beaumont and Fletcher *Comedies and tragedies*, unpaginated front matter).

'Old odd ends': Shakespeare's (scriptural) pop culture

The half-annoyed, half-admiring puzzlement that Shakespeare's verbal 'flow' provoked in contemporaries and critics is also recognizable in the onstage reactions he scripted for characters that are confronted with 'conference' as (over-)'flowing' as his own. Hamlet has often been romantically identified with Shakespeare himself, but in the graveyard scene, it is the First Gravedigger who sounds most like the exasperating joker of Shakespearean anecdotes, while Hamlet is cast as the eye-rolling listener. The Gravedigger's conversation includes all the popular genres that fed Shakespeare's textual imagination: he recycles and combines songs, proverbs, Biblical snippets, legal lore and time-honoured jests. After expounding on the legal implications of Ophelia's possible suicide and the privileges of 'great folk', he concludes:

> FIRST GRAVEDIGGER: There is no ancient gentleman but gardeners, ditchers, and grave-makers: they hold up **Adam's** profession.
> SECOND GRAVEDIGGER: Was [**Adam**] a gentleman?
> FIRST GRAVEDIGGER: He was the first that ever bore arms.
> SECOND GRAVEDIGGER: Why, he had none.
> FIRST GRAVEDIGGER: What, art a heathen? How dost <u>thou understand the Scripture</u>? <u>The Scripture says</u> '**Adam** digged': could he dig without arms? (5.1.30–38)

This joke, doubly offensive for including an awful pun and the irreverent use of scripture, meets with an understandably exasperated 'Go to!' from the Second Gravedigger. Hamlet himself, entering a few lines later, is similarly worsted: 'How **absolute** the knave is!' (5.1.140).

The half-irritated, half-admiring adjective 'absolute' for an annoying, self-regarding abuser of other people's words is highly significant; it was used by at least two contemporaries to criticize Shakespeare himself. Robert Greene, accusing Shakespeare of being 'beautified with our feathers', famously called him 'an **absolute** *Iohannes fac totum*' (sig. F^{verso}), and a despicable pickpocket in Marston's *Satires*, a possible Shakespeare figure, is called 'the **absolute** Castilio [who] doth but champe that which another chew'd' in his 'beggary' (138). A passage in *Pericles* shows the same meaning: 'I like that well: nay, **how absolute she's** in't, / Not minding whether I dislike or no!' (2.5.18–19). This is No. 14 of the meanings which the *OED* gives for 'absolute': 'free from all doubt or uncertainty; positive, decided, determined' (online edition).

Shakespeare's 'absolute' use of other people's words is even noticeable when he includes materials that are so obviously *déja lu* that it would be absurd to acknowledge them, such as proverbs and ballads. In 1887, the German philologist Moritz Wahl noted that Shakespeare incorporates hundreds of proverbs in his plays without 'indicating in any way at all what was his interest', adding markers only where he 'intended to refer to a folkloric tradition' (Wahl 'Sprachgut' 68, my translation[3]). Proverbs are a fringe category of quotation in that they cannot be marked either for author or for work: they can only be marked for quotation, presented as handed-down folk wisdom, as universally available pieces of discourse. Shakespeare uses this kind of marking for quotation quite rarely. Only about a tenth of the sayings that proverb researchers have identified in the Shakespeare canon are signalled by nouns like 'saying', 'phrase', 'adage' or 'paradox', as here: '<u>The ancient proverb</u> will be well effected: / "A staff is quickly found to beat a dog"' (*2 Henry VI* 3.1.171–172). Shakespeare was more generous with the verbal tags that announce proverbial wisdom more subtly:

> If ye should lead her into a fool's paradise, <u>as they say</u>, it were a very gross kind of behavior, <u>as they say</u> (*Romeo and Juliet* 2.4.168–170).
>
> <u>They say</u>, if money go before, all ways do lie open (*Merry Wives* 2.2.169–170).

In *Much Ado About Nothing*, the witty Beatrice develops a joke from a carefully referenced proverb, pretending an earnestness that would fit the Bible: '<u>It is said</u> "God sends a curst cow short horns", but to a cow too curst he sends none' (2.1.22–25). This marking function can be performed by other verbs as well:

> But that I <u>know</u> love is begun by time (*Hamlet* 4.7.127).
> <u>Thou find'st</u> to be too busy is some danger (*Hamlet* 3.4.40).

44   *"He should be stop'd": Too-Casual Shakespeare*

> 'Tis too much proved that with devotion's visage
> And pious action we do sugar o'er
> The devil himself (*Hamlet* 3.1.53–55).

These expressions may be combined and complemented with generic terms such as 'A man', 'no man' etc., which signal general applicability: 'Or, if thou wilt needs marry, marry a fool; for <u>wise men know well enough</u> what monsters you make of them' (*Hamlet* 3.1.149–151). Finally, such tags may give rise to new, punning jokes '<u>Some say</u> the bee stings: but <u>I say</u>, 'tis the beeswax (*2 Henry VI* 4.2.69–70).

Popular ballads and songs are as 'authorless' as proverbs yet inevitably marked for quotation by their different metre and rhyme patterns and because they are sung. With these sources, Shakespeare's 'absolute' command can be felt in the modifications which he makes to the *urtext* that exists for many ballads. Ophelia's songs 'smack very strongly of the traditional ballad' although they are not, with one exception, 'known elsewhere'. This may be because Shakespeare took '"snatches", as the Queen calls them (4.7.202), of old songs and wove them together to fit his own purpose' (Hibbard 298, note). The purpose is to express Ophelia's distraction, which fragments her memories as she is voicing her pain. The First Gravedigger, in contrast, is a stickler for the correct quotation of folklore. When he proffers the old riddle 'Who builds stronger than either the mason, the shipwright, or the carpenter?' (5.1.42–43), he treats it as a familiar set piece that must be completed with the correct answer. The Second Gravedigger's answer 'The gallows-maker; for that frame outlives a thousand tenants' does not satisfy the First Gravedigger at all:

> Cudgel thy brains no more about it, for your dull ass will not mend his pace with beating. And when you are asked <u>this question</u> next, say 'A gravemaker'. The houses he makes last till doomsday (5.1.57–61).

When the Second Gravedigger validates his brains by inventing a convincing though unconventional answer to the riddle, the First Gravedigger insists on the traditional version of the joke that must be re-enacted every time that somebody is 'asked this question'. There is no sense of an earlier author; the First Gravedigger sets himself up as virtual *auctoritas* which demands that this particular anonymous lexia be transmitted correctly. All of this is rather ironic when we consider the liberties that the First Gravedigger himself has taken with the Bible earlier in the scene.

Shakespeare's 'folksy' appropriation of Scripture often aligns his Bible quotations with proverbs and thus obscures their origin. When the First Gravedigger quotes Genesis – '<u>The Scripture says</u> "Adam digged"' (5.1.37–38) – he includes three markers to drive home the correctness of his reference: the verb 'says', the name of the source text and the proper name 'Adam'. This has inspired many modern editions to add the quotation marks given here. However, as Julie Maxwell has pointed out, no translation of the Bible contains these exact words. The 'unsubtle misquote' that the Gravedigger employs in order to make an 'occupationally motivated point' (Maxwell 63) merely emphasizes his autocratic, blunt wit and playfulness. The same is true for the possible cross-quotation in this passage: the First Gravedigger may be blending Genesis 2:15 with a combative and equally 'occupationally motivated' version of that Bible passage. John Ball, a preacher in the Peasants' Revolt, famously riffed on Genesis: 'When Adam dalf, and Eve span, who was thanne a gentilman?' (quoted in Dobson *Peasants' Revolt* 375). In any case, the First Gravedigger's inexact quotation aligns him with many other expressions of an oblique disrespect for Scripture: many Shakespeare passages that mention the Bible suggest textual or moral corruption. The lightest versions of such mistrust are just evasive: all three occurrences of the word 'psalm', for example, evoke jolly, popular musical traditions rather than the Word of God:

> FALSTAFF: I would I were a weaver. I could sing psalms, or anything (*1 Henry IV* 2.4.136–137).
> CLOWN: [B]ut one Puritan amongst them, and he sings psalms to hornpipes (*Winter's Tale* 4.3.45–74).
> MISTRESS FORD: [...] his words [...] do no more adhere and keep place together than the Hundredth Psalm[4] to the tune of Green Sleeves (*Merry Wives* 2.1.60–63).

Other passages sketch doubts lightly as in *Twelfth Night:* 'as a madman's epistles are <u>no gospels</u>, so it skills not much when they are delivered' (5.1.301–302) or in Imogen's complaint about Posthumus' failing trust in her: 'What is here? / The <u>scriptures</u> of the loyal Leonatus, / All turn'd to heresy?' (*Cymbeline* 3.4.88–89). More explicitly, Iago mocks belief in the Bible by saying that 'Trifles light as air / Are to the jealous confirmations strong / As proofs of <u>holy writ</u> (*Othello* 3.3.370–372). Richard III describes an elaborate fraud as clothing his 'naked villainy / With <u>old odd ends stolen out of holy writ</u>', telling people '<u>with a piece of scripture</u> [...] that <u>God bids us</u> do good for evil' (1.3.356–357). These passages bear out Antonio's warning that the 'devil can <u>cite Scripture</u> for his purpose' (*Merchant* 1.3.107): too carefully marked, explicit quotation of religious sources betrays a hypocrisy which protests too much. At best it indicates pedantry, as here in *Love's Labour's Lost*:

> NATHANIEL: Sir, you have done this in the fear of God very religiously; and, <u>as a certain Father saith</u> –
> HOLOFERNES: Sir, tell not me of <u>the Father</u> (4.2.172–174).

Holofernes does not give the audience a chance to hear a Patristic passage that it might not recognize; all we have of the quotation is marking for quotation.

Biblical names – as in 'Adam digged' – are perhaps the most overt and unequivocal markings for scriptural derivation; Shakespeare again manages to complicate them by including echoes of the scriptural pop culture that had brought Biblical characters to the stage, to the pulpit and into the public sphere. The First Gravedigger names Adam, but quotes his story from a popular song, not from the Bible, and Hamlet himself marks the Old Testament judge Jephthah as a character in a 'pious chanson'. Several phrases that are syntactically unexpected signal intertextuality:

> HAMLET: Oh <u>Jephthah, judge of Israel, what a treasure hadst thou!</u>
> POLONIUS: What a treasure had he, my lord?
> HAMLET: <u>Why,</u> One fair daughter and no more, The which he loved passing well.
> POLONIUS: <u>What follows, then,</u> my lord?
> HAMLET: <u>Why,</u> as by lot, God wot and <u>then, you know</u>
> it came to pass
> as most like it was
> <u>The first row of the pious chanson</u> will show you <u>more</u>; for look, where <u>my abridgement</u> comes (2.2.427–444).

In the first line, a vocative and a name evoke a world foreign to that of the play and Polonius asks for details, which may mean either that he is curious about why exactly Hamlet is interested in the story or that he does not remember the Jephthah tale, which would tally with Hamlet's surprised 'why'.[5] What is certain is that Polonius recognizes an intertextual reference, for which Hamlet provides the more precise citation, announced by the 'casual "you know" [which] may suggest that the ballad was popular' (Dávidházi 49) and by the incongruity of a verse line in a prose conversation. Polonius then asks either for the next line in the Jephthah ballad or for an explanation of why Hamlet is mentioning the ballad at all; in any case, the fact of quotation is once more acknowledged. The rhymes in Hamlet's answer ('by lot – God wot' and 'to pass – it was') indicate that he is speaking lines from a song, i.e. a quoted element, and the elusive syntax is complicated by nominalization. It is easier to parse the speech if the implicit quotation tags and quotation marks are made visible to set off the nominalized phrases from the ballad from the rest of what Hamlet says: 'Why, [what follows is] "As by lot, God wot", and then, [as] you know [comes the phrase] "It came to pass, as most like it was". All in all, the Jephthah passage is abundantly, redundantly, marked for quotation; it is made as transparent as modern citation ethics demands. And yet, Hamlet is not being straightforward with Polonius. Like Richard III, he could be accused of doublespeak in his scriptural references. Hamlet names a 'pious chanson' as his source so that the Old Testament judge appears as a character from a ballad instead of as a Biblical patriarch: we are alerted to a quotation and simultaneously distracted from its origin.

Mystery plays and homilies haunt Hamlet's disapproval of a hammy actor's 'o'erdoing Termagant [which] out-herods Herod' (3.2.14–15), which recalls the stage noisiness of the popular 'Herod of Jewry'[6] (*Merry Wives* 2.1.20). This may be a sly dig at the smooth Claudius, who out-herods the Biblical Herod (who married his half-brother's divorced wife Herodias) by murdering his brother. This crime implicates him in the Cain and Abel narrative, another popular Bible story which has several dimensions in Shakespeare's writing. At the moment when Claudius is contemplating his guilt most seriously, he simply says that a brother's murder has 'the primal eldest curse upon't' (3.3.41), evoking Cain's misery as an abstract concept. When the first fratricide's name does come up, it is with comic violence in the Gravedigger Scene, where Hamlet marvels at the callousness with which the Gravedigger bangs a skull 'to the ground, as if 'twere Cain's jawbone, that did the first murder' (5.1.79). This image comes from a popular stage version of the Biblical narrative: Abel is slain with a 'chekebon' in the Wakefield play *The Murder of Abel* (21). The simple, abstract phrase 'the first murder' seems almost calculated to obscure that memory of 'a brother's murder' which one would imagine to be ever-present in Hamlet's mind. In fact, such non-Biblical, always-already-quoted folksy echoes are an important reason why the narrative of Cain and Abel is 'the most potent Biblical story in Shakespeare's plays' (Mowat 26). In *Love's Labour's Lost,* Cain appears in a popular riddle:

> DULL: [...] can you tell me by your wit what was a month old at Cain's birth, that's not five weeks old as yet?
> HOLOFERNES: Dictynna, goodman Dull; Dictynna, goodman Dull.
> DULL: What is Dictynna?
> SIR NATHANIEL: A title to Phoebe, to Luna, to the moon. [...]
> HOLOFERNES: The moon was a month old when **Adam** was no more, and raught not to five weeks when he came to five-score (4.2.40–50).

This passage once more unites several kinds of Shakespearean sources: Dull asks a riddle, like the First Gravedigger, on which the schoolmaster Holofernes embroiders with classical mythology and when he understands that his classical names for the moon will not reach his audience, he, too, returns to folk stuff via the Bible.

'Stolen out of holy writ':
Misquoting and cross-quoting the Bible

Many quotations from the Bible, the carefully edited, jealously guarded and widely preached Word of God should be recognizable without

48 *"He should be stop'd': Too-Casual Shakespeare*

the help of familiar names and popular motifs. Nevertheless, many of Shakespeare's scriptural borrowings are just as difficult to pin down as his proverbs. Often, they seem not so much reverently quoted as 'stolen out of holy writ' (*Richard III* 1.3.356–357), used in paraphrase, twisted or out of context. Some of this difficulty is intrinsic to the source itself. Written and compiled over several hundred years, the Bible abounds in internal cross-references and echoes that make Christianity a 'fundamentally intertextual religion' (Hamlin 90). The most important feature of this intertextuality is the interpretative device of *figura*, by which the New Testament appropriates Old Testament elements as prefiguring 'types' for Christianity. *Figura* is an important phenomenon of cultural mobility which works like casual quotation: it leaves 'things standing in place' (Greenblatt 13), conserving phrases and images that are emptied of their original significance to make space for new meanings. This transformation provides multiple potential meanings and origins for any quoted element, leaving the reader to choose between more than one Old and New Testament passages in many cases. In addition to such internal correspondences, Biblical intertextuality is complicated by the popular culture of homilies and sermons, mystery plays, hymns, prayer books and carols, all of which rephrase Biblical narratives and extrapolate tenets of Christian doctrine from these stories. Finally, there is translation: by the late sixteenth century, several English Bibles were available in addition to the Vulgate. In addition to the 1560 Geneva Bible, Shakespeare could have used the 1568 Bishop's Bible, Henry VII's Great Bible and the 1604 Authorized Version. In fact, only a small number of his Biblical quotations can be identified as stemming from a specific translation (cf. Shaheen *Biblical References*). All these complications are a nightmare for source studies; for Shakespeare's associative mind, they evidently provided a congenial playing field. In Naseeb Shaheen's survey *Biblical References in Shakespeare's Plays,* for example, 371 lines in Shakespeare's comedies are identified with a possible scriptural origin, and these lines are linked to a total of 1200 Biblical verses. On average Shaheen gives three or four possible Biblical source texts for each Shakespearean reference, with up to six antecedents given for particularly elusive or allusive echoes.

Shakespeare's Biblical references are further complicated by what has been called a piece of Renaissance 'information technology' (Collinson 94). The introduction of verse numbering in the sixteenth century made it easy to move 'between the concordance and the text' (Mowat 27) to look up related passages in a volume on one's desk next to the Bible. The editors of the ground-breaking Geneva Bible, probably Shakespeare's 'favourite' (Mowat 25), were even more intertextually-minded: they added marginal editorial glosses which comment on difficult passages. Instead of pointing the reader to a separate book, the Geneva Bible fragments the layout of every individual page to accommodate the base text and its comments in a single volume. Sliding in and out of the Biblical text to check references becomes almost distractingly easy, and this multiplicity had a powerful attraction for Shakespeare. His writing suggests that he often followed the pattern of reading that the Geneva Bible's complex layout invites: a Biblical verse is repeatedly combined 'with its marginal gloss' and the resulting cross-quotation works 'more powerfully' (Mowat 28). A particularly striking instance involves, once more, the Cain and Abel story. God's reproach to Cain that 'the voice of thy brother's **blood crieth unto me**' (Genesis 4:10) has the following comment in the Geneva Bible: 'God **reuengeth** the wrōgs of his Saintes, thogh none cōplaine; for the iniquitie it selfe **cryeth for vengeance**' (cf. Mowat 29 for an image). The introduction of revenge (twice) is decidedly tendentious in a context where God threatens to punish anybody who would exert vengeance by killing Cain; but the gloss clearly appealed to Shakespeare, who fused it with the Biblical text to form the striking metaphor of spilled blood crying for vengeance. This image appears in various forms in eight of his plays (cf. Mowat 27–28), ranging from '**Blood and revenge** are hammering in my head' (*Titus Andronicus* 3.2.39), to the variant in *1 Henry VI* 1.4.151, where 'every [tear] **drop cries vengeance** for his death'. Nothing could be further from the first chapter of Genesis than such dynastic wrangling and yet these passages are verbal echoes of Cain and Abel just as much as Abel's grotesque 'cheke-bon', inspired by a paratext that had already interpreted and complicated Scripture when Shakespeare encountered it.

None of these powerful uses of Scriptural motifs are marked for quotation, in striking contrast to the suspiciously demonstrative information provided by villains and jokers. Shakespeare's characters also have a third way of handling verses from the Bible: they gloss them over or distract from their source. Gertrude's line '<u>Thou know'st 'tis common</u>; all that lives must die' (1.2.74–75) has been explained as deriving from one of at least three passages in the Bible. They include both the Old and the New Testament:

[T]he common death of <u>all men</u> (Numbers 19:29)
There is <u>no man</u> that hath power in the day of death (Ecclesiastes 8:6–8)
And <u>as it is appointed unto men</u> once to die (Hebrews 9:27)

Gertrude ignores these options for quoting the Bible and instead frames her thought by the three proverb-signalling tags 'thou know'st', ''tis common' and 'all that lives'. These markers of proverbial wisdom serve characterization: to minimize the strangeness of her quick remarriage after Old Hamlet's death, the Queen insists on the normality, even banality, of any death and avoids mentioning the portentous, authoritative Bible, which contains contradictory messages about second marriages.

This lead is followed by several *Hamlet* editions that annotate the line as an English proverb, and it is indeed so 'common' that it may seem absurd to try and identify its source at all. However, Shakespeare sets a precedent for taking it as a quotation from the Bible in *2 Henry IV* 3.2.35–36, where Justice Shallow says: 'Certain, 'tis certain, very sure, very sure: death, as the Psalmist says, is certain to all; all shall die.' This may refer to Psalm 89:48: 'What man liveth, and shall not see death? shall he deliver his soul from the hand of the grave?' or Psalm 49:7: 'Yet they cannot redeem themselves from death by paying a ransom to God.' This adds two more Biblical antecedents for the thought 'We all must die' – and none of them, in any Renaissance translation, has a wording that is exactly recognizable in Shakespeare (cf. Shaheen 441). Maybe Shakespeare was misremembering. Or making Shallow and Gertrude look as if they misremembered. Or both.

Hamlet's reasoning against suicide is another passage that is complicated by the intertextual networks of the glosses in the Geneva Bible. When he says that 'the **Everlasting** [...] fix'd / His canon 'gainst self-slaughter' (1.2.135–136), he uses an epithet derived from Genesis 21:33–34, where Abraham is said to have 'planted a grove in Beersheba, and called there on the name of the Lord, the **everlasting** God'. 'The Everlasting' is simultaneously a quotation and a respectful way of marking for derivation: Hamlet provides a 'bibliographical' reference to the author of the command that he quotes. However, Hamlet is misquoting the Bible here, or rather he is not quoting it at all. The Old Testament does not explicitly condemn suicide; this prohibition was deduced later. A gloss in the Geneva Bible gives a glimpse of this process: a suicide in 2 Maccabees 14.14 has the warning comment that 'this priuate example ought not to be followed of the godlie [...] although the autor seeme here to approue it' (Anon. *Geneva Bible* sig. BBBBB3[recto] [473]). The quotation from Scripture which Hamlet provides with an explicit marker for derivation is borrowed from an Old Testament context that is irrelevant his topic. What Hamlet makes the 'Everlasting' say is really the recommendation of a Bible editor who, moreover, knew himself to be at variance with the glossed passage, speaking against suicide 'although the autor [...] approve it'. Hamlet's marking for derivation is unmistakable, and unmistakably wrong.

Seeing that overt marking of Biblical quotations is so often suspect in Shakespeare, we might even question Hamlet's sincerity in citing 'the Everlasting' so emphatically. Immediately afterwards, if to underline his disregard for the *urtext* of God's word, he proceeds to take the Lord's name in vain:

that **the Everlasting** had not fix'd
His canon 'gainst **self-slaughter**! O God! God!

> How weary, stale, flat and unprofitable,
> Seem to me all the uses of this world!
> Fie on't! ah fie! (1.2.135–139)

Coming so immediately after the respectful citation of 'The Everlasting', the obvious infringement of the Second Commandment in 'O God God!' is quite striking, especially as it is followed by the informal, barely verbal double 'fie' two lines down. How serious, then, is Hamlet's Bible quotation? A passage in *Cymbeline* supports the hypothesis that Shakespeare's injunctions against suicide rather 'pay a visit' to the verbal surfaces of the Bible than go into its 'system' (Barthes *Roland Barthes* 74). Like Hamlet, Imogen refrains from killing herself because of the 'prohibition so divine' that is set up 'Against **self-slaughter**' (3.4.83–84), and the repetition of the striking phrase 'self-slaughter' may indicate that it, too, is a quotation. The single earlier occurrence of the phrase in the *EEBO* database is in Richard Stanyhursts's translation of Book IV of the *Aeneid*: 'Nay, nay, thye **self slaughter**: thy bad lief vnhappye death asketh' (Stanyhurst 81). Book IV was a set text in schools and the scene in which Dido expresses her despair at Aeneas' imminent departure was strongly anchored in Shakespeare's memory; he may have consulted Stanyhurst's translation out of curiosity later (it was published when he was eighteen). This would add a classical echo to Hamlet's incorrect allusion to the Bible, which is quite appropriate, given the acceptability of suicide in Roman culture. As Horatio says before he attempts to kill himself with the leftover poisoned wine: 'I am more an antique Roman than a Dane' (5.2.374).

Scripture echoes around Shakespeare's plays with classical and editorial overtones, and it is repeatedly presented as the proverbial wisdom which he so often used and which may in turn sound Biblical because it is or although it is not. Rather than consult the Bibles that he had at his disposal, Shakespeare links, fuses and confuses what his memory serves. The names and topics that would normally mark a quotation become themselves independent parts of Shakespeare's intertextual storehouse so that the content of a quotation and the marking for the quotation become mutually exclusive: his characters either quote something or talk about quoting something; it is rare to encounter both together. If a quotation is overtly marked, its substance tends to be weakened or decontextualized so that the marking is the most important part of the quotation. Richard II's strategy of deceiving with 'old odd ends stolen out of holy writ' spells out that displaying a quotation's origin while taking the quotation out of context is morally reprehensible. Thus, Shakespeare's marking for quotation always serves characterization; he marks quotation to round out the portraits of the characters who quote. Unlike his bardolatrous fans, though, he does not quote carefully. Marked and unmarked quotations alike can often be traced to several sources because Shakespeare modifies and combines phrases. The frequency and complexity of his Biblical references has been called 'intensive' (Mowat 3); '*ex*tensive' might be the better term: wide-ranging and with tenaciously preserved details, yet casually diluted in reproduction or played-up in questionable misquotation. This intertextuality embraces folk materials, scripture and even classical echoes. The following chapter, which focuses on Shakespeare's use of classical materials, will therefore have occasion to mention more Scriptural material and also some of the English quotations which are the main topic of Chapter 4.

Notes

1 Ironically, Johnson did not stop himself from saying '**A wind, or not a wind? that is the question**' during his Tour to the Hebrides (Boswell *Life of Johnson* 5:279). As Thomas Keymer aptly remarks, the eighteenth-century writer's 'golden apple, their fatal Cleopatra' was Shakespeare quotation ('In the Novel' 119).
2 In *1 Henry VI* (1. 1. 56-57), Bedford calls up Henry's ghost to protect England, whose soul will make a 'far more glorious star [...] Than Julius Caesar' and the chorus in *Henry V* evokes the 'conquering Caesar' (*Henry V* 5 Prologue 29).
3 The original German runs: 'irgendwelche Andeutung über das Interesse zu geben, das ihm zur Benützung [...] vorgeschwebt haben mag'.
4 Mistress Ford's 'Hundredth Psalm' is not Psalm 100 but a hymn tune which was created for Psalm 134 in the 1551 edition of the Geneva Psalter and and came later to be associated with Psalm 100. Eventually known as 'Old Hundredth', this melody was also used for several other hymn texts.
5 For the motivic ramifications which various versions of the Jephthah story extend in *Hamlet* and beyond, see Stevenson '*Hamlet's* Mice' and Dávidházi 'O Jephthah'.
6 'Herod of Jewry' in Shakespeare can refer either to Herod the Great (74/73 BC-4 BC), who ordered the Massacre of the Innocents, or to his son Herod the Tetrarch, who had John the Baptist beheaded. The two 'were often confused' (Shaheen 1939) or treated as the same person, a noisy, violent figure familiar from popular Mystery Plays. In *Antony and Cleopatra*, 'Herod of Jewry' refers to Herod the Great.

3 'Honey-tongued Shakespeare' and the Classics

English seneca read by candle light yeeldes manie good sentences.
Thomas Nashe (1589)

If Shakespeare's casual, irreverent copiousness met with disapproval from certain contemporary readers, there were also those who praised him effusively. Most early commendations are dominated by the topos of sweetness: Shakespeare is called 'sweet' (Covell sig. R2^{recto}) and 'friendly' (Scoloker sig. A2^{recto}) and appreciated for his 'sugred Sonnets' (Meres sig. 281^{verso}). This kind of approval came to seem so defining that a certain 'Willy' was identified as Shakespeare simply because 'Large streames of honnie and sweete Nectar' to 'flowe' from his pen (Spenser 'Teares' 69). Even though this 'gentle spirit', 'Our pleasant *Willy*', is described as 'dead of late' in this poem from 1591, the details fit Shakespeare's reputation so well that the passage came to be cited as a possible homage in collections of early Shakespeare testimonies. Nectar and honey are significant terms of praise because they evoke a popular Renaissance metaphor for quotation: the activity of the honeybee. Like bees, readers first spot and take away what is worthwhile, as do readers who mark striking passages 'from the flowers of [their] reading' in the margins of a printed volume or copy them into a 'waste book'. Then they sort the contents of the waste book into a 'commonplace book' under topical headings, just as bees put nectar from flowers into the cells of a honeycomb.[1] Once the harvest is thus sorted and structured, it can be transformed into honey, i.e. into sweet new texts. The collected 'sweet Nectar' will refresh the 'drye and withered quills' of tired writers, who are thus enabled to 'write some sweeter poetrie / That may heareafter liue a longer daye' (Anon. *Pilgrimage to Parnassus* 97). Quotation inspires new writing and makes it – as in the case of Shakespeare – appealing and durable by the integration of varied materials. In contrast with late-twentieth-century views, which stress the potential of intertextuality to distract and de-centre, Renaissance quotation was expected to enrich and sweeten a text, and so the early praise which calls Shakespeare's writings 'sweet' may imply an appreciation of his classical flower gathering. As with the Bible and the folk sources discussed in Chapter 2, Shakespeare made his classical quotations contribute a wide range of flavours to his 'honey'. Generally, Shakespeare's marking for quotation – a name, a framing remark, a Latin phrase – characterizes speakers at the expense of the quoted content. If a character points out a quotation, this is usually indicates education or its lack to the audience. I will have frequent occasion in this chapter to quote Colin Burrow's admirable *Shakespeare and Classical Antiquity*, which discusses many similar instance of the remarkable 'variety of effects' with which Shakespeare 'flag[s] up' quotations 'for special attention' (Burrow 5) and demonstrates his 'pragmatic sense of the emotional and theatrical power' (70) of overt quotations. Countless other phrases that seem derived from Latin classics are so smoothly absorbed into Shakespeare's own diction that we suspect thoughtless or even unconscious quotation. This is just as true for the third instance of casual Classicism in Shakespeare, his famous image clusters: the occurrence of these apparently random image combinations seems to have largely bypassed authorial intention.

'I read it in the grammar long ago': Shakespeare's marked quotations

Like the signals that point to quotations from the Bible, Shakespeare's overt classical quotations invariably characterize the figure who is quoting. Unlike the Bible, however, the Latin canon could not be counted on to be familiar to everybody in the audience. Shakespeare's awareness of this diversity adds an extra dimension to his marking, which caters very cleverly to a variously educated public. Unexplained Latin would have alienated the illiterate; too-clumsy help with demanding allusions would alienate those who were in no need of help. Instead, famous names are personalized to make quotations unobtrusively accessible. Virgil and Terence, who certainly had a significant influence in Shakespeare's writing are never named: their biographies yield no celebrity details. Cicero, on the other hand, is mentioned once as an author and once as 'sweet Tully' (*2 Henry VI* 4.1.144), the much-mourned murder victim and 'honest Ovid [...] among the Goths' (*As You Like It* 3.3.7–8) is the grieving poet in exile. Polonius' information that 'Seneca cannot be too heavy, nor Plautus too light' for the Players that have come to Elsinore is similarly simple. It was probably too simple: the fact that they are school authors makes them slightly embarrassing for Polonius to mention, a bit like the fact that 'Brutus killed' Caesar (cf. pp. 38–39). Like in that passage, Shakespeare slips in a conversational footnote for the uninitiated. At the same time, he makes sure that educated theatregoers will not feel affronted by this simplicity by positioning 'Seneca' and 'Plautus' after Polonius' comically breathless meander of jumbled phrases 'tragical-comical-historical-pastoral, scene individable or poem unlimited' (2.2.422–424). This makes

'Honey-tongued Shakespeare' and the Classics 55

Polonius educated but non-threateningly silly. Earlier in the same scene, Hamlet taunts Polonius with another school author:

> POLONIUS: What do you read, my lord?
> HAMLET: Words, words, words. [...] <u>the satirical rogue says here</u> that old men have grey beards [...] together with most weak hams: <u>all which</u>, sir, though I most powerfully and potently believe, yet <u>I hold it not honesty to have it thus set down</u> (2.2.208–220).

The 'satirical rogue' cited as the author of Hamlet's reading may be Juvenal, whose *Satires* were on the sixth-grade syllabus. Hamlet's improvised, evasive summary of the contents aims to insult the university-educated Polonius and at the same time slights the quoted book and author, so that readers who suspect Juvenal can feel knowing and those who do not notice do not miss anything in Hamlet's insults. This dexterous 'channelling of cultural snobbery' is typical. If Shakespeare 'quotes a hackneyed phrase he tends deliberately to tag it as hackneyed', and in order not to sound like the provincial grammar-school boy he was, he presents grammar school reading 'ironically' (Burrow 47).

I have discussed Julius Caesar in Chapter 2 as a lightly treated folk figure who was stabbed by **'Brutus' bastard hand'** (*2 Henry VI* 4.1.144), said 'veni, vidi, vici' or built the Tower of London. He appears again in this chapter on classical references because he is also the author of Shakespeare's one full and correctly referenced Latin quotation. In this passage, too, Shakespeare makes Latin accessible to all viewers and includes spectacularly dramatic results of marking for quotation that could be perceived as snobbish. In *2 Henry VI*, the Kentish rebel leader Jack Cade fulminates against education, condemning grammar schools that corrupt 'the youth of the realm' and 'talk of a noun and a verb and such abominable / words as no Christian ear can endure to hear' (4.7.40–41). When Cade has made himself 'lord' of London and sets up an impromptu court, one of the people brought before him is the unfortunate Lord Saye. Saye compliments the county of Kent in an effort to placate Cade but is incautious enough to do so in Latin:

> LORD SAYE: You men of Kent—
> DICK: What say you of Kent?
> LORD SAYE: Nothing but this: 'tis **bona terra, mala gens.**
> JACK CADE: Away with him, away with him! He speaks Latin.
> LORD SAYE: Hear me but speak, and bear me where you will.
>   Kent, <u>in the commentaries Caesar writ</u>,
>   Is termed the civil'st place of all this isle.
>   Sweet is the country, because full of riches;
>   The people liberal, valiant, active, wealthy;
>   Which makes me hope you are not void of pity (4.7.54–65).

Lord Saye's appeal to Cade's local patriotism is to no avail: on the contrary, the Latin phrase and the mention of *De Bello Gallico* probably hasten his execution, which is ordered minutes later. Hearing Latin is too much for a man who cannot tolerate education. Capital punishment for a Latin quotation is an extreme example of the vivid characterization which Shakespeare's overt quotations invariably achieve. Marking for quotation puts into relief both the well-educated aristocrat who cannot imagine the anger that his polite classical allusion will produce and the boorish rebel leader who cannot bear to be confronted with superior learning. Shakespeare may have had little Latin but he had a secure grip of 'the sociology of Latinity'. He knew perfectly well what it could mean to quote Latin and used the 'semiotic potentials' of 'classical antiquity' (Currell 'Away with him!' 31) economically and to great dramatic effect. The different dimensions of his presentation of Julius Caesar – author, legendary figure, complex tragic protagonist – are perhaps the most impressive example of how Shakespeare combined popular sources with his own classical resources to appeal to an audience which would respond to either or both without feeling over-challenged or patronized.

While Shakespeare could exploit both the popular and the learned Julius Caesar myths to appealing effect, most of his mentions of Horace smack of the schoolroom. The schoolmaster Holofernes in *Love's Labour's Lost* peppers his conversation with unobtrusively glossed Latin phrases throughout, and at one point, when he is asked to read out a letter, he breaks into Latin verse instead. Both the quotation and author would be remembered by former grammar school students in the audience:

> HOLOFERNES: Fauste, precor gelida quando pecus omne sub umbra RUMINAT, – and so forth. <u>Ah, good old Mantuan, I may speak of thee as the traveller doth of Venice,</u>
> **Venetia, Venetia,**
> **Chi non ti vede non ti pretia.**
> <u>Old Mantuan, old Mantuan!</u> **who understandeth thee not, loves thee not.** Ut, re, sol, la, mi, fa. Under pardon, sir, what are the contents? or rather, <u>as Horace says in his</u> – What, my soul, <u>verses</u>?
> SIR NATHANIEL: Ay, sir, and <u>very learned</u> (4.2.114–123).

Holofernes is quoting and praising the fifteenth-century poet Baptista Mantuanus, whose Latin *Eclogues* were standard fare in the fourth year of grammar school. After quoting an Italian tag from John Florio's language primer *First Fruits*, translating it, applying it to a Latin writer he has just quoted (rather than to a city) and humming a few notes, Holofernes is finally startled by the verse lines he sees into paying attention to the letter that he has before him. Horace's verse remains unquoted and his work implicit; his name is a marker without a quotation. He would have been too difficult; a Mantuanus quote would rope in a larger percentage of the audience than a Horace tag, and so Horace's text remains implicit here; he is just a namedrop. Holofernes is characterized as superficial, a person who takes time to elaborate on Mantuanus yet is easily distracted from Horace; at the same time the audience are spared the effort of remembering a bit of Horace.

In *Titus Andronicus*, we do get to hear two Horace verses but they are very famous and the audience is well primed. The verse is written on a tag which accompanies a present from their enemy Titus Andronicus:

> DEMETRIUS: What's here? A scroll; and <u>written round about</u>? Let's see; <u>**Integer vitae, scelerisque purus,**</u>
> <u>**Non eget Mauri jaculis, nec arcu.**</u>
> CHIRON: <u>O, 'tis a verse in Horace</u>; <u>I know it well</u>:
> <u>I read it in the grammar long ago</u>.[2]
> AARON: Ay, just – <u>a verse in Horace, right, you have it.</u>
> [*aside*] Now, what a thing it is to be an ass!
> Here's no sound jest! the old man hath found their guilt;
> And sends them weapons <u>wrapped about with lines</u> (4.2.18–28).

Shakespeare's address to multiple audiences is impressively deft and complex here. The Latin phrase 'Integer vitae' was extremely popular and offered recognition to the widest possible circle of people with grammar school experience.[3] The quotation is heavily marked as a school staple by the boorish and cruel brothers Chiron and Demetrius, while the clumsiness of Chiron's recognition and Aaron's heavy-handed mockery ensure that also Latin-less spectators can recognize and place the Latin quote; at the same time, they indicate the childish limitations of Chiron's education. Shakespeare makes it completely obvious that 'reading something in a grammar long ago does not necessarily mean that one understands it' (Burrow 25), and this insight communicates 'the thrill of privileged knowledge' (Chaudhuri 790) to the audience, who can feel with Aaron even if they never 'read something in a grammar'.

The way in which Shakespeare handles the Horace quotation on the gift-tag communicates about school memories with the audience over the heads of this characters; with admirable efficiency, he simultaneously characterizes his speakers and encourages the audience to identify with them. Aaron, who is shown as clever enough to see through the civilized surface of Titus' message, makes the audience complicit in his justified scorn for Chiron even though he is a villain himself. Titus' grandson Lucius, the schoolboy bringer of the wrapped gift and the one character who would more or less represent Shakespeare's own level of familiarity with these phrases, despises Chiron and Demetrius for their villainy and for their scant or forgotten learning. When they ask him for news, he mutters: 'That you are both decipher'd, that's the news' (4.2.8), indicating his cultural and moral superiority over these unsophisticated villains. Intent on showing up the banality of a quotation, he marginalizes its content just as Chiron and Aaron do. All three characters confirm what we could call 'Shakespeare's Law of Casual Quotation': quotations may have either meaningful content or elaborate marking. Marking completely overwhelms content in this scene: the ten quoted Latin words are far outweighed by more than thirty words which present the author's name, the technical term 'verse' and a kind of autobiographical bibliographical reference. The original book, Horace's *Carmina*, is replaced with a secondary source, 'the grammar', where Chiron in his schooldays may have encountered the line instead of reading a complete Horatian ode. Characterization is absolutely central, and for this, Shakespeare does not need quotation as much as sophisticated MARKING FOR QUOTATION. It is apt that at least one early critic speaks of the 'sugred tongues' (Weever 22) of Shakespeare's characters rather than of his sweetness.

Shakespeare exempts just one single Roman author from such fatuous name-dropping: 'sweet witty' Ovid, whose soul was said to live on in 'mellifluous & honey-tongued Shakespeare'[4] (Meres sig. 281[verso]). The *Metamorphoses* are undoubtedly one of the great presences in Shakespeare's imagination, and it is tempting to read a sense of grateful acknowledgment into the more or less informed respect with which Shakespeare's characters mention his name. In *Titus Andronicus*, the difference between the way in which Horace and Ovid are treated is particularly instructive. Instead of being quoted on a nasty gift tag like Horace, Ovid is represented by a complete volume of the *Metamorphoses*. Lavinia, raped and mutilated, needs the book to denounce her tormentors by pointing to the story of the raped and muted Philomel. The book prompts various reactions. Lucius, the clever schoolboy, is put in his place because he does not fully understand. Lavinia's agitation because he has 'read that Hecuba of Troy / Ran mad through sorrow'. Her father Titus understands that she needs a book, which reminds him of how she used to read to Lucius when he was little:

> TITUS ANDRONICUS: Ah, boy, Cornelia never with more care
> Read to her sons than she hath read to thee
> Sweet poetry and Tully's Orator (4.1.12–14).

Cornelia, Scipio's daughter and the mother of the Gracchi, is a legendary model educator that Shakespeare probably encountered in Plutarch. She is evoked as picking just the right educational reading matter: Cicero ('Tully') and the 'sweet' poetry of, presumably, Ovid. When Lavinia finally finds the volume that she needs, the boy recognizes it at once: 'Grandsire, 'tis Ovid's Metamorphosis. / My mother gave it me' (4.1.43–44). Lavinia's uncle Marcus Andronicus surmises that she has picked the book 'for love of her that's gone' (4.1.45), Lucius' mother, but Lavinia needs it to communicate her sufferings.

It is easy to imagine that the tender, educational family vignettes that prepare the gruesome account of Lavinia's suffering may be prompted by some positive memories of Ovid, a counterbalance of the Shakespearean cliché of the 'whining schoolboy [...] creeping like snail / Unwillingly to school' (*As You Like It* 2.7.152–154). A similar tenderness colours the mention of Ovid in *As You Like It*:

> TOUCHSTONE: I am here with thee and thy goats, as the most capricious poet, honest Ovid, was among the Goths.
> JAQUES: O knowledge ill-inhabited; worse than Jove in a thatched house (3.3.6–10).

The wry reference to Ovid's exile touchingly hints at Touchstone's own isolation in the forest, and Jaques adds a hint to the perhaps more familiar story of Philemon and Baucis from the *Metamorphoses*. Once more, different segments of the audience are offered points of reference. The 'less educated' Touchstone references the 'life story' of Ovid and the 'learned' Jaques alludes to the poem (Burrow 94) – and to cap it all, Jaques' allusion includes an eye-rolling putdown of Touchstone's simpler reference. In *The Taming of the Shrew*, Ovid is present in a more laboured mention:

> TRANIO: [...] Let's be no stoics nor no stocks, I pray;
> Or so devote to Aristotle's checks
> As Ovid be an outcast quite abjured (1.1.31–33).

Tranio, the schoolmaster, obviously wants to balance Aristotle's sternness with the Ovid of the *Ars Amatoria*, and Bianca's other suitor Lucentio similarly even uses it to flirt: 'I read that I profess, **The Art to Love**. / BIANCA: And may you prove, sir, master of your art' (4.2.8–9). We are invited to laugh at these characters: they are clumsy rather than evil and their references are tolerably informed. Ovid lives on in Shakespeare more intensely and explicitly than most other Roman authors do. It is apt that the one passage of praise for Shakespeare that uses not one but three 'sugar' terms to extol him should include Ovid: in Francis Meres' *Palladis Tamia*, 'the sweet witty soul of Ovid' is said to live on in 'mellifluous & honey-tongued Shakespeare' (sig. 281^{verso}). 'Mellifluous' and 'honey' specifically recall the bee metaphor; Meres is saying not only that Shakespeare continues Ovid's tradition and eminence but also that Shakespeare uses Ovid as his intertextual nectar. And Shakespeare was happier to acknowledge Ovid than many others.

'I may forget whose they are': Unmarked echoes

Classical elements that 'seem to jut out [...] as though they are designed to be noticed' (Burrow 190) are an exception in the world of Shakespeare's plays. Striking names such as Ovid, Horace or Julius Caesar, Latin scraps and the stylistically incongruous Senecan passages in *Hamlet* or *Macbeth* are far outnumbered by a considerable body of completely unacknowledged and possibly unconscious quotations. Shakespeare closes the smooth and distracting discursive surface of his own language over these borrowings so that it was easy to get the impression that 'Shakespeares best' lines were 'from all Learning [...] [c]leere' (quoted in Chambers *Facts and Problems* 2:224). The most striking wording of this perceptive, if technically mistaken, notion was penned by Leonard Digges in 1640:

> This whole booke, thou shalt find he doth not borrow
> One phrase from Greeks, nor Latines imitate [...].
> *All that he doth write*
> *Is pure his own*, plot, language, exquisite (Digges n.p.).

Digges could not be more wrong about Shakespeare's inspiration by pre-texts, but he gets one essential thing right: Shakespeare hardly ever 'borrow[s] / One phrase' as he finds it without making whatever he uses 'pure his own'. This thorough absorption is described in almost neurological detail in a letter from Petrarch's *Familiares*, where the Italian poet describes his own intertextual practice. On the one hand, ideas from texts that he had read 'only once and quickly at that' remained 'so alien to his own thoughts that [they] stood in his memory as another's'. On the other hand, phrases from writers whose works he had studied 'so thoroughly that they entered his bone marrow, not just his memory', would come 'to his pen without him recognizing the source or even the fact that they or even that they came from someone else' (Pigman 13). Quickly and superficially absorbed material tends to be accompanied by marking because the writer remains aware of quoting something, and these phrases would probably be quoted more or less *verbatim*, while whatever has been truly assimilated is no longer marked for quotation, maybe not even in the writer's mind.

Petrarch's two quotation modes can be recognized in Shakespeare's classical borrowings although overtly quoted and unconsciously absorbed texts do not account for everything that he learnt from Antiquity. Not everything that he learnt at school was thoroughly absorbed; Shakespeare quotes certain school staples in Latin, while others, such as Terence and Virgil, are never named but clearly had a profound influence (cf. Burrow *Shakespeare and Classical Antiquity*). While we have some idea of the Tudor grammar school syllabus, Shakespeare also uses a wealth of images, phrases, stories and set pieces that he found in anthologies, translations, bilingual editions, language primers and popular culture. Moreover, Latin aphorisms may have 'penetrated and enriched the vulgar tongue' (Bowring 82), becoming part of the English phrase stock that he used as a matter of course. Shakespeare's 'classical' quotations cross-quote and blur various sources as well as various *kinds* of sources. He could '"know" a classical text – or look as though he had read it' from many sources. He could have encountered it as an anthology piece or as a 'short quotation in a sermon, in the work of a learned historian or contemporary writer'. His tenacious and flexible memory could retain a phrase 'independently of [...] its original position within an ode by Horace, say; or it might be remembered as part of an essay by Montaigne' (Burrow 24). Gertrude's statement that 'all that lives must die' (*Hamlet* 1.2.75) is such a multiply remembered item. It is not only framed as a proverb – 'Thou know'st 'tis common' (1.2.74) – but has also been linked to several passages from Bible (cf. p. 49). Moreover, scholars specializing in the Renaissance uses of the classics have found in it overtones from the Latin schoolroom. Possible antecedents include Seneca's *Epistulae Morales* ('nemo tam imperitus est ut nesciat quandoque moriendum') and Cicero's *Tusculanae* ('moriendum est enim omnibus'). The word **'common'** echoes the Latin phrasing from a Renaissance anthology such as Erasmus' hugely popular and often re-quoted collection *Adagia* (cf. Smith *Proverb Lore*), where the idea appears as 'Mors omnibus **communis**'. Leonard Culman's *Sententiae pueriles* have 'Mors omni aetati **communis** est' (14). Chronologically, these sentences are 'anterior' to Hamlet; as anthology entries, they are 'never original' (Barthes 'Death of the Author' 170). Like many other Shakespeare passages, Gertrude's statement is a textual 'intersection' where always 'at least one other word (text) can be read' (Kristeva 'Word, Dialogue' 66). At least ten different sources for Gertrude's line have been mentioned in published research: Shakespeare may have read them all, and forgotten all of them.

The rich confusion of Shakespeare's reading since boyhood is reflected in the variety of scholars who have reported on his sources. A Shakespeare phrase that one specialist reader recognizes from Scripture reminds another of a proverb and a third one of a line from Virgil – and all these readers are right. The line 'there is nothing either good or bad, but thinking makes it so' (*Hamlet* 2.2.268–270), for example, has been called a proverb (Hibbard 216, note) but it has also been located in William Baldwin's much-reprinted *Treatise of moral philosophy*, which presents it as a classical quotation: '**Nothing vnto a man** is miserable, if he so thinke it: for all Fortune is good to hym, that constantlye with pacience suffereth it. Plato' (Baldwin *Treatise* sig. 218[recto]). Baldwin's *Treatise* may be misquoting: to my knowledge, the idea has not been traced to a specific Plato passage but the biographical mystery of Shakespeare's education has been a powerful motivation for scholars to trace classical references in his works. Thomas Baldwin set out to determine exactly how far Shakespeare's little Latin could have taken him while the Baconian W. M. Theobald identified hundreds of items to prove that authoring the Shakespeare canon would have taken more schooling than the man from Stratford could have had. Scores of less encyclopaedic studies have complemented these huge collections with detailed evidence for Shakespeare's use of specific authors or texts from the classical world. There is a slight danger to such research: the profound specialist knowledge that such discoveries require can lead to a concentration which loses sight of competing or complementary sources for any given phrase or motif. In contrast, the work on a database which assembles all types of sources that have been suggested for a given line encourages a vision of Shakespeare in which almost anything could have left a trace in his mind. The abundance of cross-references and potential echoes in Shakespeare's writing can greatly enrich the experience of attentive readers; on the other hand, their number and proximity dilutes the relationship of his plays with any individual pre-text, a circumstance that tends to be side-lined by researchers who are interested in Shakespeare's use of any single source.

Shakespeare's elusive, multiple intertextuality has seemed almost morally suspect; his jealous contemporary Robert Greene took it for the furtiveness of a pilferer covering his tracks, and the idea of theft also occurred to later critics. In 1751, Bishop Richard Hurd reported that Hamlet's line 'I shall not look upon his like again' (1.2.196) had been 'suspected' of 'being stolen from Sophocles' (185). Hurd's line of defence is interesting. Since the 'sole ground of suspicion' (!) is 'in the expression, "I shall not look upon his like again", to which the Greek so exactly answers', he argues that certain 'current and authorized forms of speech' are almost unavoidable. Some 'familiarity of [...] usage' that may diminish a quotation's 'natural reserve and dignity' must be expected 'in certain authors, who are not over sollicitous about these indecorums'. In this way, Shakespeare is cleared of theft and guilty merely of indecorum because

> these were the ordinary expressions of such [a common] sentiment, in the two languages, and neither the characters of the great poets, nor the situation of the speakers, would suffer the affectation of departing from common usage (Hurd 185).

Casual quotation is redefined as the natural, unaffected use of common cultural property that has made Shakespeare 'part and parcel of English-speaking culture' (Belsey *Why Shakespeare?* 1). Shakespeare is not sneakily quoting Sophocles; he is just rephrasing the woodnotes wild of a popular idiom. Or is he paraphrasing Horace? In his 24th Ode, the Roman poet is mourning Quintilius Varus and wonders when Truth and other goddesses will ever find his like ('cui Pudor [...] quando **ullum inveniet parem**'). As Bishop Hurd says: 'Thus all is derived; all is unoriginal' (110).

Richard Hurd was thinking about Shakespeare's un-originality during the historical moment when many Shakespeare lines were becoming unoriginal themselves, turning into easily recognizable quotations. The *Hamlet* item that Hurd cites as possibly 'stolen' is a case in point. In 1717, Lewis Theobald used the words to mourn the actor Thomas Betterton, who 'for his Knowledge and Justness in his Profession was **what Shakespeare makes Hamlet say of his father**: *He was a man, take him for all in all, I shall not look upon his like again*' (201). The line obviously needed referencing at that moment: author, character and situation are carefully detailed and the quoted words given in italics. In the following decades, the quotation was increasingly used in obituaries. By 1746, David Garrick was ready to use it for a little joke, celebrating a few 'never to be forgotten and paralleled Days [...] in the Month of July Anno Dom 1746'. Instead of a dead celebrity, here '*was a Time, take it for all in all &c.*' (*Letters* 1:86). The italics hint at a quotation and the casual 'etc.' implies that the addressee is in the know. Twenty-three years later, in 1769, Garrick dispensed even with the italics when he spoke about a dead friend: 'I lov'd Esteem'd & honour'd him – / **Take him for all in all &c.**' (2:655). In 1775, Garrick's friend Samuel Johnson subverted the phrase by writing about a person who was alive and well:

> I always told you that Mr. Thrale was a man **take him for all in all, you ne'er will look upon his like.** But you never mind him nor me, till time forces conviction into your steely bosom (*Letters* 2:229).

This is not a father but the addressee's husband and he is not dead. Possibly 'stolen', possibly just popular, Hamlet's line was cutting loose from *Hamlet*,[5] just as Shakespeare had 'disentangled' it (Greenblatt 82) from a folksy proverb, from Sophocles, from Horace, or perhaps from all of the above.

Perhaps the most intricate example of the mix-and-match of Shakespeare's classical intertextuality is the halo of classical reference that scholars have identified around Hamlet's friend Horatio. His name recalls the legendary Roman patriots, the Horatii, and he links himself to the classical past when he announces his intention to commit suicide with the words: 'I am more an antique Roman than a Dane' (5.2.374). Horatio's wish to die with Hamlet is the crowning expression of their friendship which is first hinted at when Horatio identifies himself and Marcellus as 'friends to this ground' (1.1.16) in his first line. Hamlet also expresses his affection for Horatio in a way that may be classicizing; when the Players arrive, he breaks off his intimate conversation with Horatio:

> Give me that man
> That is not passion's slave, and I will wear him
> In my heart's core, ay, in my heart of heart,
> As I do thee. – **Something too much of this** (3.2.76–79).

This sounds very much like Orestes in Euripides' *Electra*, who says to his faithful friend Pylades: 'Nothing in this world is better than a friend [...] but **I say no more, lest I embarrass you**' (quoted in Schleiner 40).

After his introduction of himself as a friend, the second thing that we hear from Horatio seems unclassically and unsolemnly funny. Asked 'Say, what, is Horatio there?', he says 'A piece of him' (1.1.23–24). This sounds like the kind of 'ridiculous' yet irresistible joke that Will Shakespeare should have 'stop'd' himself from making in this eerie, dark scene. However, it could also be a version of the serious topos 'you are a part of me' which had been popular since the Middle Ages in discourses of friendship and abiding memory. The name Horatio could have reinforced the topic of friendship for the first audiences of *Hamlet*, who might have associated Horatio's name with Don Horatio, the protagonist's faithful friend in Kyd's *Spanish Tragedy*, which was first performed in 1592. And perhaps, Horatio's joke is even more solemn, a classical quotation. Several scholars have been encouraged by the name 'Horatio' to comb his words for echoes from the Roman poet Horace, and 'a piece of him' was quite fruitful in this respect. It may echo a passage where Horace describes Virgil as **'half of my own soul'** (*Carmina* 1.3.8, quoted in Braden 97). Alternately, Horace's ode 'Exegi monumentum' describes itself as a monument which will make sure that **'a part of me** [the poet] will evade the goddess of death' (**'pars mei /** vitabit Libitinam') (*Oden* 182). Moreover, Shakespeare's favourite Ovid uses this conceit to pay homage to Horace in the closing line of his *Amores*, expressing the hope that **'a large part of me** will survive' ('**parsque mei multa** superstes erit'). The topic of preserving memory through language and narrative returns in the final scene of *Hamlet* when the dying prince asks Horatio to 'report me and my cause aright' (5.2.371). In this plea, memory and friendship are linked; the Horatio / Horace circle is closing.

Except it is not – there is also an Ovid connection. In the *Metamorphoses*, the 'large part' becomes more pointedly the 'better part', first in Hercules' transfiguration on Mount Oeta where 'gan **in his better part** too thryue' (quoted in Braden 96[6]) and then in the final lines where the poet again speaks of surviving in his poem: '**my better part** will be carried beyond the stars, immortal' ('**parte tamen meliore mei** super alta perennis astra ferar'). Golding's English *Metamorphoses*, first published in 1567, add a further layer.[7] Golding translates the phrase in Book XV as '**the better part of me**', and this is the wording that appears in two of Shakespeare's sonnets:

> O, how thy worth with manners may I sing,
> When thou art all **the better part of me**?(Sonnet 29, 1–2)
> My spirit is thine, the better part of me (Sonnet 74, 8).

The iambic rhythm of Golding's phrasing can also be heard in Hamlet's plea to Gertrude to examine her divided heart and 'throw away **the worser part of it**' (3.4.178). In addition, several other sonnets (18, 55 etc.) combine the topics of friendship and identity by insisting both on the poem outliving the poet and on immortalizing the poets' beloved. It is ironic that 'in using the phrase "the better part of me" the speaker is really using a "part" of someone else' by quoting (Bezzola Lambert, n.p.). All these subjects run deep through many Shakespearean texts while the verbal elements that tie them to their classical expressions are fragmented, overlapping and widely scattered. Given these many and complex alternatives, it seems overstated to suggest a truly involved 'engagement' (Jost 77) of Horatio with Horace. I prefer Sider Jost's wonderful phrase of Horatio as a 'classical possibility' (Jost 76). Among multiple, ultimately casual echoes, Horatio-as-Horace was certainly a possibility in Shakespeare's mind, if one of many.

The metamorphosis to which Shakespeare subjects everything that he remembers returns us once more to the bee metaphor, which has a digestive process at its centre. Erasmus describes how the reader transfers what he finds 'into the mind itself, as into the stomach'. The result is a complete transformation as the quoted material is 'transfused into the veins' and ultimately

> appears to be a birth of one's intellect [...] and breathes forth the vigor and disposition of one's mind and nature, so that the reader does not recognize an insertion taken from Cicero, but a child born from one's brain (quoted in Pigman 8–9).

For the final stage, the emission of what has been absorbed, Erasmus' account decorously switches metaphor from the digestive tract and the birth canal; he now speaks of breath and a birth from the head. This swerve to a classical metaphor (Athena springing from the forehead of Zeus) reinforces the message: it is completely acceptable to modify a borrowed phrase to the point of unrecognizability. Modification is not 'misquotation'; it is explicitly commended: Seneca said that after flying around like a bee we should 'digest' or 'cook up' our reading (quoted in Burrow 165). The same bias is noticeable in the comments of Francis Bacon, who extends the bee metaphor by parallels in the work of other insects. Bacon finds bees superior to ants, who 'only heap up, and use what they have collected', or spiders, who 'spin webs out of themselves'. The production of original material (spiders) and the corrected, *verbatim* reproduction of collected phrases (ants) are procedures favoured by Romantic concepts of authorship today's academic culture. In the sixteenth century, they were second-best. To the Renaissance mind, 'the true labour of philosophy' is most like that of bees, who store 'matter' after 'first modifying and subduing it' (*Novum Organum* quoted in Fischer 110–111).[8] The most striking and transformative example of Shakespeare's intertextual digestion are his image clusters, the most oblique and perhaps least conscious manifestation of his absorption of classical texts, whose raw materials Shakespeare would 'subdue' and 'cook up' again and again throughout his career.

'Not perpetrated wittingly': Shakespeare's classical image clusters

In addition to marked and unmarked quotations, there is a third kind of classical Shakespearean intertextuality, which definitely confirms Petrarch's notion that deeply studied material escapes a writer's consciousness. Shakespeare's image clusters are groups of associated images or ideas that recur in combination with almost Pavlovian reliability throughout his career, shedding or acquiring elements over time but stable and idiosyncratic enough to be recognized in many guises. First noted in the eighteenth century as a probably unconscious phenomenon, they were presented in great detail in 1946 by Edward Armstrong, who only briefly hints at the possibility that they could have a classical origin. In 1987, Barbara Sträuli described an especially persistent set of images, the 'tiger cluster', which she shows to be based on memories of Book IV of the *Aeneid*. Before reporting on her findings, I will introduce the general concept with a minor example that I have called the 'pillow cluster.' This combination includes bedding (usually represented by the word 'pillow'), an unfortunate wife, the dead body of a victim of violence and a dagger. The earliest instance of the pillow cluster, in *Titus Andronicus*, is the most dramatic one, compounding murder by sexual violence and psychological torture. Chiron and Demetrius stab Lavinia's husband Bassianus before her eyes and then decide to rape the distraught widow on her husband's dead body.

> DEMETRIUS: *drawing his **dagger**.* This is a witness that I am thy son.
> CHIRON: *drawing his **dagger**.* And this for me, struck home to show
>   my strength.
>   ***They stab Bassianus.***
> LAVINIA: Ay, come, Semiramis, nay, barbarous Tamora,
>   For no name fits thy nature but thy own!
> TAMORA: Give me the **poniard**! You shall know, my boys,
>   Your mother's hand shall right your mother's wrong.
> DEMETRIUS: Stay, **madam**, here is more belongs to her.
>   First thrash the corn, then after burn the straw.
>   This minion stood upon her chastity,
>   Upon her **nuptial vow**, her loyalty,
>   And with that painted hope braves your mightiness;
>   And shall she carry this unto her **grave**?
> CHIRON: And if she do, I would I were an eunuch!
>   Drag hence **her husband** to some secret hole,
>   And make his **dead trunk pillow** to our lust
> TAMORA: But when you have the honey you desire,
>   Let not this wasp outlive, us both to sting.
> CHIRON: I warrant you, madam, we will make that sure.—
>   Come, mistress, now perforce **we will enjoy**
>   That **nice-preservèd honesty** of yours (2.3.115–135).

These sixteen lines accommodate all the main elements of this particular cluster: the pillow, the unhappy married woman and the daggers that turn her husband into a corpse. Certain elements, like the weapons, are present both verbally and as props or stage actions. Table 3.1 gives an overview of the key words that represent the pillow cluster in *Titus* and other plays. Elements that are represented by actors or actions on stage are given in square brackets; the line numbers indicate where the word 'pillow' occurs.

Table 3.1 The 'pillow cluster'. Author's own

Pillow(s)	Other bedding	Unhappy wife	Corpse	Violence
Titus Andronicus 3.2.130		Nuptial vow (Lavinia)	Dead trunk, grave (Bassianus)	Poniard (dagger, stab)
Antony and Cleopatra 3.13.135		Gem of women, abused	Dead Caesar, morsel	Dead Caesar
Cymbeline 4.2.441	Bed, sleep	Boy [Imogen]	Dead, defunct, trunk [Cloten]	Trunk without top[a]
Cymbeline 5.3.79 (soft beds)	Soft beds	Imogen	Dead, end it, carcasses, died	Knives, slaughter
King Lear 3.4.58	Blanket, cold bed, sleep	Daughters	Spirit	Knives, throats
Lucrece lines 387 and 1620		Dear husband, alas thy Lucrece, lawful kiss	Entombed, virtuous monument [Lucrece]	[Lucrece stabs herself]
Macbeth 2.3.122 and 5.1.77	Bed	Wife [Lady Macbeth]	[Duncan]	Badged with blood
Othello 3.2.456 (bolster)	Bolster	Behold her	Death	Knives, suffocating
Othello 5.2	Bed	[Desdemona]	[Desdemona] [Othello]	[Desdemona's murder, Othello's suicide]
Pericles 3.1.73	Satin coffin	Wretched queen, terrible childbed, my dear	Coffin, the babe [Thaisa and Marina]	[Death in childbirth]
Taming 4.2.201	Bolster, coverlet, sheets	[Katherine]		Kill

[a]Cloten's decapitated corpse in *Cymbeline* is also 'a strange visual echo of [...] Priam's body lying headless on the shore' in Book II of the *Aeneid* (Burrow 84).

These combinations of images or concepts are an extremely personal element of Shakespeare's writing. They are so idiosyncratic and so stable that they can be used to restore corrupted passages or attribute contested passages to Shakespeare like a kind of semantic DNA (cf. Wentersdorf 'Authenticity' and 'Imagery'). No other writer consistently associates the elements of the dog-death-knife-hanging-hunting cluster (sixteen times in nine plays), the tiger-warrior-queen-parent-fire cluster (in sixteen plays) or the black-blanket-tragedy-heaven cluster (cf. Armstrong and Sträuli for detailed tables). In fact, why should they? Why should bedding and food be associated with each other, and with death? The associations seemed quite random already to the philologist Walter Whiter, who concluded in 1794 that Shakespeare's mind must have been 'totally unconscious of the force and principle of [the] union' between associated elements that 'have no natural alliance or relation to each other' (Whiter 65). Whiter quotes *An Essay Concerning Human Understanding*, where John Locke explains irrational associations of ideas by childhood conditioning. A child who has heard too many stories about 'goblins and sprites' from a 'foolish' nanny at bedtime will be afraid of the dark 'so long as he lives' because the ideas of evening darkness and ghosts 'shall be so joined, that he can no more bear the one than the other' (Locke *Human Understanding* 1.531 (section 2.33.10)). Such associations bypass conscious reasoning once they are established, and it has been argued that Shakespeare's clusters should not even be called a 'device': this term implies conscious artistry, whereas the process of using fixed image clusters is completely 'native to [Shakespeare's] mind' (Armstrong 119).

The most obvious memories whose imprint could explain Shakespeare's image clusters are scenarios from Elizabethan daily life. In the kite-death-food-bed cluster, for example, the first three elements may be owed to the idea of kites battening on corpses. The less obvious 'bed' element can be explained by the numerous kites that were preying on offal all over London and habitually 'padd[ed] their nests with little pieces of linen hung out to dry' (Sträuli 139). As Autolycus says: 'When the kite builds, look to the lesser linen' (*Winter's Tale* 4.3.23–24). The dog-death-knife-hanging-hunting cluster can be accounted for by the 'personal experience' of animal executions (Sträuli 138), and the practicalities of Elizabethan theatre may have provided the pattern of the black-blanket-tragedy-heaven cluster in *The Rape of Lucrece* and in *Macbeth*. The 'coarse woollen curtain of his own Theatre' becomes a blanket and 'Heavens' was the name for 'the covering or internal roof of the Stage', which was darkened by 'one piece of black baize placed at the back of the Stage' for tragedies (Whiter 154–157). Such underlying memories provide a logical connection between elements which seem completely random when they appear in the context of a play. An emotionally charged situation involving cluster elements can be imagined as triggering the other elements, which Shakespeare then worked into the emerging text in a suitable form. The new text did not usually require all the elements of a cluster but is made to accommodate them by Shakespeare's evident compulsion to reproduce these unconsciously associated elements. His artistic achievement is not in the choice of cluster elements but in the creativity with which he made these images fit into ever new contexts: 'When the moment came, thought and image rose from the pool of his memory to receive its appropriate language and rhythm' (Wilson 'Shakespeare's Reading' 20).

Shakespeare adapted the image combinations which his unconscious memory imposed on his imagination to their new surroundings with a range of (re-)creative processes. The table for the pillow cluster shows how synonyms and related terms can represent the core elements. The element 'unfortunate wife' is represented by phrases like 'nuptial vow' or 'wretched queen', by a character on stage (Desdemona, Imogen, Lavinia) or by a reference to Lear's absent and unhappily married 'daughters'. Violent death can be enacted or physically manifest in a corpse; it can also be reported or simply evoked by a word, as in Poor Tom's ramblings about the 'foul fiend' who has put 'knives under his pillows' (*Lear* 3.4.58). Technically simpler but semantically more disturbing are shifts that involve homophones and homographs. The 'beetle' in the crow-beetle cluster, for example, is a straightforward insect in *King Lear*, where Edgar looks down from the cliffs of Dover and sees 'The **crows** and choughs that wing the midway air / Show scarce so gross as **beetles**' (4.6.18–19). In *Hamlet*, when Horatio warns of 'the dreadful summit of the cliff / That **beetles** o'er its base into the sea' (1.4.78–79), 'beetle' is a verb with a quite different meaning and the crow is only present as a memory of how the Ghost 'faded on the **crowing** of the cock' (1.1.172) at his first appearance, three scenes before.

The more of these transformational steps are combined, the more irrational an individual cluster manifestation seems. In *Antony and Cleopatra*, the word 'spaniel' calls up the verb 'bark' by semantic association; both are part of the 'dog-heel' cluster. However, 'to bark' does not appear with its canine meaning:

ANTONY: The hearts
   That **spanieled** at my **heels** [...] do discandy [...] and the pine is **barked**
   That overtopped them all (4.12.22–26).

The homograph 'bark' for 'cover in tree skin' has substituted 'bark' for 'dog's voice'. Here and in many other cases, 'it is the sound of a word rather than its meaning which is significant for Shakespeare's associative activities' (Armstrong 27). Shakespeare's writing literally 'echoes' words that are in his mind. Like Roland Barthes, who describes himself as an 'echo chamber', Shakespeare 'reproduces the thoughts badly

[but] follows the words' (*Roland Barthes* 74). Edward Armstrong uses the same acoustic metaphor when he says that Shakespeare can 'arouse harmonics in our minds' (118). The sound of a word which Shakespeare repeats does not even need to be represented by the same spelling: at the end of *Othello*, the word 'heart' is substituted for 'hart', the hunted deer in the dog-death-knife-hanging-hunting cluster:

> OTHELLO: [...] in Aleppo once [...]
> I took by th'throat the circumcisèd **dog**,
> And smote him, thus. *He **stabs** himself.* [...]
> CASSIO: This did I fear, but thought he had no **weapon**,
> For he was great of **heart** (*Othello* 5.2.413–423).

Apart from the heart-hart sound effect, this passage illustrates yet another kind of transformation: The cluster element 'knife' appears as a physical object as Othello stabs himself, before Cassio speaks the synonym 'weapon'. In other passages, cluster elements are represented onlly completely non-verbally, just by a prop, by a piece of stage business or by an actor representing a human figure that is part of a cluster. In *2 Henry VI*, the bed part of the kite-death-food-bed cluster is represented by Duke Humphrey of Gloucester, who is murdered in bed and then carried on stage: '*Bed put forth, bearing Gloucester's body*' (3.2.153). Finally, cluster elements which cannot readily be accommodated by the real world of a scene – as 'death' in a comedy or a 'tiger' in most Shakespearean locations – appear as metaphors. In *The Taming of the Shrew*, Petruchio denies Katherine real food and dismantles her bed, while death and the bird of prey are metaphorically present when he calls Katherine a disobedient '**kite[s]**' or a '**falcon**' that must be starved into submission (4.1.190–196). Similar processes of modification and substitution occur with the tiger cluster, which is discussed in the conclusion to this chapter: Shakespeare is always 'the very Midas of poets, transmuting all he touched' (Wilson 'Shakespeare's Reading' 19).

The 'original' that is 'quoted' in these clusters is an event or everyday scenario remembered from childhood memory; in a few cases, passages from books which Shakespeare had to memorize in childhood have been identified as the origin of a cluster. One example is the myth of Icarus as narrated in the *Metamorphoses*, whose unconscious presence can explain a few confusingly bold metaphors. Consider this passage from *Timon of Athens*:

> POET: [...] My free drift
> Halts not particularly, but moves itself
> In a **wide Sea of wax**: no levell'd malice
> Infects one comma in the course I hold;
> But flies an **eagle flight, bold**, and forth on,
> Leaving no tract behind (1.1.55–60).

Even considering that this passage represents 'the exaggerated imagery' (Marti 67[9]) of a professional, attention-seeking 'Poet', the image of flying through a 'sea of wax' is too weird. The best explanation is that Shakespeare was unconsciously remembering Ovid's story about Icarus, a man who took **pride** in his **flying** like an **eagle** and fell into the **sea** when the **wax** in his wings melted. This 'latent Icarus imagery' (Armstrong 37) in Shakespeare's mind produced strange juxtapositions in several plays. The most striking passage is in *Cymbeline*, where Imogen opens a letter, asking the **'good wax'** of the seal for leave to break it, whereupon her husband Posthumus exclaims: 'O for a **horse with wings**!' (3.2.51). This makes much more sense if we consider that Pegasus stands in for the chariot of the sun with its winged horses, while the word 'smothering' ten lines later indicates 'some recollection of the ambitious youth drowning in the sea' (cf. Armstrong 38). The combination of wing, wax, sea and horse is only apparently random: the elements of what we could call the Icarus cluster are based on a literary template and its realizations are a kind of casual quotation at several removes.

Classical echoes are also at the root of the pillow cluster, which has served as an introduction to this section, and the tiger cluster. Both image combinations were probably fixed in Shakespeare's mind through early exposure at school: they are both based on the *Aeneid*. This paragraph reports on the tiger cluster, which Barbara Sträuli has identified in sixteen Shakespeare works, including *3 Henry VI*, *The Rape of Lucrece*, *Macbeth* and *Hamlet*. In addition to the eponymous animal, the tiger cluster includes a hard, monstrous warrior, a mourning queen, parents, tears and sometimes fire. Like the Icarus cluster, it is based on a grammar school memory, on the famous set piece in Book IV of the *Aeneid* where Dido responds to Aeneas' plan to leave her. This scene is another of Shakespeare's multiple, Protean source texts: he could have found Dido's plea in Ovid's *Heroides*, where it appears as a letter from Dido to Aeneas, in Chaucer's *Legend of Dido* and in several other reworkings of the Virgil passage (cf. Sträuli 148). The tiger cluster, though, is clearly derived from the version in the *Aeneid*. Here is Virgil in the original and in Richard Stanyhurst's 1582 translation:

Virgil *Aeneid* 92 (4.365–369)	Stanyhurst *Aeneid* 75 (4.385–389)
nec tibi diua **parens** generis nec Dardanus auctor, perfide, sed **duris** genuit te cautibus horrens Caucasus, Hyrcanaeque admorunt **ubera tigres**. [...] num fletu ingemuit nostro?	No Godes is thye **parent**, nor th' wart of Dardanus ofspring,Thow periurde fay toure: but amydst rocks, Caucasus haggish Bred the, with a **tigers** soure **milck** vnseasoned, vdderd [...]. At my **tears** showring dyd he **sigh**?

A **weeping queen** accuses a **warrior** of being as **hard**-hearted as a **rock** or as if he had a **tiger** as a **parent**: this is the source of the cluster. In 1594, the passage was quoted in two publications, the anonymous play *Selimus* and in Christopher Marlowe's *Dido*:

Marlowe *Dido* 61 (5.1.156–160)	T. G. *Selimus* sig. E4^recto (1234–1238)
Thy **mother** was no goddess, perjured man,	Thou art not false groome **son** to Baiazet,
Nor Dardanus the author of thy stock;	He would relent to heare a **woman weepe**,
But thou art sprung from Scythian Caucasus,	But thou wast borne in desert Caucasus,
And **tigers** of Hercynia **gave thee suck.**	And the Hircanian **tygres gaue thee sucke.**

Both speeches follow Virgil closely; the anonymous author of *Selimus* turns 'perjured man' into the haughtier 'false groom' and then inserts a line, while Marlowe translates almost *verbatim*. Shakespeare's reworkings, in contrast, *dis*member rather than *re*member Virgil's lines. His memory fixated on selected elements (marked in bold), and added the **mourning queen** (Dido, the speaker). The final element of the cluster, **fire**, belongs to Aeneas' memories of the Fall of Troy. The passage in Book II of the *Aeneid* where he shares these memories with Dido was another popular set piece that Shakespeare probably encountered at school: the two 'seem to have been more frequently read in Tudor grammar schools than any other passages from Virgil's' epic' (Burrow 56). The tiger cluster firmly links these two passages in Shakespeare's unconscious memory.

The Player Scene in *Hamlet* is the most obviously Virgilian realization of the tiger cluster. Hamlet asks the First Player for an episode from Book II, 'Aeneas' tale to Dido and – and thereabout of it especially when he speaks of Priam's slaughter' (2.2.471–473) and this prompts an extended elaboration of the tiger cluster, which comes from Book IV. In a **burning city**, the **monstrous warrior** Pyrrhus kills Priam 'th'unnervéd **father**' (2.2.499) while Hecuba, the **mother** and **mourning queen**, looks on in despair. Only the tiger is missing. Shakespeare's compulsion to complete his set of associations by adding a tiger to a scene of hard-hearted masculinity and royal, parental grief in Homeric Asia Minor set him a considerable challenge. The solution is elegant: the beast is outsourced into a simile:

> HAMLET: [...] if it live in your memory, begin at this line: let me see, let me see:'The rugged Pyrrhus, like the **Hyrcanian beast**,' – 'tis not so; it begins with Pyrrhus:
> 'The rugged Pyrrhus (2.2.473–477).

Shakespeare's unconscious effort to find a place for the completely irrelevant tiger is palpable in Hamlet's false start: he is trying to piece together the beginning of the Pyrrhus scene, remembers a tiger (cluster box ticked) and then starts over because the tiger really is preposterous in this context. The image combination is 'so remarkable and stylistically so gratuitous that it is impossible to believe [it] to be elaborated or maintained wittingly' (Armstrong 102). And yet, how elegant the solution: it makes Hamlet human, it stresses his education and the nostalgic value that the players have for him and it underscores the weirdness of the stylistic realm which the Players' repertory brings to *Hamlet*. Finally, 'Hyrcanian' channels a memory from Book IV of the *Aeneid* as a story from Book II is performed. The same thing happens in *Macbeth*, where the bloody warrior is on stage as Banquo's ghost and promptly triggers elements from the tiger cluster when Macbeth says: 'Approach thou like the **rugged** Russian bear, / The arm'd rhinoceros, or the **Hyrcan tiger**' (3.4.122–125). In this speech, 'Hyrcan' may also have carried a memory of the Player's speech and brought with it the adjective 'rugged' from Pyrrhus.

Shakespeare's 'inner constraint' (Armstrong 123) to assemble the disparate elements of the complete tiger cluster is palpable in many passages, especially with the elements 'fire' and 'tiger', which are harder to accommodate, and the nimbleness and flexibility of imagination that he brought to the task are remarkable. In *Coriolanus*, the **warrior** protagonist's death would be 'a **brand** to th'end of the world' (3.1.387) and the tiger is slipped into the strange adjective '**tiger**-footed rage' (3.1.399). In *Titus Andronicus*, Titus, himself the **warrior**, calls Rome 'a wilderness of **tigers**' and becomes the **mourning parent** (*ex negativo*) as he refuses to lament his daughter:

> What fool hath added water to the sea,
> Or brought a faggot to **bright-burning Troy**?
> My grief was at the height before thou camest,
> And now like Nilus, it disdaineth bounds (3.1.70–73).

Titus introduces Troy in a classicizing version of 'carrying coals to Newcastle', which seems somewhat far-fetched until the river Nile, equally far-fetched, balances out Troy to complete a Mediterranean pair of grand 'fire and water' similes. In the second act of *Titus Andronicus*, Lavinia's outraged attack on Tamora (the **queen**) accommodates the tiger cluster in a record three lines:

> When did the **tiger's** young ones teach the **dam**?
> O, do not learn her **wrath**; she taught it thee;
> The **milk thou suck'dst** from her did turn to **marble** (2.3.142–144).

In *Coriolanus*, the crazy metaphor of **mother's** milk turning to **hard** marble reappears as the (lacking) **maternal** feeling of a **hard-hearted** person when the **warrior** hero's love for his **distraught mother** has set off the tiger cluster:

> SICINIUS: He loved his **mother** dearly.
> MENENIUS: [...] There is no more mercy in him than there is **milk** in a **male tiger** (5.4.28–30).

This ticks the **mother** and the **rock** boxes in the *lucus a non lucendo* way. In Henry's description of Queen Margaret in *3 Henry VI*, the verbal echoes are more oblique:

> Her **tears** will pierce into a **marble heart**;
> The **tiger** will be mild whiles **she doth mourn**;
> And **Nero** will be tainted with remorse,
> To hear and see **her plaints**, her brinish **tears** (3.1.38–41).

Tigers, tears and marble are verbally present, the mourning mother queen is Margaret herself and the burning city is represented by the name of Nero, who has no other reason to be in this speech. *Lucrece*, finally, represents the noun 'tear' by the homograph verb 'tear':

> Stone him with hard'ned hearts harder than stones,
> An let **mild women** to him lose their mildness,
> Wilder to him than **tigers** in their wildness.
> Let him have time to **tear** his curlèd hair (*Lucrece*, lines 1978–1981).

The Protean forms and formats which the elements of a Shakespearean cluster can assume make it hard to notice the underlying connection to a literary or biographical memory

The almost unvoluntary quality of Shakespeare's image clusters, which seem to be based on deeply ingrained memories which he did not consciously draw on reinforces an important caution to scholars who are tempted to read a thematic involvement into his classical 'quotations'. Shakespeare could access the Latin classics in manifold and fragmented forms and this fragmentation was reinforced by his tendency to remember automatically, in small verbal units and along hardwired associative sequences. The shifts and modifications by which he fits his image clusters into new scenes and contexts operate on individually remembered elements and not on a conscious, integral memory of a scene, passage or situation. What conscious efforts he may have made to integrate the elements of a cluster as he was writing must have focused on the requirements of the new scene that was being created, and not on doing justice to whatever once was the original context of these elements. In this sense, image clusters, too, represent casual intertextuality. Alimented by everyday experiences, by rote-learning at school, wide (if cursory) reading and the memory training of a professional actor, Shakespeare's 'facetious grace in writting' (Chettle *Kind-Heart's Dream* unpaginated front matter) attained a distinctive combination of speed, variety and intertextual tenacity. These characteristics, confirmed by reports of his

'Honey-tongued Shakespeare' and the Classics 75

pun-riddled, skipping and unstoppably associative conversation, are beautifully caught in an epigram from 1614:

> *Shakespeare*, that nimble Mercury thy braine,
> Lulls many hundred *Argus*-eyes asleepe,
> So fit, for all thou fashionest thy vaine (Freeman *Rub* sig. K2^{verso}–K3^{recto}).

Shakespeare-as-Mercury, fleet of foot and winged like a bee, is the king of thieves who works extraneous materials into his texts to serve his poetic purposes and smooths over any incongruities that might distract a reader from his 'natural flowing wit' (Anon. *Against Too Much Reading* 14). Instead of investigating sources and meaningful intertextual networks, we are charmed into reading 'Shakespeare' in 'his vaine' and lulled into dreams by his 'nimble' language that is so intertextual and yet so much his own. The following chapter traces such casual intertextuality in Shakespeare's handling of English sources and in early Shakespeare quotations.

Notes

1. The Latin word 'florilegium' and the Greek-derived 'anthology' both mean 'collection of flowers'.
2. This verse is actually used in William Lily's elementary grammar (cf. Burrow 24).
3. The search string <integer vitae scelerisque purus> yields 52 hits in the *EEBO/TCP* corpus of sixteenth- and seventeenth-century books printed in England. The results include sermons, emblem collections, grammar primers, an English translation of the picaresque Spanish novel *Guzman de Alfarache* (1623) and Thomas Cooper's *Thesaurus linguæ Romanæ*, where the phrase is listed as an example for the use of the noun 'vita' (PPPppp4^{recto}).
4. Andrew Hadfield has suggested that 'no one would have begun a poem calling Spenser "Honey tongued"' and that the comparison makes Shakespeare not 'perhaps not quite as serious as the very best' (201).
5. Further mid-century examples include the dedication to the memoirs of a courtesan (Phillips *Apology* 1:47), a footnote to a character reference in a verse 'epistle' (Jones 'Of Patience' 11, note) and praise for a living actor in Tobias Smollett's *Peregrine Pickle* (4:110).
6. The original Latin runs: 'parte sui meliore viget'.
7. The status of Golding's translation in Shakespeare's memory is contested; Anthony Brian Taylor argues, for example, that Shakespeare would have read it after leaving school because the teachers might have seen to it that it was not available as a cheat sheet (Taylor *Shakespeare's Ovid* 4).
8. The original Latin phrases run: 'formicæ more, congerunt tantum et utuntur', 'aranearum more telas ex se conficiunt', 'Philosophiæ verum opificium' and 'materiam [...] in intellectum mutatam et subactam' (Bacon *Instauratio magna* 115).
9. The original German runs: 'Die Stelle kann nur als weiteres Beispiel für die übertriebene Metaphorik des Dichters akzeptiert werden.'

4 'Shakespeares fine filed phrase'

> *The Muses would speak with Shakespeares fine filed phrase,*
> *if they would speak English*
> FRANCIS MERES (1598)

Whatever Shakespeare read or heard, he quoted, and people in turn started quoting his texts as soon as they were performed and published. Both processes were often notably casual. Shakespeare never names the English birds with whose 'feathers' he 'beautified' (Greene (sig. F$_{verso}$)) his writing, and the borrowed feathers are so many that a full engagement with the original contexts and contents in all cases is highly improbable. This goes both for Shakespeare himself and those who used his words in the first decades. In many cases of verbal overlap, we cannot even decide who is quoting whom. Hamlet's phrase 'prophetic soul' appears in Sir Francis Hubert's *Deplorable Life and Death of Edward the Second* (sig. H8^{verso} [28]). Published in 1628, this biography seems to be one of many early quotations of this line (cf. Greenfield 'Early Seventeenth'). However, as the *Deplorable Life* was composed between 1597 and 1600, it could also have been a source for *Hamlet*. Similarly, neither *Hamlet* nor John Marston's tragedy *Antonio's Revenge* can be dated precisely enough to decide who imitates whom; perhaps both plays are based on a common source rather than one on the other. There are many works that Shakespeare definitely does quote, there are many more texts that clearly use his language, and there are many lexias whose historical trajectory we can no longer hope to determine. In hindsight, 'Shakespeare Quoting' and 'Quoted Shakespeare' around 1600 are not so much two related phenomena as an open space swirling with cross-quoted, circulating phrases.

Literary decorum in the Renaissance encouraged writers to scan classics and peruse anthologies for quotations to enrich their texts. During Shakespeare's lifetime, this habit began to extend to English sources, and Elizabethan anthologies started to include extracts from contemporary English poets. Collections from the 1590s present dozens of passages from Shakespeare's early hits *Romeo and Juliet* and the narrative poems *Lucrece* and *Venus and Adonis* and must have added considerably to the popularity of these phrases. Shakespeare 'emerges as a canonical English poet in a bound volume neither through poems nor through his plays but rather through individual "sentences"' (Stallybrass and Chartier 49 and 46). This decontextualizing effect is especially striking when passages from stage plays appear in what are essentially volumes of poetic extracts to serve new purposes that have nothing to do with dramatic speech. The subtitle of John Cotgrave's *English treasury of wit and language* describes this process in classical terms, offering 'the most, and best' of English dramatic poetry 'extracted' and 'methodically digested into common places for generall use'. The word 'digested' extends the sanction of the classical bee metaphor to the quotable snippets of vernacular texts that are presented ready for use like the Latin and Greek classics. However, as more and more living English authors were quoted, more 'proprietary metaphors' (Cook 246) emerged. In 1607, Thomas Walkington describes borrowings from contemporary texts with a lively allegory that has since turned out to have a future in copyright issues:

> If any new work that is lately come out of presse, as a barke vunder saile fraighted with any rich merchandies appeares to them, doe play vpon it eft with their siluer peeces, board it incontinently, ransacke it of euery rich sentence, full of all the witty speeches they can finde appropriateing them to their own vse (sig. 45^{verso}).

We have ample evidence that Shakespeare and his contemporary 'wit-pirates' (Donne 174) worked in exactly this buccaneering way as a matter of daily routine. Readers turned writers, texts that quote were in turn quoted, and phrases circulated as detached and often unacknowledged bits of topical 'merchandies' rather than as ponderous Quotations from Works by (Classical) Authors. Elizabethan and Jacobean literature is highly intertextual in the original sense of the word, a 'tissue of quotations drawn from innumerable centres of culture' (Barthes 'Death of the Author' 17), and this tissue is particularly dense around Shakespeare, 'the permeable Bard' (Wiggins 1). The contemporary casual intertextuality surrounding Shakespeare's works is so rich that this chapter can merely illustrate Shakespeare's way with his English sources through a few particularly a handful of particularly instructive examples. These analyses throw some light – if not a full, statistical illumination – on the process that turned Shakespeare from a verbal borrower into a lender and allowed his 'fine filed phrases' (Meres *Palladis Tamia* sig. 282^{recto}) to morph triumphantly from 'Shakespeare Quoting' to 'Quoted Shakespeare'.

Three English sources: Florio, Bright and Nashe

The English books that Shakespeare read offered him unmediated access to authorship, content and phrasing, without the translations and adaptations that conditioned his perception of the Bible and the classics. Shakespeare, however, did not avail himself of the option to provide exact and fully-marked quotations. His English sources are used in his characteristically goal-oriented way: never acknowledged, rarely *verbatim*, with minimal care for context and content and subjected to the mix-and-mash of cross-quotation. As with his classical inspirations, 'Shakespeare professionally melted [English] sources together' (Burrow 166), and a similar lack of respect is perceptible in his treatment of other people's words. Although they could have been transferred intact from recent print editions, Shakespeare adapts, distorts, displaces and re-combines them, never intent on establishing a relationship with a quoted text beyond suiting his own dramatic purposes. Texts are adapted and authors remain unnamed since living writers did not have the *auctoritas* that could serve characterization as when Shakespearean villains, jokers or pedants point out their (mis-) quotations from the Bible or from Horace (cf. Chapter 3).[1] This mode of appropriation is quite independent of the genre of Shakespeare's sources; it is uninfluenced by a topic that is relevant to a play or a model conversation that matches a scene. Whatever the contexts of the English phrases that he found useful, Shakespeare dis(re)members and 'disentangles' (Greenblatt 82) his finds from their origins. His 'wit' remained firmly 'in his own power' (Jonson 'Discoveries' 539) whether he borrowed from a language primer, an anthology, a medical treatise, a pamphlet, a poem or an epic. In the following, three examples from three different genres will show several facets of Shakespeare's verbal appropriation and its characteristic 'aggressive anonymity' (Bruster *Quoting Shakespeare* 20).

John Florio's volumes *First Fruits* and *Second Fruits* are bilingual anthologies of proverbs, dialogues and poems in Italian and English; casual quotation of such already fragmented items may seem a given. However, Shakespeare's 'power' of appropriation is noticeable even in his borrowings from such a collection of small-scale items. In a passage from *Love's Labour's Lost* that has already been mentioned in Chapter 3, Holofernes quotes and translates the first half of an Italian proverb which Florio gives as 'Venetia, Venetia, Chi non ti vede non ti pretia ma chi ti vede, ben gli costa':[2]

> HOLOFERNES: <u>I may speak of thee as the traveller doth of Venice</u>
> **Venetia, Venetia,**
> **Chi non ti vede non ti pretia**
> Old Mantuan, old Mantuan! **who understandeth thee not, loves thee not** (4.2.114–119).

Shakespeare makes Holofernes re-address his translation of the apostrophe to Venice to the poet Baptista Mantuanus, and so already adapts Florio's content. In addition, he changes the semantics. Florio translates the proverb twice, and both versions have a financial undertone that plays on the closeness of esteem / estimate and praise / price (all emphases mine):

> Who sees not Venice, cannot *esteeme* it / But he that sees it *payes* well for it (*Second Fruits* 106 and 107).

> Venise, woo seeth thee not, praiseth thee not, but who sees thee, it *costeth* hym wel (*First Fruits* 34).

Shakespeare's rendering leaves out the explicitly financial second clause and reduces the implicit monetary aspect of the first one by turning 'see' into 'understand' and 'esteem' / 'praise' into 'love'. Instead of a tourist's remark, we now have the comment of a philosopher. What remains, what is ultimately quoted, is a phrase structure, hollowed out and filled with new meaning just like 'to verb or not to verb'. The quotation is completely casual: marked by a language switch and uninterested in the original content, it deftly characterizes the speaker as a learned pedant who either knows very little Italian or feels free to improvise a translation as suits him.

More intricate transformations happen when a little set piece, a model conversation from *Second Fruits*, is worked into *Hamlet*. A 'ciuill, familiar and pleasant' exchange between 'two gentlemen in their chamber, and at the window' (*Second Fruits* 111), including talk of arms, fencing and shopping for gloves (*Second Fruits* 121), is the basis for the kind of polite exchange that the courtier Osric intends to have with his prince in Act 5 of *Hamlet*. Regrettably for Osric, Hamlet refuses to collaborate. He ridicules Osric's enthusiasm for 'French rapiers and poniards, with their assigns, as girdle, hangers' (5.2.162–163) and subverts Florio's conversational blueprint with consistent rudeness.

Second Fruits 111	Hamlet 5.2.105–116
GIORDANO. Why do you stand barehedded? You do yourself wrong.	Hamlet. **Your bonnet to his right use; 'tis for the head.**
EDWARD. **Pardon me, good sir, I doe it for my ease.**	OSRIC. I thank your lordship, it is very hot.
GIORDANO. I pray you be couered [...].	HAMLET. No, believe me, 'tis very cold [...] But yet methinks it is very sultry and hot [...].
EDWARD. I am so well, that me thinks I am in heauen.	OSRIC. Exceedingly, my lord; it is very sultry [...]
GIORDANO. **If you loue me, put on your hat.**	HAMLET. [He motions to Osric to put on his hat] **I beseech you, remember –**
EDWARD. I will doe it to obay you, not for any leasure that I take in.	OSRIC. **Nay, good my lord; for my ease, in good faith.**

Hamlet starts by conventionally asking Osric to cover himself, but he does it so abruptly that it feels like an act of condescending aggression rather than a polite offer to relax. Osric nevertheless recognizes a conversational model and correctly continues it by refusing to take off his hat as a matter of politeness. Hamlet, however, keeps going out of order so that Osric, cornered by his social superior's refusal to respect conversational etiquette, resorts to re-purposing Florio's phrases. Florio's Edward politely says 'good sir' and 'for my ease' to explain why he is not wearing his hat, then yields to Giordano's polite insistence and puts it on; Osric uses the same words to conserve a shred of dignity and keeps his hat *off*.

In the exchange between Osric and Hamlet, Florio's model of conversation is further undercut by cross-quotation: Hamlet's insistence on temperature may be echoing a well-worn joke in which a bare-headed man is forced to put on his hat but 'should haue put it of againe, to haue shewed that he was not bare in respect of them, but because of the heate' (Guazzo 30). Shakespeare-as-Hamlet once more revives an old chestnut for *ad hoc* conversational purposes, as when the Gravedigger intersperses his musings on the Bible with riddles or when Shakespeare himself produced embarrassing repartee from an admirer's bed (cf. p. 41). W. M. Theobald further suggested Juvenal's *Satire III* as a third source for 'Hamlet's mockery of the obsequious who will agree to contrary propositions' (cf. Jenkins 399, note on line 94). As always, the overall effect of Shakespeare's intertextual mangling is that his characters come to life: Osric's attempts to hold on to a stately model of conversation expose him to mockery and Hamlet, who is undermining that model, seems rude yet attractively smart.

Shakespeare's cavalier, goal-oriented treatment of his sources is most striking when the topic of a source is obviously relevant to what he is writing. From his use of Timothy Bright's *Treatise of Melancholy*, we would expect a coherent tissue of medico-psychological knowledge to underpin the portrayal of Hamlet. Instead, fragmenting casualness prevails. In the Ghost's description of his murder, the poison 'doth **posset / and curd**, like eager droppings into milk, / The **thin** and wholesome blood' (1.5.75–77). Because Shakespeare retains salient words, we recognize Bright's description of the brain as **'tender as a posset curd'** (Bright 13) even in an anatomically and grammatically modified form. The Ghost speaks of blood, not brains, and turns the compound noun 'posset curd' into two verbs. The claim that 'vnnaturall melancholie' destroys the mind 'with all his faculties and **disposition of action**' (Bright 110) resurfaces with similar imprecision, with its elements split into two different scenes: Hamlet laments that his enterprises are losing '**the name of action**' (3.1.96) and his **'disposition'** is going very '**heavily**' (2.2.320). Yet another passage is rendered by antonyms. Bright's claim that the air 'meete for melancholicke folke' is 'thinne, pure and subtile […] especially to the South, and Southeast' (Bright 257) reappears in Hamlet's quip as 'I am but mad **north-north-west**: when the wind is southerly, I know a hawk from a handsaw' (2.2.402–403). Instead of saying 'south is good', Hamlet says 'north is bad', reproducing Bright like a semantic photo-negative. In 1904, Sir Sidney Lee actually likened Shakespeare's mind to a highly sensitised photographic plate, which need only be exposed for the hundredth part of a second to anything in life or literature, in order to receive upon its surface the firm outline of a picture which could be developed and reproduced at will (291).

Lee's photography metaphor describes a process that is just as inorganic and involuntary as the acoustic reverberations in an echo chamber. Both images imply that Shakespeare could not help retaining and replicating what he encountered. And in many cases, he indeed replicated phrases with all the literary sensitivity of a photographic plate, faithfully registering details but inverting the overall image, changing its tone or blurring it. He misquotes as well as re-phrases Bright, who says that adverse winds may cause melancholy (rather than madness). Such shifts point to a memory that mostly retains verbal elements and textual surfaces even where there is an obviously relevant topic.

Shakespeare's tendency to echo verbal surfaces is especially evident when he cuts up and scatters phrases from Bright's book into different contexts. Bright says, for example, that the melancholics' 'indefatigable [practice of wit] maketh them seeme to haue that of a naturall **readinesse**, which **custome of exercise** and use hath found in them' (130). This will remind most readers of Hamlet complaining that he has 'lost all [his] mirth, forgone all **custom of exercises**' (2.2.318–320), and the quotation seems apt. However, Hamlet is referring to physical training, not intellectual nimbleness, and he is not pursuing his 'exercises' with the characteristic 'readinesse' of Bright's patients; on the contrary, he has *stopped* practising. Instead of 'mentally agile', we have 'physically inert', another semantic photo-negative reproduction of a verbal surface. Moreover, one of Bright's signifiers only turns up three acts later in Hamlet's phrase 'the **readiness** is all' (5.2.236–237), when the prince is no longer even depressed! This is an almost cubist case of fragmentation and displacement. It may of course seem far-fetched to consider the isolated word 'readiness' as a trace from *The Treatise of Melancholy*. However, all other occurrences of the word in Shakespeare's plays (fourteen in all) are all of a simple, practical nature, of the kind 'FIRST LORD: Where be our men? / SERVANT: Here, my lord, in readiness' (*Timon* 1.2.171–172). In all these passages, 'readiness' means being physically ready to go out or head into battle, whereas 'readiness' as a psychological condition is unique to *Hamlet* and may well be inspired by Bright; a tiny semantic trace which confirms the unmistakable yet superficial imprint that reading Bright's *Treatise* made on Shakespeare's memory.

In Shakespeare's echoes from Thomas Nashe's *Pierce Penniless*, we can observe yet another kind of transformation.[3] Ernest C. York, who identified most of these borrowings in 1953, assumed that Shakespeare 'was drawing on unconscious memories of *Pierce Penniless*' (371) because so many details are reproduced recognizably, while the general mood of Nashe's prose is rather changed. In two cases, Shakespeare conserves just a structural template. The 'mightie deformer of mens manners', for example, can be heard in the First Gravedigger's quip 'your water is a sore decayer of your whoreson dead body' (*Hamlet* 5.1.177–178) and Nashe's condemnation of 'Sloath in Nobilitie, **Courtiers, Schollers,** or any men' (*Pierce Penniless* sig. H1^{verso} [25]) has a structural echo in Ophelia's lament for 'The **courtier's**, soldier's, **scholar's** eye, tongue, sword' (3.1.165). *Pierce Penniless* has obvious semantic overlaps with *Hamlet*, just as does *The Treatise of Melancholy*, and in both cases, Shakespeare casually re-mastered phrases and structures and shifts between the literal and figurative uses of words. Nashe's vigorous pamphlet revels in physical detail and many of his colourful phrases reappear in *Hamlet* in less crude though still powerful contexts. Nashe's allegorical trollop with too much make-up ('**His vaineglorie** [...] he hath new painted **an inch thicke'** (*Christs teares* n. p.)) becomes shockingly serious when Hamlet addresses Yorick's skull: 'Now get you to **my lady's** chamber, and tell her, let her **paint an inch thick**, to this favour she must come' (5.1.18–191). The physical association of thick make-up – a mere metaphor for vanity in Nashe – and a bare skull really makes the phrase 'paint an inch thick' hit hard.

Shakespeare's shifting between metaphor and reality works in the opposite direction in another Nashe adaptation, Hamlet's critique of excessive drinking at court in Act 1. The underlying Nashe passage drives home the consequences of alcoholism with powerfully unpleasant images of fermentation. Hamlet, characteristically fastidious, avoids such unappealing terms although excessive drinking repels him just as much as it does Nashe. Shakespeare's eclectic mix-and-mash of bits from his source are palpable in the following passages:

Nashe *Pierce Penniless* 23
A **mightie deformer** of *mens manners* and *features,* is this *vnnecessary vice* of all other. **Let him bee** indued with neuer so many **vertues,** and haue as much goodly proportion and fauour as **nature** can bestow vppon a man; yet if he [...] is drowning his soule in a gallon pot, **that one beastly imperfection** will vtterlie **obscure all that is commendable in him**; and all his good qualities sinke like lead down to the bottome of his carrowsing cups, where they will lie, like lees and **dregges,** dead and vnregarded of any man [...] O but thou hast a foule swallow, if it come once to **carousing of humane bloud.**

Hamlet 1.4.26-39, 3.2.422-423 and 5.2.315
So, oft it chances in particular men, That for some **vicious mole of nature** in them, [...] By **the o'ergrowth of some complexion,** Oft breaking down the pales and **forts of reason,** Or by some habit that **too much o'er-leavens** The form of plausive manners, that these men, Carrying, I say, **the stamp of one defect,** Being **nature's livery,** or fortune's star, Their **virtues** else – **be they** as pure as grace,[...] Shall in the general censure take corruption From **that** particular fault: the **dram of eale.**

[N]ow could I **drink hot blood.**

The Queen **carouses** to thy fortune, Hamlet

While clearly inspired by Nashe's argument, Hamlet shies away from the chemical details of alcohol consumption except for an oblique hint at yeast in 'o'er-leavens'. Instead, he uses Nashe's abstract terms 'nature' and 'virtues'. The phrase **'carouse of human blood'** seems to have stuck in Shakespeare's mind much like Bright's 'readinesse': too crassly physical for Hamlet's argument about reason being undermined by alcohol, it was apparently too interesting to forget, and so its components appear in different contexts. In the last scene, Gertrude says: 'The queen **carouses** to thy fortune, Hamlet' (5.2.315) and then proceeds to drink the cup poisoned by Claudius. This gently lethal toast purges the verb 'carouse' of any association with excessive courtly boozing. The idea of drinking an enemy's blood is outsourced to a different scene: it becomes mere metaphor when Hamlet says, 'now could I **drink hot blood**' (3.2.422–423). Drunkenness, finally, is avoided even as a metaphor: where Nashe's drunkard is 'drowning his soule in a gallon pot', Hamlet's natural fault is 'breaking down the pales and forts of reason', a metaphor whose chivalrous overtones further damper his language.

Shakespeare's cross-quotations: Spenser, Nashe and Virgil

Shakespeare got a lot of lively language out of *Pierce Penniless* but the most wonderful instance of how he appropriates and moderates Nashe's crude, forceful phrases is an image that is neither Nashe's nor Shakespeare's. 'Breaking down the pales and **forts of reason**', the fourth line of the *Hamlet* passage quoted above, describes drink-addled Reason as a besieged fortress, and this knightly, medieval concept is introduced in the wording of a source that is about as far from Nashe as could be imagined: Spenser's archaizing epic *The Faerie Queene*. In an allegorical battle, Wrath and Jealousy 'Strong warres [...] make, and cruell battry bend / Gainst **fort of Reason**, it to ouerthrow' (253 (2.4.34)). This knightly background reinforces Hamlet's moralizing tone, as if Spenser's 'fort of reason' was holding out against the language from *Pierce Penniless* that surrounds it. Conversely, we could say that Nashe's vigorous phrasing makes the Spenser insert sound priggish. The strongest effect of the cross-quotation, however, is that of the incongruity itself – a kind of oblique marking for quotation – which makes Hamlet sound complex and impressively eloquent. The individual impact of the two incongruous sources is weakened and the main impression is not of Nashe's and Spenser's interestingly contrasting styles; what we remember is the richly ambiguous character of Hamlet's ranting. Out of two incongruous sources, Shakespeare creates an effect of aggressive yet contained sententiousness (which is then dramatically knocked out of Hamlet two lines later by the first encounter with his father's ghost). Nashe's diatribe against drinking is highly topical for Hamlet's disgust with his uncle's court but his words, collocations, structures and sound effects are completely detached from their contexts, appropriated and scattered to enrich Shakespeare's own language.

Spenser contributed many more phrases to *Hamlet*, including some extremely famous ones. '"Seems", madam? Nay, it **is**. I know not "seems"' (1.2.79) may be an echo of 'Yet inly **being** more, then **seeming** sad' (554 (3.12.16)), and the striking rhythm of Spenser's 'lesson **too too hard** for **liuing clay**' (438 (3.4.26)) reverberates in 'O that this **too too solid** flesh would **melt**' (1.2.133). This transformation is similar to the process that turned Timothy Bright's 'South, and Southeast' into Hamlet's 'north-north-east'. Shakespeare fills a remembered phrase structure with synonyms (clay-flesh) and antonyms (melt-hard) and turns it into something that means the opposite of the quoted phrase: Spenser's 'living clay' is too weak, Hamlet's 'flesh' too strong. What gives the echo away as an echo is the skeleton 'too, too' and the mood of suffering. With other phrases, we can observe associative chains as Spenser's phrase **'goodly frame'** for the castle of Temperance (351 (2.11.13) is transformed from allegory to reality in 'this **goodly frame**, the earth [with its] brave o'erhanging **firmament**' (*Hamlet* 2.2.320–326). The shift is technically the same as when Nashe's painted vanity becomes Yorick's skull; the effect is rather different because the physical counterpart, Shakespeare's starry sky, is lofty rather than shockingly decayed. Another allegorical castle in Spenser is the '**goodly frame,** / And stately port of *Castle Ioyeous*' (*Faerie Queene* 392 (3.1.31)), which Britomart and the Red Cross Knight have to leave 'ere the **grosse Earthes** gryesy shade / Was all disperst out of the **firmament**' (401 (3.1.67)). Here we can recognize Hamlet's '**gross as earth**' (4.4.49) as well as Owen Glendower's '**frame** and **huge** foundation of the **earth**' (*1 Henry IV* 3.1.16). As Colin Burrow says à propos of a Virgil reminiscence, this 'could be a deliberate effect, or it could just be an effect of a misfiring memory and an inspired pen' (Burrow 76). Sequences of tenuously and superficially associated fragments are juxtaposed and recombined as they wander through Shakespeare's memory.

Remarkably, phrases from Shakespeare's reading infiltrated even his image clusters. The first appearance of the pillow cluster in *Titus Andronicus* (cf. p. 67) includes some striking phrases that seem to be Thomas Nashe's. The horrible detail of Lavinia being raped on her husband's 'dead trunk', which becomes a 'pillow' to Chiron and Demetrius' 'lust', figures neither in Ovid nor in later versions of the Philomel rape story but in *The Unfortunate Traveller,* where Esdras rapes Heraclide and makes her husband's '**dead** bodie [...] **a pillow to his abhomination**' (sig. K4[verso]). If Shakespeare remembered 'this bizarre detail [...] from his reading' (York 371), it would explain the intensity of the scene in *Titus Andronicus* as coming straight from the impact of reading Nashe, while the horror is significantly less in later realizations of the pillow cluster. However: *The Unfortunate Traveller* was published in 1594, one year after the latest date that has been suggested for *Titus Andronicus*. Shakespeare does seem to have read the *Traveller* before he wrote *1 Henry IV*, which contains a cluster of striking verbal overlaps (cf. Coffman 318). Perhaps a common source for *Titus Andronicus* and *The Unfortunate Traveller* will be identified one day or we will learn that Nashe's book could have reached Shakespeare in manuscript a few years before publication. No such doubts exist about *The Faerie Queene*'s publication date and about the echoes from Spenser that intersect with the Player's Speech in *Hamlet*; Hecuba, the **mourning queen**, encounters Pyrrhus, the **rock-hard** Greek **warrior** and metaphorical **tiger**, in the **burning** city of Troy. These elements of the tiger cluster are derived from Book IV of the *Aeneid*; the **'rugged'** Pyrrhus is **'like th'Hyrcanian beast'** (2.2.472–475) not only because Virgil's Dido calls Aeneas tiger-bred for wanting to leave her, but also because Spenser's Pyrochles **'rudely rag'd** and **like a cruell Tygre** fared' (*Faerie Queene* 259 (2.5.8)). The names 'Pyrrhus' and 'Pyrochles' both include the Greek root for 'fire' or 'red' and Shakespeare transposes Pyrochles' personal fieriness – he 'round about him threw forth sparkling fire, / that seemd him to inflame on euery side' (*Faerie Queene* 257 (2.5.2)) – to the heat of burning Troy, which 'roasted' Pyrrhus 'in wrath and fire' (*Hamlet* 2.2.486). The massed r-sounds in 'Pyrrhus', 'rugged', 'roasted', 'Hyrcanian', 'wrath' and 'tiger' not only give the First Player a chance for theatrical elocution, but they are also phonetic traces from the *Faerie Queene*'s 'round', 'Pyrochles' and 'threw'. And, of course, the young Ed Spenser – like Will Shakespeare, Tom Nashe and Kit Marlowe – must have memorized the set pieces from Book II and IV at grammar school. Hamlet may be hinting at this shared experience when he tells the First Player that he 'chiefly loved' the speech from 'Aeneas' tale to Dido' (2.2.470–471).

Shakespeare's casual quotation practice combines two fundamentally different intertextual experiences that were first distinguished by Petrarch (cf. p. 60). With profoundly studied and absorbed works, a writer may become paradoxically oblivious to the textual details of a source or even to the fact that there *is* a source; the quoted thought is remembered and used as if it were the writer's own. Conversely, books that are read quickly, perhaps with the conscious purpose of finding things to quote, are more readily remembered and acknowledged. In contrast, Shakespeare treats all his English sources in a similar way: he often seems indifferent to or even unaware of the contexts of borrowed phrases, while his tenacious memory for surface details – sounds, words, collocations, structures – allows us to identify his borrowings even in transformation and paraphrase.[4] F. P. Wilson described this gathering process beautifully in 1953:

> We catch him dipping into that spirited piece of anti-Catholic propaganda, Samuel Harsnett's *Declaration of egregious Popish*

Impostures, and coming up with the names of Edgar's fiends [...] and a few phrases. He remembers from Sir William Segar's *Book of Honour and Arms* the first and second causes for a trial of arms and builds them into the character of Don Armado ('Shakespeare's Reading' 17).

Whether or not the contexts of Shakespeare's sources are relevant to his writing, Shakespeare twists, adapts, scatters, juxtaposes and digests quoted words; he could 'tear the heart out of a book as quickly as any man' (Wilson 'Shakespeare's Reading' 17) with a disconcerting combination of thoroughness and disconnected detail.

Shakespeare's capacious memory for details that remain identifiable can create an impression of thematic involvement which may be misleading. Abbie Findlay Potts, who identified the verbal parallels between *Hamlet* and *The Faerie Queene* discussed above, claims that these borrowings demonstrate a 'substantial kinship between this great English tragedy and the greatest ethical poem in English' (43). This seems to me somewhat overstated; for scholars who have discovered individual sources that seem topically pertinent, it is easy to forget 'how little use he made in his plays of some of the books that he looked at' (Wilson 'Shakespeare's Reading' 17). The quest for the 'fetish of literary meaning'[5] makes us overlook the possibility that Shakespeare simply 'rehearses' words (Barthes *Roland Barthes* 74). The claims that have been made about Shakespeare's professional experience are an instructive parallel. His adroit handling of technical jargon has led to suggestions that he was an 'alchemist, botanist, butcher, churchman, farmer, lawyer, mad doctor, musician, ornithologist, page, sailor, schoolmaster, skewer-sharpener, soldier, surgeon or a woolman' among other things (Blades iii–iv). However plausible these conjectures may be individually, they become almost absurd when considered together, just as the number of works that overlap verbally with the Shakespeare canon make casual quotation more likely in many cases. William Blades proposed a theory that would explain both the extent of Shakespeare's specialist vocabularies and his casual quotations: he could have worked as a typographer during his 'second lost years' (1585–1592). His erstwhile schoolmate Richard Field was the apprentice and later successor of Thomas Vautrollier, who published Bright's *Treatise of Melancholy* and *The Faerie Queene* as well as Shakespeare's first publications *Lucrece* and *Venus and Adonis*. In Vautrollier's and later Field's workshop, Shakespeare could have had thousands of pages going through his hands. Blades, who lists dozens of arcane printing expressions in the plays and sonnets in support of his hypothesis, could also have added the phrase '*Iohannes fac totum*' for 'jack of all trades' in Robert Greene's attack on the young 'Shake-scene'. One of the meanings of 'factotum' is 'An ornamental printing block with a space into which a (capital) letter can be inserted' (*OED*, online edition).

Shakespeare-the-blockhead may not prove that he ever was a jobbing printer but the image of a superficial yet detailed acquaintance with countless typeset phrases goes very nicely with his casual intertextual practice. In any case, the number of Shakespeare's casual borrowings should make us wary of weighty conclusions. His intertextual activity reveals fascinating patterns of meaning as well as evident patterns of superficiality. These same patterns appear in the texts of many writers who quote him and can be observed in impressive quantity in the work of his most persistent borrower, John Marston.

John Marston's 'play scrappes'

William Shakespeare's fellow dramatist John Marston, the contemporary who quotes him most, was active as a writer for just one intense decade between studying law and taking holy orders. From 1598 to 1607, he was a highly interactive presence in the London literary and theatrical scene. He attacked colleagues in unusually aggressive satires, took part in the 'War of the Theatres' with Ben Jonson and Thomas Dekker and co-wrote a substantial part of his theatrical output with Dekker, Jonson, George Chapman and others. Marston's relationship with Shakespeare is more elusive. His numerous Shakespeare quotations were noted early on (cf. Munro 1:29), but the *Shakespeare Allusion-Book* is 'assured' that he is not the J. M. who signed the poem 'To the memorie of M. W. Shake-speare' in the *First Folio* (Munro 1:319) and he is barely mentioned in the recent composite biography *The Shakespeare Circle*. Marston's satires may have inspired Shakespeare's Thersites, Iago and mad Lear, yet the two dramatists do not seem to have collaborated. Instead, they wrote two strikingly similar plays that cannot be dated exactly enough for us to decide whether *Hamlet* adapts *Antonio's Revenge* or the other way around (cf. Geckle 91, note 4); in fact, both tragedies may derive from the lost *Ur-Hamlet*. The somewhat mystifying suggestion that they were written 'in close collusion' (Duncan-Jones *Ungentle Shakespeare* 145) indicates how difficult it is to describe the 'obvious, though puzzling, relationship' (Potter 243) between these writers and their work. Rather than add to this discussion, I will present Marston's numerous comments on Shakespeare as an introduction to his borrowings. Like much of Marston's writing, his remarks on Shakespeare lack the sweetness for which their subject was famous: Marston's language is cryptic, highly elaborate, full of Italian phrases and musical terms, and it often has an aggressive, acerbic undertone. Nevertheless, his remarks are invaluable for their close and perceptive observation of Shakespeare's writing habits.

Marston's veiled remarks (he never mentions Shakespeare's name) are of particular interest to this study because they are all concerned with what could be called intertextuality. His satires, which were published in 1598, contain several characters that have been identified as Shakespeare. One of them is 'but Broker of anothers wit' and annoyingly '[l]aboring with third-hand jests, and Apish skips, / Retayling others wit' (*Scourge* 188, Satire 4). A certain Castilio in the third satire 'Can cut a manors strings at Primero', i.e. cheat at cards, and is described as a 'slie golden-slopt' rascal (*Satires* 138). 'Golden-slopt' means 'wearing golden breeches' and may hint at unethically gained riches; the rare fourteenth-century meaning of 'slop' given in the OED as 'charmed bag employed to steal milk from cows' would reinforce the insinuation of thieving: Shakespeare-Castilio is making off with bags of stolen gold. Marston's final dig at him is to call him 'the absolute Castilio [who] doth but champe that which another chew'd' in his 'beggary' (*Satires* 138). All these accusations of stealing chime with Greene's attack on Shakespeare for stealing other writers' 'feathers', and, like Greene, Marston uses the derogatory term 'absolute' to summarize his disapproval of Shakespeare's autocratic quotation practice.

Marston's most extended and intricate reference to Shakespeare is just as cryptic and suggestive in its outline of casual intertextual practices. 'Luscus' sounds like an enthusiastic theatregoer who comes back from 'Iuliat and Romio' with his head full of Shakespeare's phrases. The word 'lips' may indicate that he could also *be* Shakespeare: in Marston's *Pigmalion*, a character called 'Labeo' speaks an an otherwise unmarked but unmistakable quotation from *Venus and Adonis* (cf. Appendix II), and 'thick-lipped' may signal an individual physical trait that is recognizable at least in the Chandos portrait of William Shakespeare. Whatever Marston was trying to hide or hint at, the passage sketches several features of Shakespeare's writing and his success on the London scene with uncanny suggestiveness.

> Luscus, what's playd to day? faith now I know
> I set thy lips abroach, from whence doth flow
> Naught but pure Iuliat and Romio.
> Say, who acts best? Drusus or Roscio,
> Now I have him, that nere of ought did speake
> But when of playes or Plaiers he did treate.
> H'ath made a common-place booke out of plaies,
> And speakes in print: [...] speakes he not movingly,
> From out some new pathetique Tragedy?
> He writes, he railes, he iests, he courts what not,
> And all from out his huge long scraped stock
> Of well-penn'd playes (*Scourge* 226 (Book 3, Satire 11)).

Here, in a single sketch, we can see the wildly successful, theatre-obsessed, much-quoted and quotation-spouting punster who is described in other contemporary comments (cf. Chapters 2 and 3). The mere question 'what's on today' produces an unstoppable flow of language from the lips of this man who cannot but speak of the theatre and in the language of the theatre. Like William Shakespeare in Ben Jonson's anecdote about speaking 'in the person of Caesar' (cf. pp. 36–37), he ventriloquizes dramatic characters 'from out some [...] Tragedy'. The phrase about making 'a common-place booke out of plaies' may be a jealous hint at the anthologies that were full of *Romeo and Juliet* in the 1590s; it is also a reminder of how close everyday speech and theatrical dialogue could be for Shakespeare. And like Shakespeare, 'Luscus' quotes himself, fashioning jokes from his own back catalogue and recycling his own lines as he continues to write, 'scrap[ing]' the barrel of his own and other people's imagination.

Marston's comments on Shakespeare's practice betray an extremely well-informed interest, which is, however, expressed with an unmistakable edge of satirical distance. This critical undertone makes me somewhat reluctant to think that Marston was Shakespeare's 'personal friend' (Duncan-Jones *Ungentle Shakespeare* 145). Casual quotation, the 'constant repetition of phrases from memory', may as a rule have indicated that Shakespeare 'was loved and that he was honoured, and [men] paid a tribute to the way in which he excelled them' (Munro 1:xlv), but in the case of Marston, the testimony of imitation seems more ambiguous. The tension between the extensive borrowing and the repeated digs at Shakespeare make Marston's continuous quoting look less like homage than like a kind of verbal stalking. He quotes Shakespeare well over a hundred times and uses such a large number of his plot and character elements that the *Allusion-Book* identifies even weak and dubious verbal overlaps as quotations: 'as Marston certainly copied *Hamlet* in other passages, he most probably took [also this] from Shakspere' (Munro 1:xl). This propensity to borrowing was noticed already in Marston's lifetime, and he persisted in it with a certain perversity: the more he 'was accused of plagiarism, the more he seemed to delight in openly defying his critics by quoting' (Cook 121). This included accusing Shakespeare of stealing in stolen phrases. 'The absolute Castilio' echoes Robert Greene's 'absolute fac-totum'; 'Broker of another's wit' and 'Retayling others wit' may recall the phrase 'pick-purse of anothers wit' in in Philip Sidney's sonnet cycle *Astrophil and Stella* (469, Sonnet 74). Marston may even have gone as far as to blame Shakespeare for his quotations with a Shakespeare quotation, rephrasing a line in *Love's Labour's Lost*: 'He is wit's pedler, and retails his wares' (5.2.317). The conclusion is that if something sounds like a quotation and is in a text that could be by John Marston, it most probably *is* a quotation. Just one or two of these many borrowings hint at their sources. In addition to 'Iuliat and Romio' and 'Labeo', **Bettrice** the waiting-woman in *Eastward Ho*, who enters **'leading a Monkey after her'** (93), may be a dig at Beatrice in *Much Ado About Nothing*. Beatrice jokes about leading 'apes into Hell' (2.1.41) and is notoriously talkative, while Marston's Bettrice does not speak a single word and her name is not spoken by any of the other characters. She remains an oblique joke, a name locked away in a stage direction with Marston's customary cageyness.

Marston's Shakespeare quotations are a fact that is frequently mentioned but has not been comprehensively documented and there is as yet no complete scholarly edition of his works that could present them in its apparatus. Marston might have been pleased to be such a recognized but shady presence; I am nevertheless working on a complete (if open-ended) Marston-Shakespeare concordance that will include as many overlaps as possible. A selection of about one hundred tokens is given in Appendix II of this book; there are probably at least twice as many, some of which are still hiding in full sight. I have mentioned the handful that are marked for derivation; another few are marked for quotation only, acknowledging the fact of quotation in typically indirect fashion. When Ferneze in *The Malcontent* sighs at Aurelia: 'Your smiles have bin my **heaven**, your frowns **my hel** / O pitty them; **Grace should with beauty dwell**', he echoes Hermia in *A Midsummer Night's Dream*: 'O, then, what graces in my love do dwell, / That he hath turn'd a heaven into a hell!' (12.1.211–212). Ferneze's quotation seems to be recognized by the 'old pandresse' Maquerelle, who interposes before Aurelia can react: 'Reasonable perfect, bir-lady' (*Malcontent* 156). This nod of approval may 'refer to the imitation of Shakspere' (Munro 1:132).

The instinctive appreciation of Shakespeare's verbal success which John Marston had is apparent in the line that he marks for quotation most conspicuously: Richard III's desperate call for a horse in his final battle was to prove quotable indeed. In Marston's very first publication, *The Scourge of Villainie* of 1598, the phrase appears in italics and is repeated *verbatim* (*Scourge* 202 (2, Satire 7)). Seven years on, as a co-author of the comedy *Eastward Ho*, Marston could count on the line being recognized even in variation: '**A boate, a boate, a boate, a full hunderd Markes for a boate**' (133). The catchphrase may have seemed even funnier here because *Eastward Ho* is full of obvious jokes about a different Shakespeare play, *Hamlet*. In *Parasitaster* (1606), Don Zuccone, who is named for a fool, echoes his name by calling for 'A foole, a foole, a foole! my Coxcombe for a foole!' (212). The fourth appearance of Richard III's line is again *verbatim* and comes with unusually complete metatextual equipment that acknowledges the popularity of the line with, possibly, just a touch of sour grapes: '**A horse, a horse, my kingdom for a horse,** / Look the[e], I speak play scrappes' (*What You Will* 248). The phrase 'play scrappes' is a prophetical, telescopic pointer to the future of Shakespeare quotations that were to become recognizable, famous and finally annoying. Richard's line became a Jacobean running gag that could be spoken for the benefit of a stage interlocutor as well as for the sniggering audience. The playful modifications in Robert Daborne's *Poor Man's Comfort* pick up the variation in *Eastward Ho* and indicate that the phrase was still familiar in the 1610s:

> SIGISMUND: [...] where is *Europa*? see where she swims away upon a buls back; **my kingdom for a boat, for a muscle boat**; lay more sailes on (sig. D^{recto}).

By the 1620s, the joke had become annoying, as we can see in a duel scene in the Fletcher-Massinger comedy *The Little French Lawyer*.

> SAMPSON: [...] Looke up brave friend, I have no meanes to rescue thee,
> **My Kingdome for a sword,**
> CHAMPERNELL: I'll <u>sword you</u> presently, I'll claw your skin-coate too (69).

The old and crippled Champernell, patently unwise to be spoiling for a fight, is annoyed by a younger adversary's hackneyed quotation even in his senile excitement before a duel. 'I'll sword you' clearly acknowledges an exasperatingly famous tag. Richard III's line had become so familiar that Fletcher and Massinger could reduce it to a core and – like Karl Marx writing **'Das ist die question'** – still be sure that it would trigger recognition of the full quotation.

While Marston marks enough of his quotations for us to discern his interest, most of his Shakespeare borrowings are unmarked, with all the typical features of casual quotation. Marston quotes small bits *verbatim*, reproduces structures with different vocabulary – as in 'a boat, a boat' – paraphrases passages loosely around one or two salient words, cross-quotes different Shakespeare texts and recreates Shakespearean images or situations with his own vocabulary. He also displays the surest give-away of casual quotation: favourite lines that are used again and again. They can be observed in countless texts including Shakespeare's own, which reproduce 'veni vidi vici' or certain impressions from the *Aeneid* almost randomly (cf. Chapter 3). With the exception of 'a horse, a horse', all Marston's favourites are taken from *Hamlet*, which clearly obsessed him. They include **'the front of Jove'** (*Hamlet* 3.4.65), which he uses four times (cf. Appendix II) and the idea that man is distinguished from 'beasts' by his 'reason'. From Hamlet's phrase 'O God, a **beast** that wants **discourse** of reason / Would have mourned longer!' (1.2.154–155), Marston takes the two items 'best' and 'reason' and works them into quite different syntactical structures:

> PEACE: [...] What is a **man superior to a beast / But for his mind?** (*Histriomastix* 248).
> DOCTOR GLISTER: What else, sir? **I have reason.**
> DRYFAT: I know it well, I take you for **no beast** (*Family of Love* sig H$^{\text{3recto}}$).

These passages may also be echoing a second *Hamlet* passage, which says that a man who does nothing but 'sleep and feed' should be considered 'A **beast, no more**' because God, who has given us 'such large **discourse,** / **Looking before and after**' (*Hamlet* 4.4.38–39), would want us to use it. In the early nineteenth century, William Hazlitt, definitely a friendly and admiring Shakespeare quoter (cf. Chapter 6), would fuse these two passages into '**large discourse of reason, looking before and after**' and use this least three times. Another Marston favourite, Hamlet's idea that 'funeral baked meats' (1.2.187–188) could be used at a hasty new wedding, is recognizable by the salient words 'meat', 'table' and 'furnish' in the following phrase in *Eastward Ho*: '**the cold meat left at your wedding, might serve to furnish their Nuptiall table**' (119). In *The Insatiate Countess*, it is candles rather than food that are used up on an unexpected second occasion: '<u>Learne of a well composed Epigram</u> [...] **The Tapers that stood on her husbands hearse, / Isabell**' advances to a second bed' (*Insatiate Countess* 8). The careful introduction of this concept as an 'epigram' could be taken as defiantly casual marking for quotation only.

The phrase 'second bed' in *The Insatiate Countess* adds a cross-quotation to Marston's rephrasing of 'funeral baked meats': there is a hint of the Player Queen's 'A second time I kill my husband dead / When second husband kisses me in bed' (*Hamlet* 3.4.207–208). Such echoes, which hint at an intimate familiarity with the quoted texts, are quite frequent in Marston. Maria's sigh in *The Family of Love*, 'Oh that **this flesh could like swift mouing thoughts transfer it selfe**, From place to place, vnseen and **vndisolued**' (sig A^{3verso}) fuses the *Hamlet* line 'that **this too, too solid flesh** would melt, thaw, and **resolve** itself into a dew' (1.2.133) with 'as **swift** / As meditation or the **thoughts** of love' (*Hamlet* 1.5.35–36), 'phonetically' recalling Hamlet's 'resolve' in 'vndisolued' (Olive 77). Sometimes, it is impossible to decide which of two similar Shakespeare lines Marston may have had in mind. '**The abstract of the spacious world**' (*Family of Love* sig. A^{3verso}), for example, may echo '**Brief abstract and record of tedious days**' (*Richard III* 4.4.2) or '**Abstract and brief chronicle of the time**' (*Hamlet* 2.2.550–551). In *The Malcontent*, finally, we find the rather crazy conjunction of Hamlet's insult to Polonius 'You are a fishmonger' (2.2.190) with his description of his father's ghost as 'Armed at point exactly, **cap-à-pie**' (1.2.210):

MENDOZA: Then we agree?
MALEVOLE: As Lent and **fishmongers**. Come a *cape a Pe*, how in forme? (182)

This is not the only example where Marston condenses Shakespeare to a very effective brevity. In *Richard II*, Aumerle describes tears as the effect of a sharp wind rather than emotion, saying that he did not shed any tears 'except the northeast wind, / Which then blew bitterly against our faces, / Awaked the sleeping rheum and so by chance / Did grace our hollow parting with a tear' (*Richard II* 1.4.6). In *Antonio and Mellida*, Marston condenses this very effectively when Mellida is trying to hide that she is deeply moved by hearing about a man who sighed for her in his last words. Her cousin asks: 'what makes my Lady weepe?'; she says very curtly: '**Nothing** sweet *Rossaline*, but **the ayre's sharpe**' (20). In my final example, Marston fuses two passages from *Macbeth* and quotes a structure. The semantic basis is the metaphor 'it would take an ocean to wash the blood of my victims off my hands':

Macbeth 2.2.78-81 and 5.2.53-55
MACBETH. [...] Will **all** great
   Neptune's ocean wash **this blood**
Clean from **my hand**? No, **this my**
   hand will rather
The **multitudinous seas incarnadine**,
Making the green one red.
LADY MACBETH. [...] **All the**
   perfumes of Arabia will not
   sweeten **this** little **hand**.

Insatiate Countess 69
DON SAGO. Although **Neptolis** cold,
   the waves of **all the northerne sea**,
Should flow for ever, through **these**
   guiltie **hands**,
Yet the sanguinolent staine would
   extant be.

Marston's paraphrase is simpler than the originals, making Don Sago less hysterical than Macbeth with his rhetorical questions and Lady Macbeth with her 'little hand'. The most interesting aspect of this passage is a structural echo. Shakespeare famously juxtaposes Latinate and Anglo-Saxon vocabulary in Macbeth's speech, contrasting the *recherché* 'incarnadine' with simple 'red'. Of this effect, Marston copies just the template 'extremely rare four-syllable word for "red"', substituting Shakespeare's verb 'incarnadine' with the rare adjective 'sanguinolent', a word that is 'not part of normal discourse and would be unknown to most people' (*OED*, online edition). It belongs in Band 2 of 8 in the *OED*'s categorization for frequency, while 'incarnadine' is in Band 3 (i.e. sightly more familiar); once again Marston is taking 'sweet' Shakespeare to a knottier extreme.

Quoting into quotable Shakespeare

The relationship between Shakespeare's and Marston's works is not limited to Marston quoting from Shakespeare. In some cases, it may have been the other way around, and like everybody who had been to grammar school, they had a certain classical heritage in common and liked to quote a variety of English sources. At the moment, it is not possible to say just how frequently Marston cross-quotes Shakespeare with other texts because his sources have not been investigated with the same thoroughness as Shakespeare's. Some of the overlaps that have been annotated as Marston's Shakespeare quotations may indeed echo earlier sources which Shakespeare himself used. This is quite obvious in the mysterious exclamation of the 'drunke' Quicksilver in *Eastward Ho*: 'Eastward Hoe; *Holla ye pampered Jades of Asia*' (101). The italics are original and probably indicate a quotation, possibly from *2 Henry IV*, where Pistol says:

> Shall pack-horses and **hollow pampered jades of Asia**, which cannot go but thirty mile a day, compare with Caesars and with cannibals and Troyant Greeks? (2.4.165–168).

'Holla ye pampered jades' for 'hollow pampered jades' would be quite clever of Marston; but as it turns out, he and Shakespeare were both quoting Marlowe's *Tamburlaine*: '**Holla, ye pampered jades of Asia!** What! can ye draw but **twenty miles a day** [...]?' (2:236). The creative twist is the contribution of Shakespeare, who created the combination 'hollow pampered jades' and coupled the tired 'jades' with equally dejected-sounding 'pack-horses' to make it all work.

The same three plays – *Tamburlaine*, *Hamlet* and *Eastward Ho*, with an additional Spenser echo – intersect even more strikingly in Ophelia's mad scene:

Hamlet 4.5.73-78
OPHELIA. We must be patient, but I cannot choose but weep to think they should lay him i'th'cold ground. My brother shall know of it, and so I thank you for your good counsel. Come, my coach. **Good night**, ladies, **good night**. Sweet ladies, **good night, good night.**

Eastward Ho 117-118
HAMLET. What Coachman? my Ladyes coach, for shame; her ladiship's ready to come downe;Potkinn. Sfoote, <u>Hamlet</u>; are you madde? whether run you now? [...]
<u>GERTRUDE</u>. Thanke you good people; my coach for the love of Heaven, my coach? in good truth I shall swoune else

The names 'Gertrude' and 'Hamlet' make it clear that Marston, Jonson and Chapman are taking off Shakespeare's hit tragedy; Hamlet the hysterical footman is mainly there so that Potkinn can shout at him: '<u>**Hamlet**</u>; are you **madde**?' Like the silent Bettrice, 'Hamlet' is a Shakespeare joke, a marker for derivation. Hamlet, Potkinn and Gertrude then quote phrases from Ophelia's mad scene – or, possibly, from Shakespeare's sources. Ophelia's call for a vehicle has reminded at least one scholar of the moment in *The Faerie Queene* when '**Suddein** vpriseth from her stately place / The royall Dame [Lucifera], and for **her coche doth call**' (83 (1.4.16)). The difference is that the proud and false Lucifera is aiming to impress her guests; she does not want to escape with her coach but to show it off. Ophelia's emotional state is much closer to that of the enslaved, suicidal Turkish queen Zabina in *Tamburlaine*:

ZABINA: [...] Let the souldiers be buried. Hel, death, Tamburlaine, Hell! **Make ready my Coch**, my chaire, my jewels, **I come, I come, I come!** (172).

Here is the lonely, desperate woman calling for a protective shell and means of escape; here are Ophelia's hysterically repeated phrases though not her gentle, distracted courtesy. Did Shakespeare get this from Marlowe (1590), or from Spenser (1596), or from both? Did Spenser get it from Marlowe? We may never know. What we do know is that the dialogue in *Eastward Ho,* which is reminiscent of Spenser's Lucifera and could be spoken by Marlowe's Zabina, is marked for derivation from *Hamlet.* Despite the striking parallel passages in recently published and highly successful works, the passage is clearly a casual, flippant *Hamlet* joke: Ophelia's tremulous call for a coach has become, like so many phrases, a Shakespeare 'meme' – a little bit of Marlowe that will be forever Shakespeare.

What has been quoted will be quoted: Shakespeare quotation looks both ways. This Janus-faced aspect is reflected in the historical ambiguity of quotation marks. Such signals included spacing, contrasting fonts like italics and black letter and typographical signals such as inverted commas, asterisks or the 'index', a hand with an outstretched index finger. Inverted commas were usually placed only at the beginning of the quoted/quotable phrase, signposting the beginning of a quotable statement while the length of what follows – a quotation, a unit of reading and of (re-)writing, a lexia – is determined by the reader. There has been a scholarly debate[6] about whether the various quotation markers signal 'indebtedness' (Hunter 171) for quotation from an earlier work or whether they alert readers to *sententiae*, i.e. to generally recognizable sayings that are recommended for memorization and further use: quotations waiting to happen. In the seventeenth century, there was still a considerable range of interchangeable typographical devices which signalled intertextual inserts, quotable phrases and even direct speech. Only around 1700 did emphasis and quotation become 'distinct' (King 41). Joseph Aickin's *English Grammar* of 1693 says that quotation marks show 'an author to be quoted' while an 'index pointeth forth something worthy to be remarked' (sig. F3^{verso} [70]). When 'inverted commas for literary citation' became standard, they were 'double [i.e. closed]' signs (King 53), which indicated also the end of a quotation and thus took a bit of terrain back from self-willed readers. But really, it does not matter. An anthology piece is repeated out of context because it is considered important enough to be repeated in yet further, later contexts, and that is what Polonius does. The quotation marks in the *First* and *Second Quartos* of *Hamlet* do not so much 'fence in a passage as property of another' as 'advertise its appropriability' (De Grazia 57). They indicate that a passage had been considered quotable before and inviting readers and future writers to use as much or as little of the following as they please. Whether quotation marks indicate passages worth quoting or words quoted from somebody else is a question of considerable historical interest; from the perspective of radical intertextuality, the difference does not matter very much. Both are, inevitably, always already read. Marked, 'extraordinary passages' or 'notable passages' (Jones 45) are extraneous to the printed context in two ways: they are taken from a different book and will appear again in more books. Shakespeare's works in this sense are true textual intersections: the difference between markers for quotedness and for quotability is blurred or even uninteresting if both represent casual intertextuality.

Shakespeare's success, his talent for creating memorable phrases and the recent fashion of including English authors in anthologies facilitated the detachment and re-use of quotable phrases from his works. This tendency is already visible in the first print editions of his works, where inverted commas signal 'extraordinary passages' (King 45) as ready to cut-and-paste. The *locus classicus* of quoted-into-quotable is Polonius' advice to his son Laertes. The *First Quarto* acknowledges the quotability of the lines from 'Be thou familiar' to 'to thine own self be true' by putting them in inverted commas (and the *Second Quarto* similarly favours Laertes' advice to Ophelia in act 1, scene 3). It re-enacts the popular Renaissance genre 'mirror for princes', may be borrowing from other elaborations of that model and includes many individual phrases that can be traced to other sources. It is framed as 'these few precepts' and it is shot through with markers of universal applicability like 'every man', 'each man', 'they in France' or 'This above all' (1.3.74, 75, 79 and 84). Such phrases indicate that this speech is quoted from authoritative sources and that it should be quoted in the future: quotedness constitutes quotability. Indeed, this profoundly re-hashed speech has been claimed to be Shakespeare's 'most often memorized passage' (Bennett 'Characterization' 12).

Sources that have been identified for Polonius 'few precepts' include Lord Burghley's *Certaine precepts or directions, for the well ordering and carriage of a mans life*, which may have furnished the word 'precepts' to Polonius' introductory phrase; passages of advice in Hesiod, in Greene and Massinger and in a letter from Sir Henry Sidney to his son Philip. Like Polonius' speech, Sidney's letter is a sequence of imperatives framed by an opening address and a personal conclusion: 'Well (my litell Philippe) this is ynoughe for me, and to much I feare for yow' (Sidney 'Learner' 133). In addition to a model template, these sources also offered single phrases to Shakespeare's memory, as did John Lyly's recent *Euphues* narratives, *Euphues: The Anatomy of Wit* and *Euphues and His England*, to an extent that has led to a description of Polonius' speech as 'a cento of quotations' from Lyly's books (Dowden 141). The phrase **'these few precepts I giue thee'** (Lyly *Euphues England* sig. 11[verso]) is an alternative source for Polonius' opening; 'Let thy attire be **comely but not costly**' (Lyly *Euphues Anatomy* 16) became '**Costly** thy habit as thy purse can buy, / **But** [...] rich, **not** gaudy'. The words 'costly' and 'attire' in conjunction appear also in several other passages like 'Let your attire be comely but not too costly' (Lyly *Euphues Anatomy* 142); 'be not quarrellous for euery lyght occasion' (Lyly *Euphues England* sig. 13[recto]) becomes 'Beware / Of entrance to a **quarrel**' and so on. In all these lines, we recognize Shakespeare's casual transformation of what he found. What complicates the assignment of such sources to individual lines is the way in which some of these writers quote each other. Lord Burghley may be echoing *Euphues* when he advises his son Robert not to be 'lavish of thy tongue' (Lyly *Euphues England* sig. 11[verso]) and reminds him that 'euery one that shaketh thee by the hand, is not ioyned to thee' (cf. Bennett 'Characterization' 3). Both phrases could also be Shakespeare echoing Lyly directly. When he picks up structural patterns, we can be more sure: Sidney's 'Be you rather **a Herer, and Bearer** away of other Mens Talke, then **a Begynner or Procurer** of Speeche' (Sidney 'Learner' 132) probably inspired 'neither **a borrower** nor **a lender be**', shifting a syntactic pattern to the expression of a different piece of advice. A final complicating factor is that all these writers used a common source that could also have been Shakespeare's: a piece by the fourth-century Greek rhetorician Isocrates that was extremely popular in sixteenth- and seventeenth-century Europe in Erasmus' 1517 Latin translation *Ad Demonicum*. This text had a success story in Spain which is intriguingly similar to that of Polonius' speech: Calderón's *El alcalde de Zalamea* (1640), which conquered the Spanish national canon much as *Hamlet* did the English, includes an Isocrates passage that came to be 'best known out of dramatic context' (Beardsley 189), just like Polonius' admonitions. In England, *Ad Demonicum* saw at least three translations in the second half of the sixteenth century. It has been thought that these admonitions, particularly those that Polonius addresses to his son, are tedious or even ridiculous because they are such unoriginal 'commonplaces', a hoary 'collection of weary maxims' (Garber 38). Thanks to the powerful integrative force that Shakespeare's writing exerts on its 'submerged and dispersed' (Lynch 117) sources, Polonius' speech is one of the 'most admired distillations of practical wisdom in all Shakespeare' (Bennett 'Characterization' 12). The quoted wisdom was not his but he made it quotable – and quotable as his.

The unique phenomenon of 'Quoted Shakespeare' emerging from 'Shakespeare Quoting' was guessed at already in Shakespeare's lifetime. Francis Meres, who hinted that Shakespeare's sweetness was owed to his Latin sources because 'the sweet witty soul of Ovid' lived on in 'mellifluous & honey-tongued Shakespeare' (*Palladis Tamia* sig. 281[verso]), also seems to have anticipated how Shakespeare's own words, in turn, would live on in new texts: 'The Muses would speak with Shakespeares fine filed phrase, if they would speak English' (sig. 282^{recto}). John Davies of Hereford, who used Shakespeare's words extensively (cf. p.), used another classical comparison to write of Shakespeare's quotability: he calls him 'our English Terence' (*Scourge of Folly* Epig. 159, 76). This is more than praise for writing enjoyable comedies; Davies' compliment has an intertextual implication. Terence's plays were set grammar school texts because their accessible, pleasantly straightforward Latin contained an unusual amount of material that was suitable for being 'copied into commonplace books and memorized' by literate people: 'sententiae, the epigrammatic comments on the human situation in, for example, a comedy of Terence' (Frye 238). So, the epithet 'our English Terence' indicates that Shakespeare was an exceptionally quotable writer as well as a successful playwright. The same comparison also appears in 1614 in Thomas Freeman's 'Epigramme 92', which likens Shakespeare's brain so fittingly to the mobile Mercury (cf. p. 75). Freeman, too, evokes Terence to describe Shakespeare as both quoter and quotable:

> [his] wit winds like Meander,
> Whence needy new-composers borrow more
> Than Terence doth from Plautus or Menander (sig. K3^{recto}).

Shakespeare-as-Terence has a threefold identity. He is a borrower who uses Plautus and other sources, a writer who produces 'sweet' poetry and a lender who offers eminently quotable texts and 'fine filed phrase[s]' to 'new-composers'. As his fame grew, Shakespeare quotation was institutionalized and even adaptation and parody were caught up in this and became generically stable yet casual in the eighteenth century.

Notes

1 Only Chaucer's near-classical status as 'of all admired' is acknowledged in the Prologue to *Two Noble Kinsmen* (line 13).
2 'O Venice, Venice, he who does not see you does not appreciate you but who sees you pays dearly' (my translation).
3 For these and several other 'tricky' parallels with *Hamlet* and *Macbeth* which are 'very easy to miss' cf. Davenport 374.
4 Jason Lawrence provides an interesting bit of additional evidence for Shakespeare's casual use of Florio. If his quotations from *First* and *Second Fruits* are put in the order of the two Florio volumes, they are also in the order of Shakespeare's works from the earliest plays through to *Othello* (cf. Lawrence 123–124). He seems to made his way through Florio, using whatever he encountered for whatever he was writing at the time.
5 This lovely phrase is Ina Habermann's.
6 Cf. King 'Small-Scale Copyrights', de Grazia 'Quotation Marks' and Hunter 'Marking of *Sententiae*'.

5 'The old parody': A Post-Shakespeare Genre

> *The serious question with him*
> *was the old parody of, 'To marry, or not to marry'.*
> AGNES MARIA BENNET (1797)

Like casual quotation, casual Shakespearean verse parody has met with ambivalent criticism. Both quotation and parody repeat familiar elements out of context, gain a certain attention from association with that original context and are taken to confirm the original's prestige by their number. Simultaneously, quotation as well as parody *lose* prestige by the damaging comparison with the hopelessly superior originals. With casual quotations, this perceived inferiority has led to scholarly indifference; parodies have been studied but most publications register a certain defensiveness in the face of general scorn. In 1758, when Tobias Smollett was reviewing the Shakespearean cento *Madrigal and Trulletta*, he claimed that parody and burlesque require only 'a very modest capacity [...] even in the highest degree of perfection they are capable of attaining' (*Works* xxxvi). In the nineteenth century, scholarly defensiveness focused on the fear that parodying Shakespeare might be irreverent. In 1885, Walter Hamilton felt the need to insist that publishing a collection of verse parodies did not imply 'the slightest disrespect [...] to the immortal bard' (Hamilton *Parodies* 2:144). In the early 1980s, Jonathan Bate took considerable trouble searching the (not yet digitalized) archives to find Shakespeare parodies 'in magazine verse' because he considers them one of the 'most striking developments' in the popular response to Shakespeare ('Parodies' 7). Indeed they are. And yet Bate concludes that those products of 'hack writer[s]' ultimately represent 'a mean and limited thing when set beside the magnanimity and breadth of the plays themselves' (76 and 89). More recently, Sayre Greenfield has rounded off a discussion of eighteenth-century tokens by observing that Shakespeare's meaning 'lingers in the reader's mind only as a point of contrast to indicate how far the subject matter has *descended*' ('Outside Britain' 241, emphasis mine). Collected to document the fame and quality of their models, Shakespeare parodies are simultaneously seen as devalued by these models; expectations of Shakespearean signification are inevitably disappointed by the 'descent' that his passages have undergone. Such comparisons risk blinkering scholarly enquiry. Instead of setting them up to fail in competition with Shakespeare, I have attempted to read eighteenth-century verse parodies on their own terms. Paradoxical as it may seem, these truly casual parodies are in no way predicated on the comparison with Shakespeare; they largely ignore him.

Shakespearean verse parody from the mid-eighteenth century onwards is an intertextual genre of a very particular kind. These poems do not work in a relationship with the speeches they rewrite. They relate to each other and to other quotable and much-quoted items. Therefore, comparing several dozen versions of 'To be or not to be' *to each other* is much more instructive than comparing them to the Shakespearean original. This approach does more justice to how these texts think of themselves. All of these poems signal a certain awareness of each other, and the relationship to the original is strikingly relaxed. It is often hard to draw 'the line between "imitation" and "parody"' and to decide whether we see 'deference to its models' or 'parodic intent' (Dentith 105). Samuel Taylor Coleridge put the difference as follows: 'Parodies on new poems are read as satires; on old ones (the soliloquy of Hamlet for instance) as compliments' (quoted in Bate 'Parodies' 75). Coleridge echoes the old idea that quoting the classics without marking is fine while using the words of contemporary writers without acknowledgment is theft.[1] The 'Imitations' and 'Parodies' that are discussed in this chapter are neither deferential nor mocking; they remain casually neutral and so eschew parody's 'inherent danger' of becoming 'too aware of the affective force of the original' (White 'Another Response' 181). If anything, the title 'imitation' announces a playful literary aspiration that invites complicit readers to share a clever pleasure. As Beate Müller has remarked, competitions 'in which readers were asked to discuss topical issues [...] in the form of a passage from Shakespeare' practically turned the writing of such texts into a 'spectator sport' (Müller 131).

The increased familiarity that is evident in such unassuming recyclings was favoured by the process that was turning Shakespeare into the 'national poet' after the Restoration. The 1737 Licensing Act censored new play texts and resulted in a surfeit of Shakespeare performances, which by the 1740s accounted for nearly a quarter of all London stage productions (cf. Scouten 192 and Dobson *National Poet* 3) and gave his plays a wider audience. Any 'celebrated speech' (Rider 648) was too familiar to invite literary aggression. What Stephen O'Neill, writing about YouTube adaptations of Shakespeare, describes as 'the normative condition of the Bard as he is consumed in [twenty-first-century] global culture' is also true for these poems: they show 'Shakespeare sampled and enmeshed within popular culture' (O'Neill 55). And their writers were as aware of each other as are Shakespearean YouTube communities.

'The old parody': A Post-Shakespeare Genre

The seventy-six rewritings of 'To be or not to be' (published between 1744 and 1837 and available on *HyperHamlet*) that are discussed in this chapter are linked by a sophisticated network of contexts and meanings. Many of these connections do not depend on the force field of *Hamlet*; they develop topical subjects, hint at non-Shakespearean templates and link each token to its peers. When the names 'Shakespeare' or 'Hamlet' are included, it is in the way that Roland Barthes has described: naming a quoted source 'dispenses the reader from following to its conclusions the system of which it is the signifier' (*Roland Barthes* 74). Respectfully confident *vis-à-vis* their original, these parodies acknowledge their source so that they can set it politely aside. They are above all intent on their own themes and intensely aware of each other and so belong to the casual intertextuality that is explored in this book.

Casual quotation and casual parody

The link between casual quotation and casual parody is most evident in rewrites of 'to be or not to be' because, apart from being a famous set piece, the speech contains a number of individual lines that have 'made it' as famous quotations in their own right. Moreover, its generalizing structure has made it the most frequently adopted model for parodic rewritings. The earliest specimen sets the tone for these exercises: verbally ingenious and fashionably topical, it offers a decidedly cavalier take on *Hamlet*:

> **To wed or not to wed, that is the question**
> **Whether** 'tis happier **in the mind** to stifle
> **The** heats and tumults **of outrageous** passion,
> Or with some prudent fair in solemn contract
> Of matrimony join – **to** have – **to** hold
> **No more** – and by that have **to say we end**
> **The heart ach, and the thousand** love sick pangs
> Of celibacy – **'twere a consummation**
> **Devoutly to be wish'd** (Anon. 'The Bachelor's Soliloquy' 1744, lines 1–9).

Like dozens of other parodies and like thousands of casual Shakespeare quotations, this text is remarkable for the combination of formal adherence to the original and emotional distance from that original's concerns. Thirty-plus iambic pentameters starting out with 'to verb or not to verb' ignore the content of Hamlet's speech while preserving a sequence of catchphrases and syntactical patterns like the double infinitive 'to die – to sleep'. These phrases enforce a general adherence to the structure of Shakespeare's argument. First, the options 'to-verb' and 'not-to-verb' are briefly elaborated. 'Not-to-verb' (death, in Hamlet's case) seems immediately preferable since it offers escape from the familiar and certain suffering of 'to verb' and is paraphrased by further infinitives ('to die: to sleep'), which seem attractive, 'devoutly to be wish'd'. Then comes the turning point, the 'rub': another infinitive transforms the attractively unknown 'not to be' into a menace: 'to sleep, perchance to dream / ay, there's the rub'. The list of all-too-familiar earthly pressures in lines 16–23 cannot counterbalance this new fear of the unknown: the unfamiliar 'not to be' remains so terrifying that it 'makes us rather bear those ills we have / Than fly to others that we know not of.' In Shakespeare, the result is a stand-off; no decision is taken and the outcome 'to be' is achieved by inertia, by paralysis and not-doing. This overall structure is only superficially preserved in many parodies; the outcome, depending on the topic and the speaker persona, may be quite determined and even positive, while Hamlet's phrasing is preserved in impressive detail as part of a literary game.

Literary cleverness rather than *Hamlet*-referentiality is particularly noticeable in poems that are concerned with literary production. 'To write or not to write' was first used in 1747 in a soliloquy reprinted in 1754 and 1768 and then in versions that appeared in 1763, 1769, 1776 (two versions), 1786 and 1810. The related question 'to print or not to print' was addressed in 1758, 1793 and 1799[2]; all these items were reprinted at least once. The earliest token, the 1747 'Parody on the Speech of To be, or not to be, in Hamlet', is remarkable for its verbal ingenuity.

> To write or not to write! That is the Question!
> Whether 'tis nobler with the Pen to scribble
> The Flights and Fancies of outrageous Nonsense;
> Or to lay down the Quill, or forbear to tire
> The Patience of the world? To write! to scrawl!
> And by that Scrawl to say we utter all
> The Horrid Stuff and the thousand foolish Whimsies
> Labouring in the Brain – tis a Deliverance
> "Devoutly to be wish'd." To write! to scrawl!
> To scrawl - perchance to blot! – "ay, there's the Rub,"
> For on a strict Review, what Blots "may come"
> When we have scribbled all the Paper o'er,
> "Must give us Pause". – "There's the respect,"
> That stops the weak, presumptuous hand of Fools (Anon. 'A Parody'
> *British Magazine* 1747, lines 1–14).

The awareness of verbal parallels is so strong that strings of words that are preserved *verbatim* are put in inverted commas. The more characteristic phrases whose structure is preserved and completed with new lexical items – 'with the Pen' for 'in the mind' in line 2 etc. – are not marked although those manipulations are essential for creating a recognizable parody. In any case, the highlighting of quotation-within-parody underscores the closeness of the two intertextual practices.[3]

While Hamlet's discursive blueprint and its verbal surface are cleverly and pointedly respected in the 1747 'To write or not to write', the poem changes the logic of the conclusion:

> the itch of writing for the Stage [...]
> **'puzzles the Will'**
> and makes us rather risque all Ridicule,
> Than shun the Muses, and forbear to rhime.
> Ambition thus makes Asses of us all; [...]
> and Petit-maitres, of great Skill in Dressing,
> Ev'n from the fav'rite Mirror **'turn away'**,
> To gain the name of Author (Anon. 'A Parody' (1747), lines 25–32).

The two phrases that are marked here originally refer to the turning point of Hamlet's soliloquy, the sudden paralysing worry about the afterlife which makes the thought of dying unattractive and suicide impossible. In the parody, these phrases describe the inability of would-be authors to abstain from hackwork that will only make them ridiculous. Scribblers will scribble, heedless activity prevails: instead of losing 'the name of action', the misguided 'Authors' fight to 'gain' a professional name. The most famous constituents of Hamlet's soliloquy are signalled with quotation marks and casually used *against* its own famous argument! A short 'vocal Paraphrase on Hamlet's Soliloquy' takes this dismemberment to its absurd conclusion in 1795:

> Then, till we quit **this Mortal coil**,
> To reach **that undiscover'd bourne**,
> Where terminates all human toil,
> and **whence no trav'ller can return**
> Let smiling Hope expand the breast,
> and all from doubt and dread be free;
> Since *Jove* has order'd for the best,
> What'er's *To Be* or not *To Be* (Brush, lines 33–40).

Hamlet's phrases, carefully preserved, are re-ordered to reinforce a hopefulness that is a parody of the original in the worst sense of the word. As so often, *Hamlet* serves as 'literature's greatest bazaar; everything available, all warranted and trademarked' (Kermode 125): wholesale adaptation, cocky imitation and affectionate parody disintegrate into fragmented quotation before our eyes.

The title of the next 'to write or not to write' piece (1763) uses a formula which became a stock feature of later parodies: 'The Poet's Soliloquy'.

104   *'The old parody': A Post-Shakespeare Genre*

This seems an aptly proto-Romantic title for a text which weighs 'The impatient longings of a tow'ring soul' and a 'heart aspiring to immortal fame' against the battle with 'the critic's rage' (Ashley, lines 2–5). The conclusion that the poet will not publish because 'foolish fears make cowards of us all' is a very Hamletian thought, but Hamlet is nowhere acknowledged. If this refusal to mark a quotation, implicitly declaring the text to be 'not Hamlet's', was a gesture of artistic independence, it did not have a future: the idea of the non-Hamlet speaker persona was soon imitated and turned into a fad, witness the following selection of later titles:

> Old Tunbelly's Soliloquy.
> The Adventurer's Soliloquy: A Parody.
> The Dental Soliloquy.
> The Soldier's Soliloquy. A Parody.
> The Subaltern's Soliloquy.
> The Young Farmer. A Parody.
> The Young Student's Soliloquy.
> The Presbyterian Parson's Soliloquy; Or a Parody of Hamlet's celebrated Soliloquy.
> The Spouter's Soliloquy.
> The Journeyman Tailor's Soliloquy.
> The Housewife's Soliloquy: A Shakespearean Parody.
> The Student's Soliloquy, In Imitation of Shakespeare's Hamlet.[4]

All these poems announce their personae[5] and topics ahead of any marking for quotation; only five of them have any such marking at all ('A Parody') and just three mention their source by name. Instead, the title patterns indicate a clear priority: readers are referred to other texts of the same kind rather than to the Shakespearean source.

'To Wed or Not to Wed'

The most striking instance of the 'horizontal' relationship between parodies that use similar effects are the pieces that address the enormously topical 'Marriage Question'. Before the Matrimonial Causes Act of 1857 made divorce possible without a ruinously expensive Act of Parliament, the gravity of 'to wed or not to wed' could be fairly said to have approached that of 'to be or not to be', and the debate about it reached a peak in the Romantic period, as is exemplified in the quotation from *The Sylph* mentioned in the introduction to this book. Passages like the following became endemic:

> LAETITIA RAYNER: **To wed, or not to wed, – that is the question** – lose no time; for, as I take it, we are all just now in the cue to vote for the affirmative (Cumberland *Box-Lobby Challenge* 58).
>
> My first View, was only to make a dear little Mischief between him and my Rival; but now I have reason'd within myself, *pro and con*,

to wed or not to wed, was the Question; and would you believe it, I am now absolutely determined for the former (Gibbes *A Woman of Fashion* 2:130).

In both passages, The Question is asked by a young woman, which means that the *Hamlet* reference is even more casual than usual. The Question is not a real question here because heroines of courtship novels always want to marry. The question is whether to wed or not to wed *a particular suitor*, a detail which the *Hamlet* template does not accommodate. The marriageable girl's task of choosing a husband wisely determined its own, hugely successful literary genre, the courtship novel. This genre started with a bang with Samuel Richardson's *Pamela* and enjoyed steadily increasing success for a century that ended with the 'Silver Fork' novelists of the 1830s. In between, courtship novels scaled literary peaks in the works of Frances Burney and Jane Austen – and entered the 'To be or not to be' arena. 'The Maid's Soliloquy' of 1783 ends with the resolve to 'venture marriage let what will befall'. Even if men are 'by nature fickle', the 'pitied state of stale virginity' is clearly worse than the '**dread of something** yet untried' (Anon. 'Maid's Soliloquy', lines 13, 7 and 28). In a poem which is called 'To Marry or not to Marry' but not otherwise based on *Hamlet*, the female speaker chooses a different outcome. Those who would like to should 'pray make haste and marry' but,

> if that's true, which I've just said,
> I think this truth will follow
> That, could you sink the phrase 'Old Maid',
> By Jove! you'd beat 'Wives' hollow (Anon. 'To Marry', lines 79–86).

This deconstruction of spinster stereotypes is wonderful. Sadly, this confident bachelorette is an exception; the freedom to truly decide whether 'to wed or not to wed' is reserved for the masculine genre of Bachelor's Soliloquies.

The first of many 'Bachelor's Soliloquies' was published two years after *Pamela*, in 1742, and such poems continued to be written as long as courtship novels were, into the 1830s. The bachelors voice the male part in the marriage debate: the men start talking back! And as ever in casual parody, they are not talking back to *Hamlet*: the real target are those popular women's narratives that inevitably end with the right marriage. In contrast, the bachelor soliloquies reach an interesting range of different conclusions; the speakers accept or decline marriage for a variety of reasons that are very different from Hamlet's indecision. A woman's question is always whom to wed; when asked by a male, the question 'to wed or not to wed' has many answers. Only the first specimen, the founding text, as it were, replicates Hamlet's fearful indecision.

'The old parody': A Post-Shakespeare Genre

> To wed or not to wed, that is the question;
> Whether 'tis happier in the mind to stifle
> The heats and tumults of **outrageous** passion,
> Or with some prudent fair in solemn contract
> Of matrimony join – **to have** – **to hold** –
> **No more – and by that have to say we end**
> **The heart ach, and the thousand** love sick pangs
> Of celibacy – **'twere a consummation**
> **Devoutly to be wish'd** – in nuptial band
> To join till death dissolves – **ay there's the rub,**
> **For in that space what dull remorse may come,**
> **When we have** taken our solemn leave of liberty,
> **Must give us pause. – There's the respect**
> **That** slacks our speed in sueing for a change
> Else – **who would bear the scorns and sneers** which batchelors
> When aged feel, the pains and flattering fevers
> Which each new face must give to roving fancy
> **When he might rid himself at once of all**
> **By a bare Yes. Who would** with patience **bear**
> To fret and linger out a single life
> **But that the dread of something yet untry'd,**
> Some hazard in a state **from whose strict bond**
> Death only can release **puzzles the will**
> **And makes us rather choose those ills we have,**
> **Than fly to others which we** fancy greater
> This last reflection makes us slow and wary,
> Of curtain lectures jealousies and cares,
> Extravagantly great entailed on wedlock,
> Which to avoid the lover checks his passion,
> And, miserable, dies a BATCHELOR (Anon. 'The Bachelor's Soliloquy' (1744)).

This poem preserves many phrases as well as the argument and mood of the original. The decision to marry is prevented by a vague fear of unknown ills, while the readily imaginable miseries, 'scorn and jeers' of bachelor life cannot prevail over 'dreadful thoughts' of marriage. Horribly afraid of both options, the poor man reins in his desires and makes a miserable end. So far, so *Hamlet*. However, the structure of the argument is turned on its head. For the bachelor, the worst outcome is 'to verb' (to get married), whereas in *Hamlet* the unknown horrors belong to '*not* to verb' (not to be, death). Hamlet's misery is 'to be', while the bachelor finds himself unable 'to marry', even if death, in a *Hamlet* echo, would promise release from the miseries of both marriage and singleness.

'The old parody': A Post-Shakespeare Genre

The first 'Bachelor's Soliloquy' seems to have struck a chord: it was republished at least thirteen times until 1805 and imitated many times. The radically different mood of the second 'Bachelor's Soliloquy' (1758) indicates, though, that it was the general idea rather than the sad conclusion which caught the public imagination. Here we have a bit of a woman-hater:

> **To wed, or not to wed – that is the question:**
> **Whether 'tis better** still to rove at large
> From fair to fair, amid the wilds of passion;
> Or plunge at once into a sea of marriage,
> And quench our fires? – **To marry,** – take a wife,
> **No more – and by** a wife **to say we** quell
> Those restless ardours, all those nat'ral tumults
> **That flesh is heir to;** – 'tis a consolation
> **Devoutly to be wish'd.** – Marry, – a wife,
> A wife, – perchance a devil: – ay, there's the rub;
> [...]
> Thus forethought **does make bach'lors of us**
> And hence the face of many a willing maid
> **Is sickly'd o'er with the pale cast of** languishment;
> And many a youth **of no small pith and moment,**
> With this regard, spends all his days in whoring,
> **And** damns **the name of** husband (P-o. 'The Bachelor's Soliloquy').

While the first Bachelor has to 'check' his 'passion' to live alone, the second finds his 'wilds of passion' stifled by wedlock. The 'undiscovered country' of marriage that follows the (assumed) sexual gratification of the honeymoon inspires only dread, while single life offers a 'well-known, simple path'. Hamlet's 'ills we have' appear as a familiar and pleasant lifestyle. The refusal to go into the unknown and risk 'A wife, – **perchance** a devil' will inconvenience not so much the roguish bachelor as the maid who is left to suffer '**the pale cast of** languishment'. Hamlet's worries are divided up between two protagonists, and shying away from marriage is a positive choice. Gleefully violating social norms and a literary template simultaneously, this bachelor does not passively 'lose the name of action' but actively 'damns the name of husband'. Eight reprints bear witness to the attraction of this scenario, even if some editors felt the need to tone down the risqué final lines. A version from 1795 substitutes more decorous synonyms: 'spends all his days [a-] wenching and shuns the name of husband' (Anon. 'Parody on Hamlet's Soliloquy' (1795), lines 34–35) and one from 1784 uses ellipses: 'With this regard, spends all his days in wh---g, / And d---s the name of husband' (Anon. 'The Bachelor's Soliloquy' (1784) 308).

108   'The old parody': A Post-Shakespeare Genre

The third Bachelor soliloquy is George Tousey's 'The Bachelor's Deliberation. A Parody of the Soliloquy of Hamlet, (To be or not to be) versified'. This poem, too, comes down squarely in favour of the single life in 1768, though with a rather different motivation. The liberty of 'wenching' or 'whoring' is of no interest; the attraction of bachelorhood is the promise of peace and quiet:

> Charges and Discord, Jealousy and Strife,
> **Ills** which **all** center in the name of Wife;
> These to avoid, a single life we chuse,
> By Prudence urg'd to shun the Marriage noose (Tousey, lines 28–30).

This passage retains just two words from *Hamlet* and is 'versified' in heroic couplets rather than blank verse. This departure from Shakespeare is owed to cross-adaptation: the rhyming couplets are derived from a second template. The rhyme scheme as well as the opening line are taken from a 'Soliloquy in Imitation of Hamlet', which was written nineteen years earlier by the Jacobite poet William Hamilton. Hamilton starts out in a Hamlet voice to express his dismay after the defeat of the Jacobite forces in the Battle of Culloden:

> My anxious soul is tore with doubtful strife,
> And hangs suspended betwixt death and life;
> Life! death! dread objects of mankind's debate;
> Whether superior to the shocks of fate,
> To bear its fiercest ills with stedfast mind,
> To Nature's order piously resign'd,
> Or, with magnanimous and brave disdain,
> Return her back the' injurious gift again ('Soliloquy', lines 1–8).

After more such complaints, a friend turns on the speaker, urging him in the name of 'God, Nature, Reason' to abandon his 'rash resolves' for suicide and end 'crown'd in heaven' (lines 27–28 and 40). The 1768 'Bachelor's Soliloquy' adapts Hamilton's opening as follows:

> My anxious mind is torn with doubtful strife,
> While hopes and fears alternate vex my life;
> **Whether 'twere best** to act the Stoic's part,
> And bar fond Love all entrance to the heart (Tousey, lines 1–4).

For the rest, the poem follows Hamlet's structure and argument, integrating (unlike Hamilton) several recognizable catchphrases like 'This makes **us rather bear the ills we know**, / Than rashly venture on new scenes of woe' (lines 23–24) into its rhyming couplets. The intertextual echo chamber is reverberating in multiple ways here: the poem rewrites Hamlet's soliloquy as well as Hamilton's version of it (with more *Hamlet* phrases) in a rhyme scheme that was fashionable in the 1760s, and then fits all this to the best-selling 'Bachelor' template.

In the fourth bachelor piece, 'A Parody on Hamlet' from 1792, the misogyny intensifies: the speaker decides against marriage because he fears being cuckolded. The section corresponding to Hamlet's 'who would bear' elaborates on the attendant humiliations, the 'jeers and taunts of men, / The cuckold-maker's wrong, the general sneer' (Philomeides, lines 15–16). The male aggression imagined here prepares the reader for the shocking realization that the alternative to marriage is not celibacy. Nobody would put up with 'The insolence of an unfaithful wife' once they have realized how much more simply satisfaction can be come by: 'When he himself possession may procure / For half a crown!' (lines 18–21). Instead of passive resignation to bachelorhood, here is a determination to obtain the sexual perks of matrimony elsewhere, for money. This is a far cry from Hamlet's resignation, and in fact the poem ends after a mere twenty lines with the financial and sexual analogue of the 'bare bodkin' that could bring Hamlet's problems to a violent end. After this high-water mark of rakishness (the piece was never reprinted), regrets and fears both become noticeably more decorous. In a piece from 1808, fear of scoldings, obnoxious children and 'vast expenditure' inspire the 'serious thought' and 'melancholy resolution' of remaining single: ultimately it is 'economy [that] makes bach'lors of us' (Hawkins, line 24) and 'the name of husband' (line 33) is lost with a resigned passivity that recalls the first soliloquy from 1744. As the post-Napoleonic attempts to 'make the world safe for conjugality' (Walker 71) begin to take effect in the 1810s and 1820s, the bachelors offer ever less resistance and their fears become domesticated. They run from a dread of being 'henpeck'd' (Twiss, line 10) to that of finding a 'scold' (Anon. 'Parody on Hamlet' (1824), line 9). By 1824, the 'horrors' included 'The cook's conceit, a curtain lecture, / The apothecary's visits, or **the wrongs** / A patient husband from his wife must take' (Kean, lines 17–19) and 'the dread of sundry fits of gout / and **other ills that** need a woman's care'. It is only natural that 'man's natural bacheloric **hue**' should be finally '**sickly'd o'er** and kill'd' (lines 23–24 and 29–30). Being single is a sickly thing, and so this bachelor will marry for his health. After eighty years of bachelor soliloquies, the eighteenth-century rake has dwindled into a proto-Victorian husband. Only a few of these parodies take their cue from Hamlet's indecision; they all provide their own different answers to that burning question that is so unlike Hamlet's.

Cross-adaptation: Whose soliloquy is it anyway?

Whether the outcome is singleness, whoring or wedlock, the 'bachelor's soliloquies' are completely dominated by their topic. This is announced already in the titles, where the genre marker 'bachelor's soliloquy' usually precedes any mention of Shakespeare or *Hamlet*. In titles like 'A Parody of Hamlet's celebrated Soliloquy', the adjective 'celebrated' hints at Shakespeare's fame but simultaneously reminds readers that this fame is reflected by, and owed to, the many parodists who have been inspired by it. These rewrites validate both Shakespeare and each other. Any 'anxiety of influence' or intertextual context in mid-eighteenth-century parodies concerned not so much Shakespeare as the lively contemporary competition and the opportunity for reprints. The 1744 poem was republished in 1748 in the second edition of a peculiar booklet called *The Bachelor's Recantation*.[6] This pro-marriage pamphlet maintains that the 'Contempt of Matrimony in either Sex is big with the greatest Evils' (Single iii) and adds various items of supporting evidence in an appendix. These pieces include 'A Young Lady's Recantation of Her Resolution to turn Nun', 'The Doctor confuted: Or, NO Cure for Love' and a 'Maid's Soliloquy' of which more later. The 'Bachelor's Soliloquy' is included without any mention of Shakespeare in the table of contents; readers flicking through a magazine number or a miscellany of jokes, 'amusements' and set pieces were obviously expected to turn pages for the Bachelor, not the Bard. As a matter of fact, the first edition of *The Bachelor's Recantation* came out in 1731 and may well have inspired the first Hamlet-Bachelor's Soliloquy, which appeared years later and was then included in the second edition of the *Recantation*. Bachelor covers Bard. This fact is reflected in the title of the 1744 piece. 'The Bachelor's Soliloquy in imitation of *a* celebrated speech of Hamlet' (my italics) bestows the definite article, an indication of public familiarity, on the bachelor poem, while 'To be or not to Be' is still 'a' speech, not 'the' speech.[7] Similarly, a poem on 'Female Celibacy' was advertised in 1813 as by 'the Author of the "Bachelor's Soliloquy"' – and this 'Soliloquy' is not at all related to *Hamlet*. It laments a birthday that is 'With no kind gratulations blest' and a loneliness which welcomes death: 'Why then, without a tear, / I *yield the worm its prey*' (Jackson 'Soliloquy', lines 7 and 78–80). Welcome death, Hamlet's great subject, is present while Jackson's identity as an 'author' is owed to a poem title that he has borrowed from a group of poems on marriage, some of which happen to incorporate the surface structure of Hamlet's soliloquy. In this web of cross-quotation, we can indeed wonder whose soliloquy we are reading.

In 1809, a new literary bachelor specimen complicated the intertextual field even further when the evangelical educationalist Hannah More published a gender-flipped courtship novel, *Coelebs in Search of a Wife*. In an enlightening inversion of the rakes and oafs who are disqualified from marrying Austen's and Burney's heroines, the pious Coelebs rejects a number of unsuitable potential brides such as the hysterically accomplished 'Miss Rattle' before finally hitting on Miss Right. The refreshing re-shuffle of popular elements made *Coelebs* an

'The old parody': A Post-Shakespeare Genre   111

immediate bestseller and added another literary template to the referential network of prenuptial soliloquies. In March 1809, well before the twelve impressions of *Coelebs'* first year were out, an anonymous poet capitalized on its popularity by publishing a 'Coelebs' Soliloquy' after the *Hamlet* pattern. Reversing More's narrative, the speaker remains literally 'coelebs', choosing 'The holy joys of some sequester'd cell' over marriage because he is a poet and fears for his literary pleasures:

> Yet, **who wou'd bear** the follies of a spouse, [...]
> When he, *unbound*, **might his** *quietus* **make**
> **With** studying Plato?
> **Thus marriage does** deter my **tow'ring soul** [...]
> and all in air dissolve! (Menander, lines 15, 20–21, 28 and 33).

Even if this Coelebs sounds repressed rather than rakish, the poem represents the triumph of the bachelor motif over the courtship novel and over Hannah More's piety. The phrase 'tow'ring soul' is also used in the 1763 'Poet's Soliloquy' mentioned above and underscores the subversion of More's ideal of Christian marriage, which is declined for literary reasons. *Hamlet*, among all these competing voices, recedes further from view.

As in Shakespeare's own quotation practice, cross-quotation weakens the link to any single source in the soliloquy parodies, making intertextuality more casual. In cross-*adaptation*, as in the Hamilton and 'Coelebs' pieces, the effect is even stronger. An absurdly close rewrite of Hamlet's soliloquy from 1751 starts like this:

> **To be or not to be; that is the Question!**
> Death either robs this Clod of feeling Earth
> of Sense; or there is **something after Death,**
> **Some undiscover'd Country, to whose** Coast
> Th' unburthen'd Soul, without Obstruction fails.
> But if no Wreck of Sense survive the Grave;
> **If Death be Sleep;** a Sleep where Dreams ne'r fright
> No Thoughts disturb us, **'tis a Consummation**
> **Devoutly to be wish'd, to die! to sleep!** (Rider, lines 9).

One wonders what the point could be of rewriting a famous passage so closely, especially considering that the title does not mention *Hamlet*. Instead, the poem is called 'Socrates on Death. Translated from Plato's Apology in Shakespeare's Manner'. This title sends several competing intertextual messages. The announcement of the topic, 'Socrates on death', is in the style of thematically sorted anthologies and marks the following text as an isolated set piece worth memorizing. The subtitle refers to the passage in Plato's *Apologia* where Socrates explains that fear of death is unnecessary. An introductory remark elaborates on this connection:

> The Similitude which this Passage bears to the celebrated Speech in Hamlet, will vindicate the Attempt of translating it in Shakespeare's Stile, and it may serve as a Proof that he understood more Greek, than the Generality, even of his Admirers, will allow (Rider 648).

This comment is one of many attempts to save Shakespeare's educational credentials. It is hard to understand, though, how the 'translation' (strange word!) of a Plato passage into an Elizabethan pastiche modelled on a Shakespeare text of which said Plato passage is supposed to have been the model should argue that Shakespeare knew more than a 'little Greek'! As the Greek text that Shakespeare probably quoted through a Latin translation appears rewritten in Shakespeare's style, intertextuality is coming full (casual) circle.

The 1763 'Poet's Soliloquy', which I have briefly mentioned, implicates Socrates' death as recounted by Plato and then adds a more recent literary hit. The minimal verbal twists are of the by now familiar kind, and syntax and even mood are rather more carefully preserved than in other versions.

> To write! – or not to write! – that is the question
> Whether 'tis better **in the mind to suffer**
> The impatient longings of a tow'ring soul
> A heart aspiring to immortal fame;
> Or to take pen **against** the critic's rage,
> And by opposing end them? (Ashley, lines 1–6).

While the previously discussed *Hamlet* imitation is called 'Socrates on Death', this one has the subtitle 'A Parody of Cato's celebrated Soliloquy'! Joseph Addison's tragedy *Cato* (1712) does feature a soliloquy in which the eponymous hero ponders suicide – and this soliloquy contains a number of phrases adapted from *Hamlet*. 'The wide, **th'unbounded** Prospect' (56) for the immortality of the soul recalls Hamlet's 'undiscovered country' while 'I'm weary of Conjectures – **This must end 'em**' echoes 'and by opposing end them' (56). Even Cato's resolution to commit suicide, so different from Hamlet's inability to take any kind of 'action', is couched in terms of Hamletian indecision when Cato becomes fatally 'Indiff'rent in his Choice **to sleep or die**' (57). No such decisiveness is evident in the 'Poet's Soliloquy', which ends with the regret that the inability to write should condemn poets to 'oblivion'; and yet Addison's tragedy was so popular half a century after its first performance that it seemed opportune to replace the name 'Hamlet' by 'Cato' in a rewriting of 'To be or not to be'. In fact, searches for <celebrated speech> in the *Eighteenth*

Century Collections Online database turn up far more hits connected with *Cato* than with *Hamlet*. The phrase 'tow'ring soul', by the way, is from Addison's *Cato*, and may be borrowed from *Cato* in 'Coelebs' Soliloquy': Cato's Sempronius describes Cato as a 'tow'ring Soul' who remains superior 'Midst all the Shocks and Injuries of Fortune' (Addison 30). And this echoes Hamlet's 'heart-ache and the thousand natural shocks / That flesh is heir to' (3.70–71).

Cato's soliloquy itself, to complete the convolutions, contains further layers of intertextuality. Its own indebtedness to *Hamlet* of course goes unacknowledged. In contrast, there is a nod to Plato in the stage direction 'Cato, *solus, sitting in a thoughtful posture: in his hand Plato's book on the Immortality of the soul. A drawn sword on the table by him.*' A book as the prop of a soliloquizing actor has its own intertextual history in turn. It may echo Hamlet entering 'poring vppon a booke' in the *First Quarto* (sig. D4^{verso}), where he may be meant to read the soliloquy from an unidentified volume, and it then reappears in a *Hamlet*-free 'Maid's Soliloquy'. Published in the appendix of the 1748 *Bachelor's Recantation*, this piece carries the subtitle 'Act V, scene I of Cato Imitated' and describes the girl as entering '*alone, with* Milton *in her Hand, open at this celebrated Passage*'. This time, the 'celebrated passage' is the 'hymn' 'Hail, wedded Love' from Book IV of *Paradise Lost* instead of *Hamlet* or *Cato*. As is to be expected, the maid's doubts are soon overcome and she declares in Miltonian tones: 'I wed – my liberty is gone forever, / but Happiness from Time itself secur'd' (Single 22 and 23). Such convoluted and always casual intertextuality is maybe best described by the terms that Stephen O'Neill uses to write about YouTube videos, whose 'logic of media smash-and-grab positions *Hamlet* as an amalgam of texts to be readily combined with other texts rather than as any anchoring or single textual authority' (O'Neill 83). In this endlessly reverberating echo chamber, *Hamlet* may be the element that we recognize most readily, but it is just one element among many.

From imitation to genre

Like Shakespeare's own texts, eighteenth-century parodies of his speeches obscure their primary source by cross-quotation and cross-adaptation. Even the titles of these pieces, which at first glance seem to foreground marking for derivation, include decontextualizing links to other texts. An item from 1826 is called 'A **Touch of the Sublime** and Beautiful: *Translated [!] from Hamlet's Soliloquy*' (Anon. 'A Touch'), combining overt marking for Shakespeare with an unmarked echo from Byron, who winks at his readers in Canto V of *Don Juan*: 'Let this fifth canto meet with due applause, / The sixth shall have a **touch of the sublime**' (588). An 1810 version of 'To write or not to write', which appeared in the *Hibernia Magazine*, has the title 'A Parody on Hamlet's Soliloquy on

Death'. This is as full a bibliographical reference as could be wished. It is, however, also the exact title of a soliloquy debating whether 'to shave or not to shave', which had appeared in *Walker's Hibernian Magazine* thirteen years earlier (Barbatus 'Parody')! Moreover, the mini-summary 'on Death' evokes another important habitat of Hamlet's speech outside *Hamlet*: the literary anthology. Many such collections, including volumes of *Beauties* dedicated exclusively to Shakespeare's works, grouped their contents under topical headings to facilitate their use in the Renaissance tradition of the commonplace book. In such anthologies, 'To be or not to be' appears under a number of different general titles. Such headings may include simple abstract terms such as 'Suicide' (1783, 1796, 1800), 'Life and Death weigh'd' (1752, 1791) or 'Futurity' (1702, 1718, 1737, 1756); others combine this information with marking for quotation such as 'Hamlet's Meditation on Death' (1749, 1758, 1764, 1768, 1778) or 'Soliloquy of Hamlet on Life and Death'. This context means that a title like 'A Parody on Hamlet's Soliloquy on Death' would have prepared its first readers for an anthology piece rather than for a spoof on a tragedy.

Cross-quotation and references to anthologies indicate an intertextual process that is predominantly 'horizontal', i.e. looking to recent texts of a similar kind, and which keeps a noticeable distance from the 'vertical' dimension reaching towards a single historical model. Fully formed genres have no 'points of origin except those which are retrospectively designated as origins' (Culler *Pursuit of Signs* 117), and these parodies represent the complementary process: they implicitly diminish and obscure Hamlet's 'designation' as the origin which it technically is. Alistair Fowler's classic *Kinds of Literature* distinguishes genres from '[e]laborations of an original' because such elaborations have this original 'as their context, rather than each other' (127). In this respect, eighteenth-century soliloquy parodies do qualify as specimens of a genre: their 'radial' relationship with *Hamlet* as a centre is indeed outweighed by the 'circumferential' (127) relationship to peer specimens, which 'relates a literary work to a whole series of other works', the 'constituents of a genre' (Culler 'Presupposition' 1394). This 'horizontal' element is reinforced by serial publication. 'Coelebs' Soliloquy' was published as 'Imitations of Shakespeare No. 2: Coelebs' Soliloquy'. This title is intriguingly complex. It announces a Shakespeare parody, a token of the popular 'X's Soliloquy' and 'Bachelor's Soliloquy' genres and references a current bestseller that itself inverts a highly successful novelistic genre and advertises a topical social issue. Finally, the title locates this text in a mini-series of 'Imitations of Shakespeare' in the *Universal Magazine*, which in its turn emulated a series which had run in the *Gentleman's Magazine* from June 1793 to December 1802.[8] Such 'cycles and series tend in turn to become genres' (Frow 139) because they encourage the perception of texts as parts of a contemporary group of texts rather than as individual works. Historically, genre is 'almost always constituted by way of imitation (Virgil imitates Homer, Mateo Aleman's *Guzman* imitates the anonymous *Lazarillo*)' (Genette 7); after this start, imitation of an influential text produces new realizations of an 'architextual' model (as Genette calls it) which is abstracted from the founding original. *Hamlet* verse parodies practice rewriting as a transaction within a community of rewriters and so exemplify the process of 'genrification'. This term was coined by the film historian Rick Altman for the process which turns descriptions of individual tokens into a genre term, as when the word 'Western' went 'from adjective to noun' (52). Similarly, every 'So-and-So's Soliloquy' implies that there may be many more speaker *personae*, just as there are countless Westerns that are not defined by their relationship to *The Great Train Robbery*.

The close affinity of eighteenth-century parodies with casual Shakespeare *quotation* is evident in parody titles that include additional quotations and in the typographical acknowledgment of 'uber-quotes' within adaptations. The marriage question, which was so often associated with Hamlet's famous question, brought the two even closer together. In an anonymous epistolary novel from 1776, the worries of a confused young woman fuse and expand several lines from the soliloquy,

> arguing *the Point*, **Whether 'tis nobler in the Mind to suffer** continual Mortifications, **or, by a loveless Marriage, end them. To wed, or not to wed?** For, (would you believe it?) the Man has actually askd *that important* **Question**, in Spite of Poverty and Dependence (*Husband's Resentment* 1:38–39).

This passage is effectively a mini-adaptation within the body of the novel. Thirty years later, the Hamletian marriage question was so trite that it became its own parody:

> **The** serious **question** with him, at the moment the fair widow as seriously asked him, which of three Marquisses, the Earls and four Barons he would advise her to think on for Kattie, **was** *the old parody of*, '**To marry, or not to marry**' (Bennett *Beggar Girl* 3:68).

'To marry or not to marry', a casual reworking of a famous Shakespeare line, has itself become famous, and worse than famous: to say 'to marry or not to marry' is to parody all those who have uttered this version of the *Hamlet* line before. It becomes evident that casual Shakespeare references, whether overworked quotation or generic parody, do not primarily work 'as an intersubjective transaction between author and [parodist]'; what is paramount is the relation 'between one [parodist] and another' (Price 'Poetics of Pedantry' 80). Casual parody and casual quotation both reflect a familiarity with Shakespeare's turns of phrase which was so intense that it induced self-consciousness. It became difficult to quote without turning into the parody of an affected pedant and it became, conversely, possible to write Shakespearean 'imitations' with an 'ethos' that was neutrally 'respectful' or 'playful' (Hutcheon 63). Scorn and mockery were reserved for the political or social problems which are criticized; what is still called 'parody' is nothing but a formal 'vehicle' (Hutcheon 58) which does not have any kind of relationship with the Shakespearean original.

Charles Lamb had a point when he complained in 1811 that the soliloquy was torn 'inhumanly from its living place and principle of continuity in the play'. He was, however, mistaken in concluding that this treatment made the speech into 'a perfect dead member' (Lamb 192). Once removed from the 'body' of Shakespeare's play, Hamlet's speech did not only stay alive; it became extremely, prolifically, fertile, as if liberated rather than amputated. This development is profoundly typical of the many Shakespeare items that have truly 'left the book' (Engler 55). It may seem wittier to write 'he shuffled off his mortal coil' instead of 'he kicked the bucket' or 'he cashed in his chips', but it is not more of a *Hamlet* interpretation. The quotation has shed author, context and quotation marks and turned into an idiom which helps us to avoid saying 'he died'. In the same way, the model 'Somebody's soliloquy – to verb or not to verb' has become a formal pattern of expression, the blueprint of a genre. The reader's experience of such a 'parody' is not determined by *Hamlet* resonances but by the awareness that this text belongs to a host of others that have followed the same pattern before. This is also the determining factor in the tide of casual Shakespeare quotations that washed over English letters from the mid-1770s: all these writers know that they are quoting Shakespeare and that many other have quoted him and will quote him – and most of them care very little.

Notes

1 This idea is Carol Leininger's.
2 In 1786, John Wolcot worried about the censorship that would limit his choice 'To eat or not to eat' depending on whether he would be prepared 'To write, – to lie; – / To lie! – perchance to pay' ('Peter Pindar's Soliloquy' 2, column D).
3 The explicitness of such marking for intertextuality is even stronger in a parody that was published in the same month. Starting with 'To drink or not to drink', it arranges the italicized *Hamlet* text and the rewriting in alternating lines: '*To be or not to be, that is the Question* / To drink, or not to drink? – that is the Question. / *Whether 'tis nobler in the mind to suffer* / Whether 'tis better for a Man, to suffer / *The slings and arrows of outrageous fortune,* / The Pangs and Horrors of outrageous Thirst' (Anon. 'A parody' *Newcastle General Magazine* 1747, lines 1–6).

4 Full texts and bibliographical references can be found at www.hyperhamlet.unibas.ch. A little subgenre flourished around 1803: 'Bonaparte's Soliloquy at Calais', 'Bonaparte Solus' and 'Buonaparte's Soliloquy on the Cliffs at Boulogne' are spoken by Napoleon, who is considering whether 'to invade or not to invade'.
5 Other political issues include parliamentary elections (1805; 'to stand'), the poll tax (1795; 'to pay') and many others. For a detailed discussion see Bate 'Parodies'.
6 The importance of the bachelor topic is confirmed by the twenty reprints which the 1744 and 1758 parodies went through until the 1820s, while only half of the over fifty non-bachelor soliloquies discussed here were reprinted even once.
7 The casual indefinite article is the same as in Samuel Pepys' diary eighty years earlier, when Pepys spent an afternoon in 1664 'getting <u>a speech out of Hamlett</u>, '**To bee or not to bee,**' <u>without book</u>' (13 November 1664, emphasis mine). A hundred years later, Pepys would certainly have used the definite article.
8 The author, Reverend Thomas Ford, who habitually laced his sermons with Shakespeare quotations, also published more than fifty Shakespeare parodies as 'Master Shallow'. Five of them (numbers 6, 21, 32, 39 and 42) riff on 'To be or not to be'. Overall, the *Gentleman's Magazine* published at least 22 *Hamlet* parodies, thirteen of which on 'to be or not to be'. Romeo's apothecary speech accounts for thirteen out of sixteen numbers from *Romeo and Juliet* and 'Seven Ages of Man' for eleven out of thirteen tokens from *As You Like It* (cf. Bate 'Parodies' 79).

6 Peak Casual: Romantic Routine

> *Shakespeare's celebrated passages are in half the books we open.*
> JANE AUSTEN

When Lionel Verney, the 'Last Man' of Mary Shelley's apocalyptic novel published in 1826, writes down his story after surviving a shipwreck in which his last three friends have perished, he always aims for 'words capacious of the grand conclusion' (338). To describe how his friend Adrian, son of the last king of England, went mad for love, Verney borrows words from Shakespeare and from Percy Shelley's friend Bryan Procter:

> Have those gentle eyes, those '**channels of the soul**', lost their meaning, or do they only in their glare disclose the horrible tale of its aberrations? Does that voice no longer '**discourse excellent music?**' **Horrible, most horrible!** (37).

This is a veritable feast of cross-quotation: three-and-a-half quotations in two-and-a-half sentences. There is a phrase, 'channels of the soul' from Procter's narrative poem *The Broken Heart*; a blended echo of two *Hamlet* lines about the recorder, which can 'discourse most eloquent music' (3.2.389–390) and has 'much music, excellent voice' (3.2.398), and finally Old Hamlet's description of his own murder: 'O horrible, O horrible, most horrible!' (1.5.87). Only two of the borrowed phrases are given in quotation marks and none of the original contexts have anything to do with the love-madness that is Lionel Verney's subject. This is what I have come to call Romantic Routine: Shakespeare quotation at its most intense and at its most casual. In the decades around 1800, when Shakespeare's influence on reverential – and referential – poets was arguably at its greatest, his phrases appear in English prose with a frequency that makes meaningful reference improbable in most cases. They are cross-quoted with other texts, quoted imprecisely and often, though inconsistently, signalled by quotation marks. This mode of using Shakespeare was, apparently, so endemic that it persists even in the notes of the last man on earth. While '"[d]ecorative" [...] rather than referential' forms of quotation are 'increasing' (Garber 38) in the early twenty-first century, the casual use of Shakespeare *decreased* over the nineteenth and twentieth centuries, after having gone absolutely viral around 1800. This early peak is the subject of this chapter.

Quotation as a mass phenomenon

Thousands of Shakespeare quotations from the late eighteenth and early nineteenth centuries can be called 'routine' because they are numbingly frequent and unobtrusive. They only came to my attention through the 'distant reading' that was enforced by working on *HyperHamlet*. As I oversaw the editing of hundreds of eighteenth- and nineteenth-century text extracts for the database, I was struck by what seemed a unusual density of Shakespeare references around the turn of the nineteenth century and by the apparently random nature of many tokens. Something special seemed to be going on there. To test this hunch, I first set aside materials in which quotation or citation are generic givens: I excluded quotations that occur in anthologies, works of literary criticism, *Hamlet* parodies and works that are suffused with *Hamlet* motifs and characters, such as Walter Scott's *The Bride of Lammermoor* or William Wordsworth's verse tragedy *The Borderers*. This first filtering left a collection of 3,400 *Hamlet*-quoting extracts that were written between 1700 and 1900, all taken from texts which did not 'need' to contain Shakespeare quotations. A closer analysis of this material confirmed that the decades around 1800 were indeed special. Two distinct shifts in quotation practice could be identified in the 1770s and the 1830s, bracketing a period of 60 years which is represented by 2,400 tokens. These text passages will be referred to as the *Romantic Routine Corpus* or *RR Corpus* for short; the conveniently alliterative word 'Romantic' being shorthand for 'written between the mid-1770s and the mid-1830s'. A quantitative analysis of this material revealed distinct patterns of casual use which can be found both in 'the world of the canon' and 'the archive of the Great Unread' (Caselli 6). The results can be considered reasonably representative for Romantic Shakespeare quotation because *Hamlet* was the most-quoted Shakespeare play by a distinct margin: the indexes of scholarly editions indicate that this play accounts for between 15% and 20% of all Shakespeare echoes in the Romantic period.[1] So until a complete *HyperWill* database becomes available, the *HyperHamlet* sample remains a serviceable basis for a data-based investigation into the Romantic epidemic of Shakespeare quotation.

The defining pattern of use that distinguishes Romantic Routine from the quotation habits that came before and after concerns the MARKING of intertextual insets. First, the average ratio of items with MARKING

FOR QUOTATION is 56%, which is significantly higher than in other periods. Of the twentieth-century tokens on *HyperHamlet*, for example, only 35% alert their readers to intertextuality in any way. In contrast, the typical Romantic Shakespeare quotation is an explicitly signalled intertextual act. Second, these signals rarely include any information on the origin of a borrowed phrase. A mere 14% of the items in the *RR Corpus* include a mention of *Hamlet* or of a character from the play, and just 6% indulge in the 'self-congratulatory' naming of Shakespeare; only a tiny minority of tokens attempts to 'claim cultural authority' (Keymer 118) by overt MARKING FOR DERIVATION. Even more obviously than the verse parodies discussed in Chapter 5, Romantic quotations mark an intertextual presence and simultaneously obscure or gloss over the identity of the pre-text: the characteristic mode of the Romantic period is MARKING FOR QUOTATION ONLY.

The historical evolution of the Romantic marking patterns is visualized in three graphs (Figures 6.1–6.3), which show the relative frequency of characteristic indicators for a given period. In each graph, the solid black line at the top represents the percentage of quotations recorded for a given period that show MARKING FOR QUOTATION. The dotted and dashed lines show the percentage of marked quotations that have or do not have MARKING FOR DERIVATION. The percentage of texts that mention Shakespeare or a name from *Hamlet* is indicated by the dotted line; the remaining marked quotations are MARKED FOR QUOTATION ONLY and are represented by the dashed line. Figure 6.1 shows these defining indicators by decades.

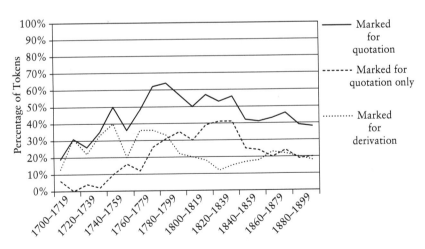

Figure 6.1 Defining Romantic Routine. Marking of Shakespeare quotations in percent of all quotations in the *RR Corpus*: the eighteenth and nineteenth centuries by decade. Author's own.

This graph has two main features that stand for the defining characteristics of Romantic Routine: the overall rise and fall of the solid black line and the crossings of the dotted and dashed lines. Romantic Routine is, first of all, a period in English letters when the majority of Shakespeare quotations are marked, the years when the solid black line is above 50%. Second, Romantic Routine is the time when the majority of marked quotations are marked for quotation only so that the dashed line (quotation only) is *above* the dotted line (derivation). The six decades of Romantic Routine as a historical phenomenon are represented by the surface between the two crossings of the dashed and dotted lines in the 1770s and 1830s. Before that period, MARKING FOR DERIVATION was always more frequent than MARKING FOR QUOTATION ONLY and in the later nineteenth century, marking of any kind returned to a generally low level, without discernible distribution patterns for quotation / derivation.

While MARKING FOR QUOTATION overall increased until the mid-eighteenth century and then stayed above 50% for several decades, MARKING FOR (Shakespearean) DERIVATION peaked in the middle of the eighteenth century when bardolatry reached its first high. The quotations in Sarah Fielding's novels are a case in point. Written between 1744 and 1759, these texts mark almost all of their quotations: the ratio of 29 out of 31 tokens in the *RR Corpus* would easily meet the first criterion for Romantic Routine. However, Fielding's quotation practice does not fulfil the second criterion of predominant MARKING FOR QUOTATION ONLY, for she names Shakespeare (seven times) and *Hamlet* (eighteen times) far too often. The following passage from the preface to *The Countess of Dellwyn* is typical:

> And if any one should think **I am tracing this Matter too curiously,** I, who have considered it in various Shapes, can only answer <u>with Hamlet, on Horatio's making the same Objection to his philosophical Reflexions, in the Scene of the Grave-digger</u>, that, in my Opinion, I can truly say, – **not a Jot**; it being no more than the natural Result of examining and considering the Subject (xlii–xliii).

This quotation is casual: the *Hamlet* phrase is split up and modified and its context is irrelevant to Fielding's topic, which is prose composition. The marking for derivation, on the other hand, is pre-Romantically elaborate, giving the name of the speaker, the addressee, the scene and the context of the dialogue: 'no kind of intertextual reference is more formal [...] than the direct quotations of a mid-eighteenth-century novel' (Rumbold *Eighteenth-Century* 17).

As the familiarity of popular phrases was increasingly assumed, MARKING FOR DERIVATION became less frequent; writers increasingly foregrounded the act of quotation itself until MARKING FOR QUOTATION

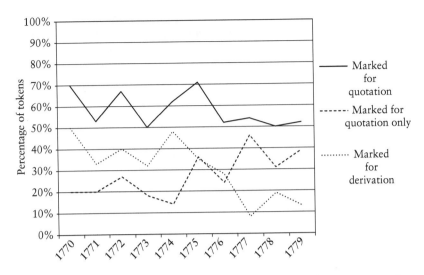

Figure 6.2 The onset of Romantic Routine. Marking of Shakespeare quotations in percent of all quotations in the *RR Corpus:* the 1770s by year. Author's own.

ONLY overtook MARKING FOR DERIVATION in 1776. Figure 6.2 provides a close-up of that moment, showing the distribution of different kinds of marking by year.

The mid-1770s watershed in Shakespeare quotation may be partially explained by the defeat of perpetual copyright in 1774, which made a difference between the legal status of older and more recent published works. 'Timeless gleanings from the backlist' were more frequently reprinted (Price *Anthology* 67) and signals to the readers lightened as quotations became more frequent. Marking could now be merely typographical, as in James Boswell's diary: 'Westminster Hall seemed to me "**flat and unprofitable**"' (*Private Papers* 13:152); it could consist just of an archaism, as in Hannah Robertson's autobiography: 'How weak are human resolves. – **Frailty, thy name is woman**' (8); or it could be a throwaway tag indicating a cliché, as in this report on a suicide from the *Times*:

> The case excited considerable interest from the artful and cunning method the poor maniac had resorted to to destroy himself, proving the old adage, that '**some men have method in their madness**' (Anon. 'Singular Suicide' 3).

After several decades, the popularity of MARKING FOR QUOTATION ONLY had run its course, and by the 1840s, items marked for derivation were back in the lead. As can be seen in Figure 6.3, the ratio of

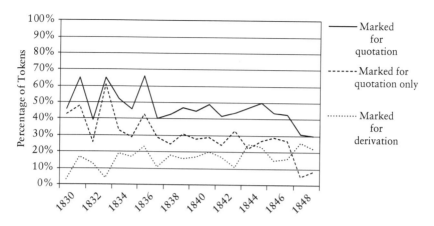

Figure 6.3 The end of Romantic Routine. Marking of Shakespeare quotations in percent of all quotations in the *RR Corpus*: the 1830s and 1840s by year. Author's own.

MARKING FOR QUOTATION overall oscillates throughout the 1840s; for a cut-off date for Romantic Routine, I selected the distinctive and lasting drop in overall MARKING FOR QUOTATION (the solid line) in 1837, which offered the serendipitous bonus of having 'my' era end with the beginning of Victoria's reign.

The significance of the 1776–1837 timespan is confirmed by two observations on eighteenth-century reading. Michael Gardiner speaks of 'reading and massification' between 1771 and 1831, when worries about revolutionary upheavals in France and the doubling of the British population prompted attempts at a 'disciplining of reading' (Gardiner 25). The success of these efforts resulted in an increased collective tendency to self-censorship and a certain discursive uniformity. The mass tendency to casual quotation could be explained as part of this. Franco Moretti's analysis focuses on the chronological centre of this period, 'the traumatic, fast-moving years between 1789 and 1815' (*Distant Reading* 20), which saw the rise of extensive reading with 'one-volume-per-day consumption'. Moretti claims that without such speeded-up reading 'there would have been no rise of the European novel' (176); it may also have encouraged the use of quickly absorbed catchphrases.

Defined by the predominance of MARKING FOR QUOTATION ONLY, Romantic Routine has a number of other features which indicate the characteristically loose connection between the quoted phrases and their original context. Quotations are split, blended and modified to fit new contexts; they can be triggered by acoustic memories of rhythm and sound and they frequently involve cross-quotations from inside and outside the Shakespeare canon. In addition, individual writers have favourite lines that they use again and again. These characteristics can be found already in Shakespeare's own writing and in the use of his texts that was made in the early seventeenth century by writers such as John Marston. Many of these textual overlaps have been very carefully investigated and documented in philological publications. Romantic casual quotations have figured less prominently in research and criticism, as became obvious when the *HyperHamlet* team was assembling this part of the corpus. Our starting points for research were the footnotes in the great twentieth-century scholarly editions of Romantic literature. The Princeton Coleridge, the Cornell Wordsworth, Jerome J. McGann's *Complete Poetical Works of Byron* or the Edinburgh Edition of Scott's Waverley novels point out every imaginable literary allusion with great care. The complementary digital research – running *Hamlet* lines through databases such as *LION, ECCO* and *The Romantic Era Redefined* – managed to unearth only a small handful of additional *Hamlet* quotations that these editions do not annotate. In recent, less lavishly curated editions, casual quotation does not fare so well. Pickering and Chatto's *Collected Novels and Memoirs of William Godwin* (1992), for example, point out just 57 of at least 75 *Hamlet* quotations in the radical novelist's work. 56 of the 57 quotations that did catch the editors' attention are marked for quotation by Godwin, which suggests that his texts were scanned for quotation marks or the word 'Hamlet' as part of the editing process. This procedure would risk missing the unmarked borrowings that Godwin's ideal reader would have noticed. Although MARKING FOR QUOTATION ONLY is the most typical format of the Romantic decades, a complete picture of Romantic Routine must include the substantial percentage of quotations which are slipped in without any signals and depend completely on complicit readers for recognition.

A writer who is particularly badly served by a lack of in-depth editorial attention is Mary Shelley, whose intense cross-quotations are a highly characteristic feature of her work. In the dense passage that opens this chapter, only the two phrases in quotation marks are annotated in the 1996 *Novels and Selected Works of Mary Shelley*. A footnote points out that 'discourse excellent music' is taken from *Hamlet* and that it leaves out the word 'most' from the *First Folio*'s wording 'discourse most excellent music'. However, it goes completely unmentioned that 'horrible, most horrible' is also a *Hamlet* quotation! And this is not an isolated oversight. The following paragraph from *The Last Man* combines two unmarked *Hamlet* quotations with an allusion to the *Aeneid* and a nod to the Bible:

> [I]n **my heart of hearts**, I made a vow to devote life, knowledge, and power, [...] to him alone [...] Methought the time was now arrived, when, **childish occupations laid aside,** I should enter into life. **Even in the Elysian fields,** Virgil describes **the souls of the happy as eager to drink** of the wave which was to restore them to this **mortal coil** (32).

These jumbled riches are not caught by the footnotes, which do explain that the Elysian Fields come from Book VI of the *Aeneid* but point out neither the unmarked *Hamlet* phrases 'mortal coil' and 'heart of hearts' nor the echo from 1 Corinthians 13:11: 'when I became a man, I **put away childish things**'. Readers of such densely intertextual passages cannot be meant to scamper off in every direction to hunt for the meaning of every casual quotation. But they are certainly meant to recognize the fact of a quotation, and a modern edition should give twenty-first century readers a chance to appreciate this aspect of Mary Shelley's writing. Research into Romantic-era Shakespeare quotation clearly has some way to go, also because only very few of the casual quotations that did make it into footnotes have then received more sustained scholarly attention. With a few significant exceptions, such as the work of Leah Price and Kate Rumbold on eighteenth-century novels, anthologies and the Silver fork novelist Susan Ferrier, the mass of casually recycled phrases in the literature of the Romantic decades still awaits discovery and exploration.

Elegant routine:
William Hazlitt, the 'Shakespeare prose writer'

William Hazlitt's essays are the best introduction to the characteristic features of Romantic Routine because they offer a large sample of knowledgeable, fluidly elegant quotation. His prolific intertextuality was controversial: Thomas de Quincey maintained that having one's 'verbal memory infested with tags of verse and "cues" of rhyme is in itself an infirmity' ('Lamb' 381), while William Bewick called Hazlitt 'the Shakespeare prose writer of our glorious country' as a compliment on his 'truth, style, and originality' (Bewick 42). Both remarks have a point. At an estimated 2,400 quotations from Shakespeare alone, many of Hazlitt's borrowings must be facile. It seems even random whether Shakespeare came to his mind or not: a two-part article, published on 29 September and 13 October 1816, is 'packed with Shakespearean quotations' whereas the stand-alone piece he published on 6 October 'does not contain a single one' (Bate 'Hazlitt's' 26). Casual as it was, Hazlitt's extensive quotation habit gave him a tremendous facility: his quotations are always done with a reader-friendly elegance and never worked in to impress, in keeping with the communicative, conversational and all-embracing quality of his essays. Hazlitt's light and fluent marking is quintessential Romantic Routine, taking marking for quotation to an extreme by marking a staggering 87% of his *Hamlet* quotations (the *RR Corpus* average is 56%) and marking 81% of his marked quotations for derivation (the *RR Corpus* average is 77%). The reader is not instructed, just given a chance to catch an intertextual moment by the gentle nudge of quotation marks. This is well-done Romantic Routine at its most typical. Other characteristic features such as the blending of unrelated *Hamlet* snippets, cross-quotation with other works, the quotation of sounds and structures rather than words and the routine use of favourite lines are all amply and elegantly illustrated by Hazlitt's essays.

The quotation routine of William Hazlitt and his contemporaries includes many kinds of blending and 'juxtapos[ing] without justifying' (Price *Anthology* 94). They run from sentences that are reduced to a short phrase through blended lines from different Shakespearean scenes all the way to cross-quotation between Shakespeare and other sources. In the simplest cases, distinctive words from a clause are short-circuited, as when 'though I am native here / and to the manner born' turns into **'native to the manner here'** (*Selected Writings*, 8:248 'Elia and Geoffrey Crayon'). In longer passages, memorable key words or key phrases are pulled together across stretches of less famous blank verse. The following passage from Hamlet's 'to be or not to be' soliloquy was repeatedly subjected to this treatment by Hazlitt and others:

> [...] ay, there's the rub
> For in that sleep of death what dreams may come
> When we have shuffled off this mortal coil,
> Must give us pause: there's the respect
> That makes calamity of so long life (3.1.73–78).

The initial **'there's the rub'** seems to have been a kind of 'uber-quote', which serves as the springboard for various leaps across the speech. In his spoof *Modern Novel Writing*, William Beckford skips two lines to write **'Aye, there's the rub / Must give us pause'** (2:179) and William Hazlitt leaves out three to make **'Aye, there's the rub, that makes calamity of so long life'** (*Collected Works*, 3:127 'Western and Brougham'). This shortcut became a fixed item in Hazlitt's memory; it appears at least two more times:

> Yet **'there's the rub that makes absurdity of so long life'** (*Collected Works* 6:37 'Genius and Common Sense').
> **'There was the rub'** that made philosophy of so short life! (*Selected Writings* 7:90 'William Godwin')

A newspaper article from 1772 takes the condensation even further, reducing half the soliloquy into one line: **'To be or not to be, a Bankrupt, that's the rub'** (Anon. 'Review'). This kind of pulling-together of salient words is reminiscent of the inverted commas that highlight especially quotable lines in the first print editions of Shakespeare's works (cf. p. 96) or phrases that are quoted *verbatim* in this eighteenth-century adaptation of 'To be or not to be' (cf. Chapter 5):

To write! to scrawl!
To scrawl – perchance to blot! – "ay, there's the Rub,"
For on a strict Review, **what Blots** "may come"
When we have scribbled all the Paper o'er,
"Must give us Pause" (Anon. 'A Parody' *British Magazine* 1747, lines 9–14).

In this poem, not only the quotemarked extracts are from *Hamlet*, otherwise the parody would not be recognizable as such, but the impression is also that impatient or overfamiliar Shakespeare users would be happy simply to skip from one such 'uber-quote' to the next.

The telescopic short-circuiting of key phrases can also happen across a whole play, as when 'discourse of reason' (*Hamlet* 1.2.154) and 'large discourse' (*Hamlet* 4.4.38) are blended to make **'large discourse of reason'** (Lloyd *Edmund Oliver* 2:38–39). Two sets of quotation marks signal that Hazlitt knew what he was doing when he combined 'in my mind's eye' (*Hamlet* 1.2.193) with 'in my heart's core' (*Hamlet* 3.2.78) to 'Notice we have taken, but it has been **with** "our mind's eye," "our heart's core"' (*Collected Works* 11:366 'Old Actors'); another passage, however, juxtaposes the two lines without marking: 'But they saw [the charms of nature] **in their mind's eye**: they felt them **at their heart's core**' ('Sir Joshua Reynolds' 95). In these passages, we see Hazlitt picking up a structure rather than a word or a phrase: he remembers two instances of the construction 'in my something's metaphorical body part' from two different *Hamlet* scenes. This kind of structural or rhythmical quotation that lines like 'a horse, a horse, my kingdom for a horse' have inspired can also be based on the sound of a single word. In an essay on Edmund Burke, William Hazlitt juxtaposes echoes from *Hamlet* and from *Othello*:

He was not **'native to that element,'** nor was he ever **'subdued to the quality'** of that motley crew of knights, citizens, and burgesses (*Collected Works* 3:326 'Character of Mr. Burke').

The *Hamlet* phrase is shortened from 'native and endued unto that element', and the memory of the word 'endued', which Hazlitt did not put on the page, probably triggered the *Othello* phrase, by acoustic association. Desdemona's tender admission that her heart is 'subdued / Even to the very quality of my lord' (*Othello* 1.3.285–286) has nothing to do with the conservative statesman Edmund Burke, and neither has the death of Ophelia, who seems to Gertrude 'native and endued' to the water in which she drowns (4.7.204–205). Hazlitt is just using phrases. Even in the one passage where the 'element' is physical water, the context is ludicrously different: it concerns the physical constitutions of the Italians and the Swiss.

> The sanguine Italian is chilled and shudders at the touch of cold **water**, while the Helvetian boor [...] is 'native and endued unto that element' (*Selected Writings* 8:156 'Hot and Cold').

This flippant moment makes quite clear that Ophelia's tragic end was not on Hazlitt's mind even if the water that he mentions is as real as that which drowns her. This kind of cross-quotation truly 'decentraliz[es] literary culture' (Price *Anthology* 3).

Not all Shakespearean blendings and cross-quotations have Hazlitt's practiced, near-automatic elegance. Here is a much clumsier passage from the scandalous memoirs of the courtesan Harriette Wilson, who was famously told to 'publish and be damned' by her most famous client, the Duke of Wellington:

> Soon, we find too, **a certain falling off**, in our own powers of human life, a subjection to common accidents, to ill health, and to indigence, which **sicklies o'er the rich colouring of passion, with the pale cast of humanity** (*Memoirs* I:54).

The way in which Hamlet's 'pale cast of thought' is doubled as 'rich colouring of passion' and 'pale cast of humanity' is trying too hard, even if Harriette Wilson came by her quotations honestly: she was 'absolutely charmed with Shakespear' (1:26), 'mad' for reading his plays (2:142) and discusses several passages quite earnestly. A late-night letter that Mary Wollstonecraft (Mary Shelley's mother) wrote in 1787 manages cross-quotation in a less cloying way:

> I am both sick and sleepy – it being past the *witching time of night* – and I have been thinking '**how stale, flat, and unprofitable**' this world is grown to me – you'll [...] tell me, as a friend once before did, alluding to music, that I mistook a flat for a natural (*Letters* 136).

Wollstonecraft's cross-quotation is technically similar and her marking (italics vs. quotation marks) is slapdash, but the shortness of the two (*verbatim*) extracts, the self-deprecating musical pun at the end and the topical, unforced use of the two Shakespeare bits provide a lightness that saves her quotation from pomposity. This is clever, casually easy cross-quotation.

Cross-quotations that range beyond the Shakespeare canon are harder to bring off but Hazlitt, as ever, manages the most outrageous combinations smoothly. Here is a passage that uses the Bible (2 Samuel 2:7), *Paradise Lost* (2.599) and *Macbeth* (1.5.56–57) along with Hamlet's 'discourse of reason' (1.2.154) to discuss Robert Southey:

> [W]e [...] have little hesitation <u>in saying</u> to Mr Southey, **'Thou art the man'**. We know no other person in whom **'fierce extremes'** meet with such mutual self-complacency [...]; who lives so entirely in the **'present ignorant thought,'** without <u>the smallest</u> **'discourse of reason looking before or after'** (*Selected Writings* 4:157–165 'The Courier').

If one were to read all of this out loud, it would flow without any problems, and sometimes Hazlitt rises to charming combinations, like this lovely gesture of rise-and-fall through *Hamlet, Henry V* and Hazlitt's own words in 'The Prose Style of Poets':

> [The poet] **'treads the primrose path of** dalliance' [*Hamlet* 1.3.54], or ascends **'the highest heaven of invention,'** [*Henry V* Prologue 2] or falls flat to the ground (*Selected Writings* 8:7).

The bathos – 'flat' indeed – of the last, finally Shakespeare-free, phrase is wonderfully appropriate and the general quotation marks and light archaisms make Scripture, comedy, epic and tragedy all sound the same. When Hazlitt differentiates the markings more carefully, the effect is less smooth and almost macaronic:

> The writers, instead of 'outdoing termagant or out-Heroding Herod,' were somewhat precise and prudish, gentle almost to a fault, full of candour and modesty,
>   'And of their port as meek as is a maid!'
> There was none of that **Drawcansir** work going on then that there is now; no scalping of authors, no hacking and hewing of their **Lives and Opinions**, except that they used <u>those of</u> **Tristram Shandy, Gent.** rather scurvily; which was to be expected (*Collected Works* 6:216 'On Criticism').

This accords the typographical courtesies of indentation and offsetting to a quotation from the *Canterbury Tales*, gives mere quotations marks to the immediately preceding, heavily adapted Shakespeare extract and introduces two further works by character names. The phrase 'Life and Opinions', which is marked just by capital letters, is only revealed as the first half of the title *The Life and Opinions of Tristram Shandy,*

Gentleman in hindsight, and the speaking name of Drawcansir, the blustering character from George Villier's *The Rehearsal* (1671), further contributes to an old-fashioned air – Romantic Routine with an eighteenth-century flavour.

Hazlitt's Shakespeare quotations are palpably unconcerned with the complete works of art from which they are borrowed. Gracefully accomplished or whimsically obvious, they always remain firmly casual in their relationship to their source. Critics who have investigated them in detail speculate that many of Hazlitt's quotations could be 'fruitfully [...] unpacked' to reveal 'complexity and depth' (Natarajan 104 and 103). Jonathan Bate claims, for example, that Hazlitt's description of London, in which 'the metropolis gradually grows and emerges out of its original obscurity in "the mind's eye"' ('Travelling Abroad' 533), purposely introduces a context of 'ghostly presences' through the *Hamlet* context: Such 'associations in the past [...] must' strike a 'reader with well-tuned ears', who remembers 'that Hamlet first saw the ghost of his father in his "mind's eye"' ('Hazlitt's' 32–33). This is nicely observed but overlooks the fact that 'mind's eye' was a favourite line, which Hazlitt used at least twenty-one times. Some examples are discussed above; here is one more which describes the extremely un-ghostly Falstaff:

> [He] carries a most portly presence **in the mind's eye**; and in him, **not to speak it profanely,** 'we behold the fulness of the spirit of wit and humour bodily' (*Selected Writings* 1:186 'Henry IV').

Falstaff's obesity being such a very physical attribute, 'eye' seems not even to be a pure metaphor here, especially in combination with the irreverent pun on Colossians 2:9–10: 'For in [Christ] dwelleth all the fulness of the Godhead bodily'. The allusion is highlighted by quotation marks and the archaic word order 'humour bodily', and excused by the apologetic *Hamlet* phrase 'not to speak it profanely': both *Hamlet* and the Bible are presented obliquely and with a certain levity. The incorrect quotation marks are intriguing: they include the verb phrase 'we behold', which does not occur in the passage from Colossians but has a Biblical ring to it that works as a subtle, impressionistic marker for derivation. Such quotations may well make us suspect that they 'no longer carr[y] the weight of [their] original context' (Bate 'Hazlitt's' 32).

Narrative routine:
Shakespeare's voices in Romantic novels

However indifferent to their sources, Romantic quotations are integrated into the surface of their host texts in ways that are highly sensitive to generic issues, including that of narrative voice. While mid-eighteenth-century novelists use elaborate, overt Shakespeare quotation to characterize their protagonists, later writers work their borrowings in more smoothly. In direct speech, lightly marked quotations can have a rather artificial effect, as in this passage from Susan Ferrier's *Marriage* (1818):

> 'I vanish', said Mrs. Apsley, snatching up her tippet, ridicule, &c. 'and, **like the baseless fabric of a vision, leave not a wreck behind**'. 'Fare-thee-well at once – **Adieu, adieu, adieu, remember me!**' cried the last of the band, as she slowly retreated (422–423).

The speakers in this little scene are not Shakespeare-spouting eccentrics, who cannot refrain from using the phrases of 'our great poet'. They are completely normal people and so the conspicuous archaisms, the dramatic repetition of 'adieu' and the quotation marks feel unnatural. Quotations that have 'neither origin nor context' (Price 'Poetics of Pedantry' 78) are standard for Romantic Routine but the generalized use that Ferrier's characters make of them is rather disturbing; one Ferrier character actually calls her own sentiments 'all at second hand' (Price *Anthology* 101). Such second-hand language works better with narrators, where it is often done with considerable nuance. At the beginning of this chapter, I have defined Romantic Routine by the relative frequencies of MARKING FOR QUOTATION, MARKING FOR DERIVATION and MARKING FOR QUOTATION ONLY. The same parameters can be used to compare quotation in different fictional and nonfictional voices (this time as average percentages for the period 1776–1837) in order to find out, for example, whether MARKING FOR DERIVATION is used more frequently in dialogue or in third-person narration. In Figure 6.4, this distribution is represented by a cluster of three columns for every kind of voice. The black columns indicate the percentage of items that are MARKED FOR QUOTATION. The other two columns in every cluster show how MARKING FOR QUOTATION is distributed between the period-defining MARKING FOR QUOTATION ONLY (dashed) and MARKING FOR DERIVATION (dotted) for six different kinds of voice. The four clusters on the left represent direct speech, first- and third-person narrators and the 'narrators' of non-fiction. The two clusters on the right compare marking in real letters and in the epistolary novels that were so frequent in the period under consideration.

This analysis confirms the defining features of Romantic Routine and provides further insight into how these features are realized in different kinds of writing. The most important defining characteristic holds throughout: MARKING FOR QUOTATION ONLY tops MARKING FOR DERIVATION everywhere. The second defining feature, a value for MARKING FOR QUOTATION of over 50%, is not found throughout; it is an average value which turns out to be owed to the high percentage

132 Peak Casual: Romantic Routine

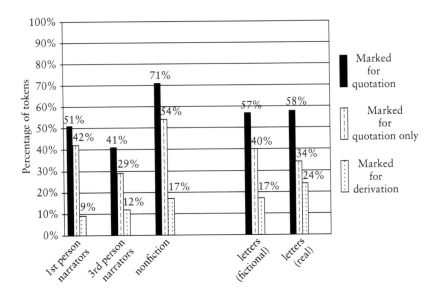

Figure 6.4 The voices of Romantic Routine. Marking of Shakespeare quotations 1776 to 1837 by genre and voice. Author's own.

of marked quotations in non-fictional texts (including fictional letters, which imitate the discourse of real letters). 71% for MARKING FOR QUOTATION in nonfiction comes comparatively close to modern academic practice, although the low value for MARKING FOR DERIVATION of course does not conform to twenty-first-century bibliographical requirements. Fiction has a set of its own, very different standards: MARKING FOR QUOTATION remains well below 50% in poems, plays and novels. The lowest level of MARKING FOR QUOTATION of all is to be found in dialogue, i.e. the representation of spoken language in plays and in passages of direct speech in prose fiction. This makes sense because the largely typographical devices of MARKING FOR QUOTATION ONLY are not really congenial to the rendering of direct speech and because overt marking in conversation has a strong impact on characterization. Like Shakespeare, Romantic literature uses these devices sparingly but to good effect.

Other patterns of distribution are more surprising. For example, the highest value for MARKING FOR DERIVATION both in relative and absolute terms occurs in letters. This may indicate the communicative value of MARKING FOR QUOTATION: rather than worry about the potentially clunky effect of pointing out works and authors, letter-writers are intent on enabling their addressees to share intertextual references and do not preoccupy themselves so much with style. Novelists penning fictional letters, on the other hand, keep their marking for derivation a bit lower, possibly because they are keeping one eye on contemporary standards of elegant writing. On the whole, though, the counts for genuine and fictional letters are extremely similar: the balances of MARKING FOR QUOTATION ONLY and MARKING FOR DERIVATION are closer than those of any other two voices, and the values for MARKING FOR QUOTATION are essentially identical at 58% and 57%. It can be fairly said that the pastiche of letter-writing in Romantic fiction is generally done with impressive realism. This accuracy may reflect the origins of the epistolary novel genre in the model letters for real use that Samuel Richardson published before he hit on the idea of constructing narratives out of fictional correspondence.

In contrast, narrative voices are very much their own thing in their treatment of intertextual insets. I expected third-person narration to be closest to non-fiction and first-person narration to resemble dialogue but as it turns out, first- and third-person narrators are more similar to each other than to anything else. First-person narrators, who mark just over 50% of their borrowings and have an extremely low rate of MARKING FOR DERIVATION (9%) are perhaps the most typical kind of casual Romantic quotation, but both first- and third-person narrators accommodate casual quotation very well. This may be due to their characteristic mix of features of spoken and written language, which has no models in real-life discourse: narrative voices do not need to mimic realistic conversation or respect the sober conventions of expository writing. This can result in an exuberant freedom. Here are two specimens by William Godwin (1799) and his daughter Mary Shelley (1826):

> [T]hat, which I had never regarded but as **'a ribband in the cap of youth'**, I now determined to have resort to, and to try the experiment at least, whether it might not be made to afford me **'yeoman's service'** (Godwin *Deloraine* 266–267).

> Were our proud dreams thus to fade? Our name was written 'a little lower than the angels;' ['Thou madest him a little lower than the angels', Hebrews 2:7] and, behold, we were no better than ephemera. We had called ourselves the **'paragon of animals'** and, lo! we were a **'quintessence of dust'** (Shelley *Last Man* 4:309).

And here is Maria Edgeworth writing in the third person in 1809:

> Mrs Dareville [...] gave full scope to [...] **all the insolence of fashion. Her slings and arrows,** numerous as they were and **outrageous,** were directed against such petty objects [...] that [...] it is scarcely possible to register the **hits,** or to describe the nature of the wounds. **Some hits, sufficiently palpable,** however, are recorded for the advantage of posterity (*The Absentee* 31).

This casual, freewheeling sequence of associations is the kind of flow that Ben Jonson thought 'should be stop'd' ('Discoveries' 539) in Shakespeare's writing and conversation. 'Insolence of fashion' seems to remind the narrator of Hamlet's soliloquy; cue 'slings and arrows', which then acquire the adjective of 'outrageous fortune', and finally, the fighting metaphors prompt memories of the duel and Osric's 'palpable hit' from Act 5 of *Hamlet*.

Intertextuality and voice are most interesting to observe in passages where characters are reported as quoting or remembering Shakespeare phrases. Who is quoting *Hamlet* when the narrator of Mary Wollstonecraft's *Wrongs of Woman* says that the protagonist 'descanted on "the ills which flesh is heir to", with bitterness' (81)? And what about Matilda in A. A. Hutchinson's *Exhibitions of the Heart*?

> 'Oh he was indeed beloved by all who knew his transcendent virtues!' sighed Matilda, 'for
> **"He was a man, take him for all in all, I shall not look upon his like again."'**
> She wept and repeated Hamlet's words over and over several times (4:317–318).

Matilda adapts Hamlet's phrase to her own first person singular and does not add any marking to its slightly archaic ring. We can assume that she does not lift two fingers of each hand in a twenty-first-century 'quote-unquote' gesture. So are the quotation-marks-within-quotation-marks there for the benefit of the reader? And does Matilda know that she is using 'Hamlet's words' or does the narrator add this information over her head? In Maria Edgeworth's *Manœuvring*, a Hamlet quotation does not quite make it into speech:

> '[...] Often and often [Colonel Beaumont] said in his letters to me, that he wished his wife to marry again after he was gone [...] I only hope that your choice may fulfil – may justify –' Mr Palmer stopped again, something in Shakspeare, about preying **on garbage**, ran in his head (Edgeworth *Manœuvring* 116).

We can only guess what Mr. Palmer is thinking here. He may be thinking 'Shakespeare' or not; he may or may not be aware of the word 'lust' that is the link between the topic of marriage and the *Hamlet* passage 'So, lust [...] Will sate itself in a celestial bed / And **prey on garbage**' (1.5.62–64). These lines would be a rather nasty comment to make on the potential remarriage of an acquaintance so it is possible that Mr Palmer is consciously or unconsciously censoring himself while the narrator is commenting on Mrs. Beaumont's plans – to readers who remember that the quotation is about an ill-advised second marriage. My final example is a first-person narrator who tells us about a quotation he nearly made. Frank Osbaldistone in Walter Scott's *Rob Roy* is recounting a tense conversation with his future wife Diana Vernon, during which some movement behind a wall-hung tapestry makes him suspect an eavesdropper:

> 'It is nothing,' said she, faintly; 'a rat behind the arras.' '**Dead for a ducat**,' would have been my reply, had I dared to give way to [my] feelings (244–245).

Diana is talking of a real rat as an excuse, but the phrase 'behind the arras' reminds Frank of Polonius, who hides '**Behind the arras**' (3.3.30) to spy on Gertrude and Hamlet in the closet scene, and is then mistakenly killed by Hamlet with the cry: '**Dead for a ducat, dead**' (3.4.28). Diana is an uncommonly smart teenager but it is not clear whether she is offering Frank the *Hamlet* cue on purpose. In any case, Frank speaks 'his' part of the quotation only in his mind because it would expose his angry suspicion. Using Shakespeare's words would mean 'to give way' to his feelings. In this, he also expresses his creator's attitude: in 1826, Walter Scott wrote in his journal: 'When I want to express a sentiment which I feel strongly, I find the phrase in Shakespeare' (26).

Historicizing routine:
Walter Scott's Shakespeare quotations

Narrative voices and the sentiments that they express with the help of quotations are fascinatingly complex. In historical fiction such as Walter Scott's, where fictional characters live in a different relationship to Shakespeare from that of their narrators and readers, these complications are compounded. Hutchinson's Matilda, Ferriers' Mrs. Apsley and Edgeworth's Mr Palmer all inhabit the same historical period as their narrators and their real readers, while Walter Scott adapts his Romantic Routine to stories that are set anywhere between the eleventh century and the early nineteenth. In all these tales, Scott quotes Shakespeare with a frequency that approaches Hazlitt's more closely than that of any other writer,[2] and demonstrates a remarkable sensitivity to the historical development of quotation. As part of an imaginary early-seventeenth-century dialogue, a word like 'thee' is part of the fictional world: in an essay or farce from the 1790s, such a word would be an anachronism and constitute marking for quotation. Scott was clearly aware of these gradations. In his medieval novels, he uses Shakespeare phrases to fit the generically archaizing dialogue, as when Cedric says in *Ivanhoe*: 'The ghost of Athelstane himself would **burst his bloody cerements**, and stand before us to forbid such dishonour to his memory!' (375–376). The narrative voice of these tales, on the other hand, does often mark its quotations, as if to remind the readers – over the heads of the medieval or Renaissance characters – that they are consuming a story that is mediated by an early-nineteenth-century consciousness: 'John easily attached to his person [...] the numerous class of **"lawless resolutes"**, whom the crusades had turned back on their country' (*Ivanhoe* 66). Such winks can be quite elaborate, as in *The Abbot*:

> Doctor Lundin [...] had even, <u>like the Prince of Denmark</u>, caused [the actors] to **insert**, or according to his own phrase to infuse, here and there, **a few pleasantries of his own penning**, on the same inexhaustible subject (250).

This novel is set in the mid-sixteenth century when *Hamlet* was still to come, so this quotation is clearly aimed at Scott's readers.

After *The Abbot*, the next novel in the chronology of fictional time is *Kenilworth*, set in 1575, and here Scott switches over to using *Hamlet* phrases in the dialogue as 'Elizabethan' elements. They are of course not marked as Shakespeare quotations; Scott just puts in a few subtle hints that make attentive readers complicit with his contemporary narrative voice. The Earl of Sussex uses the First Gravedigger's rough language as a sporting country gentleman of the Tudor era would, genially riffing on the phrase 'A whoreson mad fellow' (5.1.181):

> I wish the **gamesome** mad fellow no injury. Some of **his whoreson** poetry (I crave your Grace's pardon <u>for such a phrase</u>) has rung in mine ears as if the lines sounded to boot and saddle (147).

The apology for the rude phrasing is part of the pretty faultless Elizabethan pastiche and can at the same time bring a smile to the faces of nineteenth-century readers who can feel that Shakespeare is being criticized for his coarse language. The Gravedigger's ditty, too, is marked in this double-faced way, when the faithful servant Wayland Smith says: 'but **age has clawed me somewhat in his clutch**, <u>as the song says</u>' (247). The reference to a traditional folk song is plausible for a servant and simultaneously marks a quotation for readers who know their *Hamlet*. Hamlet / Shakespeare himself appropriated the Gravedigger's song from Thomas Vaux's poem 'The Aged Lover Renounceth Love', which was first published in *Tottel's Miscellany* in 1557; we could imagine Scott imagining Wayland having heard it from his master.

In novels set in the 1660s or later, in a world after Shakespeare, Scott's characters quote *Hamlet* as Shakespeare's play, like Sir Henry Lee in

Woodstock: 'Take a foil, man – **I walk here in the hall, <u>as Hamlet says;</u>** and 'tis the breathing-time of day with me – Take a foil, then, in thy hand' (156). Other passages seem to indicate Scott's awareness that such overt Shakespeare quotation was not really a 'done' conversational thing in the mid-seventeenth century. Simple Phoebe is made nervous by Sir Henry's obsession:

> '[...] Ah! he is a fellow would take the earth like a rabbit if he had been here, never may I stir but he would have countermined them ere now, and
>> "Tis sport to have the engineer
>> Hoist with his own petard."
>
> <u>as our immortal Shakspeare has it</u>.' 'Oh Lord, the poor mad old gentleman,' thought Phoebe – 'Oh, sir, had you not better leave alone <u>playbooks</u>, and think of your end?' uttered she aloud, in sheer terror and vexation of spirit (281).

Phoebe's disapproval of 'playbooks' may be triggered by the adjective 'immortal', which she perceives as blasphemous rather than bardolatrous, exactly as a mid-seventeenth-century country girl should. *ECCO* and *LION* searches confirm that expressions like 'immortal Shakespeare' 'the divine Shakespeare' were hardly used before 1758. The idea of *reading* 'playbooks' rather than attending a performance is reinforced by the layout: the use of indentation is incongruous for representing spoken language and this incongruity emphasizes Sir Henry's pompousness because it displays the *Hamlet* phrase as a quotation on a printed page. This subtle signal is backed up by overt narratorial disapproval:

> [A]s many others do, he was wont to quote [Shakespeare] from a sort of habit and respect, as a favourite of his unfortunate master, without having either much real taste for his works or great skill in applying the passages which he retained on his memory (59).

Scott is overdoing the quotation a bit here: such an elaborate comment is not fully convincing for a mid-seventeenth century setting, where one would *not* find 'many others' habitually quoting; the elaborate description of this 'habit' may in fact indicate that Scott was aware of it unusualness. Sir Henry's heavily conscientious marking for derivation would fit the mid-eighteenth century much better. This possibility adds an extra layer of meaning to the moment when Sir Henry's son says: '**The proverb<u>, as my father would say,</u> is somewhat musty**' (186). Does he know that he is quoting Shakespeare, or is he merely repeating a phrase that he has heard his father use *ad nauseam*?

138 *Peak Casual: Romantic Routine*

Those of Scott' novels that are set after the mid-eighteenth century turn quotations in dialogue into plausible, period-appropriate Romantic Routine. The 'Antiquary' himself, as befits his occupation, demonstrates his familiarity with the archaizing phrases he likes to use:

> And now, Lovel, my good lad, be sincere with me – **What make you from Wittenberg?** – Why have you left your own country and professional pursuits, for an idle residence in such a place as Fairport? – **A truant disposition**, I fear (*Antiquary* 104).

Lovel's personal situation here is similar to that of Horatio, who has recently returned to Elsinore; the Antiquary knows what he is quoting. Finally, in his only contemporary novel, Scott is the perfect ethnographer of his own society. *Saint Ronan's Well* has the highest number of *Hamlet* quotations (twenty compared to fifteen in the runner-up, *The Antiquary*) and the mimicry of society interactions is perfectly done. Here is a bit from the conversation of one Lady Penelope Penfeather:

> not at all the disgusting sort of person that you give a sixpence to while you look another way – but some one that seemed to have seen better days – one that, *as Shakspeare says*, **could a tale unfold** – though, indeed, I have never thoroughly learned her history (Scott *Saint Ronan's Well* 306).

This is the breathless chatter that Jane Austen, Maria Edgeworth or Susan Ferrier capture so well. When the tragic heroine Clara Mowbray is speaking, the quotation-laden female dither morphs into something more disturbing:

> **It is not as you would seem to say, by your winking** at Lady Binks – it is not, indeed – I shall be no Lady Clementina, to be the wonder and pity of the spring of St Ronan's – No <u>**Ophelia neither –** though I will say with her</u>, **Good night, ladies – Good night, sweet ladies!** – and now – **not** my coach, my coach – but my horse, my horse! (69).

The combination of Hamlet's annoyance at Rosencrantz and Guildenstern's innuendo with Ophelia's call for a coach creates a certain tension which anticipates the deadly madness that will overtake Clara (cf. Buck 188). The portent strangely weakened, however, by the intrusion of what is possibly the most hackneyed Shakespeare quotation ever. Richard III's call for 'a horse, a horse' was already a joke to John Marston in the early 1600s (cf. pp. 90–91) and was still a joke in 1799 when Henry James Pye used it in his novel *The Aristocrat*:

> Young Hawthorn on this occasion would certainly have quoted Shakespeare if he had ever read him, and have roared out in the words of King Richard, 'A horse! a horse! my kingdom for a horse!' He, however, heartily bewailed his want of one in plain prose (247).

Henry James Pye's 'Young Hawthorn' has the dignity of his own words, while Scott makes Clara Mowbray slip into a trite quote. Interestingly, Pye makes quoting Shakespeare dependent on *reading* him rather than an anthology.

Self-conscious routine: 'Shakespeare, who just now is much in fashion'

However strong the feelings, however sophisticated the voicing, however relevant the situations – the effortless default mode of routine quotation was always lurking at the desk of Romantic writers. In Scott's *The Bride of Lammermoor*, most of the 80-plus *Hamlet* echoes occur in the first ten chapters, where Scott was 'concentrating hard on drawing the parallels' (McCombie 419) between his plot and that of *Hamlet*. Then Scott fell ill and after a recovery that left him dependent on opiates, he dictated the rest of the book. In those later chapters, he no longer bothered with the thematic coherence of quotations and reverted to 'simply verbal and syntactical echoes' (McCombie 426). So even when he was, broadly speaking, rewriting *Hamlet*, Scott could lapse into casual quotation. In the same way, poets like Shelley, Keats, Coleridge, Byron and Wordsworth, whose poetry has a highly charged and sophisticated relationship with Shakespeare, practiced casual quotation in their letters, essays and diaries. Like Keats, they all 'knew certain episodes so well that he could allude to them easily, almost without realizing the indebtedness' (White *Keats* 117), and many of these writers, like Hazlitt, use favourite lines, maybe the most telling give-away for casual quotation. The *RR Corpus* contains 87 items by Lord Byron, who quoted just three *Hamlet* lines twice; Coleridge's 75 entries include thirteen versions of 'discourse of reason' and seven of 'mind's eye', and Wordsworth uses a different *Hamlet* line for every one of his 42 quotations. Scott (243 entries) liked 'yeoman['s] service' (sixteen times) and became touchingly fond of the First Gravedigger's phrase 'old age has clawed me in his clutch' to comment on his and other people's health after he himself had turned 50. William Hazlitt's favourite 'mind's eye' has been mentioned; another is 'a consummation devoutly to be wish'd', which he uses at least eleven times. All these writers combine a tangible respect for and intimate knowledge of Shakespeare's work with an unmistakably casual prose routine.

The tension between explicit respect and a persistent superficiality in the use of Shakespeare's words irritated readers as well as the practitioners themselves. A 'Letter to the Editor' lamented already in 1777 that Shakespeare 'is become a public Nuisance in every Company [because of] the Fashion, in this Country, to "gulp down every Drop of this immortal Man"' (quoted in Dobson *National Poet* 231). Fifty years later, Maria Edgeworth complained about 'The everlasting-quotation-loving bore', who 'usually prefaces or ends his quotations with – "As the poet happily says", or, "as Nature's sweetest woodlark justly remarks;" or, "as the immortal Milton has it"' ('Bores' 326–327). Together with the poetry-reciting bores who 'slowly but surely' deprive any phrase of 'spirit, sense, and life', the obnoxious quoters destroy any pleasure in literature:

> Poor Collins's Ode to the Passions, on and off the stage, is **torn to very tatters. The Seven Ages of Man** – and 'All the world's a stage, and all the men and women in it' – gone to destruction. **The quality of mercy is strained, and is no longer twice blest.** We turn with disgust from **'angels and ministers of grace'.** Adam's morning hymn has lost the freshness of its charm. The bores have got into **Paradise – scaled Heaven itself!** and defied all the powers of Milton's hell ('Bores' 325).

For all its hyperbolic sarcasm, this quotation-studded passage perpetuates the casual practice that it ridicules. Lines from the *Merchant of Venice* ('the quality of mercy is not strained' / 'twice blest' 4.1.190) are made to serve both as terms of abuse and as metonyms for the famous speeches they are from. The phrase 'tearing to tatters' seems appropriate at first glance, but while Hamlet refers to tasteless overacting on stage, Edgeworth describes how meaning disintegrates in excessively repeated drawing-room recitation. Milton is actually misrepresented: the phrase 'scaled Heaven itself' is mentioned next to a hint at *Paradise Lost* and does sound Miltonian but is in fact taken from Sarah Fielding's novel *The Cry* (1754): 'My imagination **scaled Heaven itself** and dethroned the very gods' (2:327). Her annoyance makes Edgeworth step up the density of the very quotations that she deplores, and her novels and letters, like everyone else's, are full of casually borrowed phrases and cross-quotations. Even as they were sneering at Shakespearean quotation overkill, writers of the Romantic period perpetuated the phenomenon. Like the ambivalent critics of Shakespeare's own puns and quotations and like the Jacobeans who observed the spread of his 'play scrappes' (Marston 'What You Will' 248) yet spread more of those phrases themselves, the

Romantic Shakespeare quoters were aware that they were contributing to what they were complaining about. There was just one single writer who was critical of casual quotation without ever practicing it herself: Jane Austen.

Notes

1 This is confirmed by the figures for William Hazlitt's works: about 500 of his 2,500 Shakespeare quotations are from *Hamlet* (cf. Bate 'Hazlitt's' 26).
2 The 260 Scott items in the *RR Corpus* may indicate an even larger overall number of Shakespeare references than they would with other writers because Scott is unusual in quoting the Scottish play more frequently than *Hamlet*.

7 Jane Austen: 'I must keep to my own style'

The overwhelming majority of English authors that were active in the decades around 1800 quote Shakespeare in a way that is completely indifferent to the larger design of his texts and their own. Even those writers that make fun of the faddish practice perpetuate it in their own texts. The one spectacular exception is Jane Austen. Linguistic or literary routine is what this most sophisticated and circumspect of writers was utterly incapable of; from her teens, she shows an unmistakable, fastidious dislike of Romantic Routine. Austen's treatment of casual quotations confirms, *ex negativo*, their popularity because she handles them exactly like other literary fads: with explicit mockery, with indirect criticism and, most characteristically, by simply and completely avoiding them in her own language. Austen's narrative voice is never distorted by the *verbatim* inlays and coy quotation marks that were so fashionably ubiquitous. In marked contrast even with the Romantic poets, who quote Shakespeare casually in their letters and diaries, Austen kept her published work as well as her private correspondence completely free from casual quotation, demonstrating an independence of spirit that is unique in her time.

Austen's scorn for pointless literary and social conventions, which has facile quotation as one of its objects, is most explicit in her early writings, the teenager's *juvenilia* and *Northanger Abbey*. *Northanger*'s introductory account of Catherine Morland's childhood targets the instrumentalization of literature as a mere source of educational platitudes. Catherine is a tomboy who only likes books if 'nothing like useful knowledge could be gained from them' (7), draws very badly and is allowed to give up the most time-consuming part of female education when she is just nine: 'The day which dismissed the music-master was one of the happiest of Catherine's life' (6). When she is in full 'training for a heroine' in her mid-teens, the peak of her musical achievement is 'to listen to other people's [musical] performances with very little fatigue' (8). From 'fifteen to seventeen', Catherine is forced to read 'all such works as heroines must read to supply their memories with those quotations which are so serviceable and so soothing in the vicissitudes of their eventful lives'; but primed as we are by the stories about her happy, unheroic childhood, we realize that reading books for quotations must have been just as tediously ineffectual for this particular teenager. Austen's announcement that Catherine 'learns' from a long list of quotations must be ironic.

> From Pope, she learnt to censure those who
> 'bear about the mockery of woe.'
> From Gray, that
> 'Many a flower is born to blush unseen,
> 'And waste its fragrance on the desert air.'
> From Thompson, that
> –'It is a delightful task
> 'To teach the young idea how to shoot' (7).

Austen lists these idiotically incoherent snippets with unmistakable glee: Catherine's intelligence will certainly require more than pious commonplaces about wallflowers in order to develop! Nourished by banal quotations, her mind is more likely to 'shoot' pale tendrils along a constricting literary trellis. The sequence of Shakespeare bits that rounds out the list is just as absurd:

> From Shakespeare she gained a great store of information –
> amongst the rest, that
> – 'Trifles light as air,
> 'Are, to the jealous, confirmation strong,
> 'As proofs of Holy Writ.'   [*Othello* 3.2.370-372]
> That
> 'The poor beetle, which we tread upon,
> 'In corporal sufferance feels a pang as great
> 'As when a giant dies.   [*Measure for Measure* 3.1.88-90]
> And that a young woman in love always looks
> – 'like Patience on a monument
> 'Smiling at Grief.'   [*Twelfth Night* 2.4.126-126]

> So far her improvement was sufficient (7).

Shakespeare quoted, education done.

Some critics have detected allusive meaning in these quotations, for example in the lines from *Othello* that might foreshadow the jealousy over Henry Tilney which sours Catherine's friendship with Isabella Thorpe (cf. Taylor 'Jane Austen' 113). As Kate Rumbold remarks, such an approach necessitates certain 'contortions' in extended, 'quotation-filled' novels: 'even if Clarissa "echoes" Isabella, has "traces" of Juliet, is "like Ophelia" and "has parallels" with Desdemona, she cannot live out all their fates' (*Eighteenth-Century* 6). In fact, the 'poor beetle' and Iago's snipe at quotations from Scripture rather distract from Othello's jealous passion. If we do want to think that Austen was quoting meaningfully here, we could consider that she is quoting a villain who is talking about fake news. The 'patience on a monument' passage would perhaps resonate most with an Austenian 'young woman in love', were it not that the tomboy Catherine Morland is so unlike the desperate Viola-as-Cesario in *Twelfth Night*. Moreover, 'Patience on a monument' had been quoted in more than 50 novels before 1780 (cf. Keymer 119), and appeared on the third page of Beckford's *Modern Novel Writing* in 1796, two years before Austen started drafting *Northanger Abbey*. The prevalence of Romantic Routine in Gothic fiction makes it more probable that Austen selected these extracts to show them up for being hackneyed and crazily irrelevant to a young woman's life. The opening reminder that Catherine is the heroine of a novel underlines Austen's double critique of routine quotations: they were both a literary nuisance and a questionable educational tool in real life. The conclusion that Catherine's 'improvement was sufficient' (7) after absorbing these absurd fragments is a wonderfully understated send-up of the idea that decontextualized quotations could nurture 'the young idea'.[1]

The chapter epigraph is another hugely popular intertextual device which Austen never uses, not even in her youthful spoofs. In formal terms, epigraphs are highly characteristic of Romantic Routine: they are invariably marked for quotation because whatever text appears as an epigraph is by definition quoted, while marking for derivation is optional and may be light ('Anonymous') or even fictitious, as in several lines from 'Old Ballads' that Walter Scott wrote himself. Frequent in Romantic novels and abundant in those Gothic tales that are the focus of *Northanger's* satire, chapter epigraphs often emphasize their intertextuality by archaisms or a foreign language. Eleanor Sleath, for example, quotes Ariosto in Italian and Horace in Latin in *The Nocturnal Minstrel*, to provide local and historical colour and to 'attach herself to a tradition of literary value' (Grundy 194). Jane Austen had little time for such cultural placeholders and felt no need to annex literary value from outside her texts. She suspected 'pedantry & affectation' in the Latin name of *Coelebs in Search of a Wife* and wondered 'Is it written only to Classical Scholars?' (*Letters* 172). The most conspicuous user of foreign-language tags in Austen's novels is one of her most cringe-making creations, Mrs. Elton in *Emma*, who keeps referring to her husband as 'caro sposo' (232) or even 'cara sposa' (197). Emma mentions this habit when she is more than usually annoyed with Mrs. Elton, calling her 'a little upstart, vulgar being, with her Mr. E., and her *cara sposo*' in her mind (181). The incorrect Italian ending 'car*a*' may be Austen's mistake, a typo or Emma's own mistake – or it may be Emma ridiculing Mrs. Elton's faulty Italian. In any case, the discursive tic, which was already old-fashioned in 1815 (cf. Rogers 75), is set out for our scornful amusement. Jane Austen's own narrative voice, in sharp contrast, completely eschews foreign language phrases nor does she use epigraphs – unless the quotations in the first chapter of *Northanger Abbey* are seen as getting 'a novel's worth of epigraphs over with at once' (Price *Anthology* 91) and as implicitly announcing Austen's ironic distance from the Gothic and other fashionable genres.

Apart from having a fatuous epithet and a tedious wife, Mrs. Elton's *caro sposo* himself represents a general category that Jane Austen disliked intensely: Mr. Elton is the epitome of the obsequious vicar. Interestingly, the two pet hates – silly clergymen and silly quotations – are associated in one of the few letters in which Austen discusses her writing. After the success of *Emma*, Austen famously declined a suggestion from the royal librarian James Stanier Clarke that her next project should be a novel about a clergyman. One of the difficulties she adduced in her refusal is the need to make such a character 'occasionally [i.e. on suitable occasions] abundant in quotations and allusions'. To mask her dislike of such abundance, Austen politely pleaded female ignorance, saying that

> a woman who, like me, knows only her own mother-tongue, and has read little in that, would be totally without the power of giving *such quotations*, since a Classical Education, or at any rate a very extensive acquaintance with English literature, Ancient & Modern [...] would be] quite Indispensable for the person who w^d do any justice to your Clergyman (*Letters* 306, emphasis mine).

This is polite nonsense, of course. If Austen's education was not 'Classical', she had the opportunity for 'extensive' reading in English, and abundance 'in quotations and allusions' would not have been technically beyond her. She simply did not *want* to 'give' quotations and the fact that clergymen were expected to do so was just one more reason for her not to write about a vicar.

The connection between vicars and quotations is further elaborated on in Austen's facetious 'Plan of a Novel, according to Hints from various Quarters', which was inspired by Stanier Clarke's request. The heroine of this plan is the daughter of a widowed clergyman. She can 'understand modern Languages' and converses with her father 'in long speeches, elegant Language', which, it is safe to assume, would include quotable, anthologized lines. When misfortune has driven father and daughter to 'Kamschatka' and the father finds 'his end approaching', he throws himself on the Ground, and after 4 or 5 hours of tender advice and parental Admonition to his miserable Child, expires in a fine burst of Literary Enthusiasm, intermingled with Invectives against holders of Tithes ('Plan of a Novel' n.p.).

The phrase 'Literary Enthusiasm' means 'extreme emotion expressed in literary style' rather than 'enthusiasm for literature'. Like the quotations in *Northanger Abbey*, the term ridicules both a literary stereotype and the reliance on facile quotation in real-life conversation. Austen's 'regulated hatred' (Harding 346) for the latter is confirmed in a letter she wrote to her sister Cassandra in November 1815, a month before writing to Stanier Clarke:

I have been listening to dreadful Insanity. – It is Mr. Haden's firm beleif that a person *not* musical is fit for every sort of Wickedness. – I ventured to assert a little on the other side, but wished the cause in abler hands (Letters 300).

This passage recalls the much-quoted warning in *The Merchant of Venice* that a 'man that hath no music in himself' is not to 'be trusted' (5.1.92–97), and thus Haden's statement of 'belief' offered Austen two clichés as easy targets: sentimentality about music[2] and the mindless use of second-hand sentiment. The distance that Austen takes both from Shakespeare's statement and its platitudinous re-use is comic: she was fond of Haden, who was of great help when her brother Henry was ill, and the hyperbolic phrasing 'dreadful insanity' may well reflect a flirtatious conversation with the young physician, but she does not hesitate to call him out over a banal quotation.

In addition to open mockery, Austen voices her criticism of facile quotations indirectly in the way in which weak or amoral characters use or defend them and in the resistance to quotation that is put up by morally reliable characters. Quotations are presented as a secondary, non-genuine form of discourse that can be as suspicious as other forms of hypocrisy. In *Emma*, the heroine's own quotations accompany her maturation process and in *Mansfield Park*, the recitation of anthology pieces from plays is practiced along with amateur theatricals, as will be seen later. I will start with the brighter *Pride and Prejudice,* where vapid quotations are more straightforwardly funny. Mary, the studious one of the five Bennett sisters, has old-fashioned preferences such as the study of Baroque basso continuo and the keeping of a common-place book into which she copies 'extracts':

They found Mary, as usual, deep in the study of thorough bass and human nature; and had some new extracts to admire, and some new observations of thread-bare morality to listen to (41).

Her father mocks Mary's hobby in his usual, irresponsibly satirical vein:

> 'What say you, Mary? for you are a young lady of deep reflection, I know, and read great books and make extracts.' Mary wished to say something very sensible, but knew not how (6).

Quotations will evidently not help this awkward young woman to make small talk. When Fitzwilliam Darcy uses a quotation to advance conversation – early in the novel, when his graceless pride is still prominent – he is put down with similar alacrity by Mr. Bennett's favourite daughter. Elizabeth deflates Darcy's allusion to *Twelfth Night*:

> '<u>I have been used to consider</u> **poetry as the *food* of love**', said Darcy. 'Of a fine, stout, healthy love it may. Everything nourishes what is strong already. But if it be only a slight, thin sort of inclination, I am convinced that one good sonnet will starve it entirely away.' (31).[3]

Like her creator, Elizabeth does not just laugh at a quotation; she mocks a whole over-used literary genre.

Penny Gay aligns this scene with Rosalind's 'wonderfully freewheeling and charismatic [...] scenes', where 'quasi-pedagogic authority [...] rewrites the rules of courtship' for Orlando (Gay 465). This is elegantly put; I suspect that it slightly over-reads the quotation from *Twelfth Night* and undervalues the realism with which Austen represents this conversation. Surely Darcy is too well-educated for a 'slightly pompous *mis*quotation' (Gay 465, emphasis mine) of 'If *music* be the food of love'? It seems more probable that he is making a purposely *modified* quotation. This intentional, if simple, piece of wit could be the first tentative acknowledgment that Darcy has recognized a fellow mind capable of appreciating a clever lack of literary piety. We could then re-read Elizabeth's comment as her first response to his intelligence; while she is still basically laughing at him, she may also have a first inkling of mutual respect for a humorous peer. Darcy is of course not cured of intertextual pomposity in a single conversation; ten pages later, he declares that it is 'the study of my life to avoid those weaknesses which often expose a strong understanding to ridicule'. Elizabeth's incredulous smile goads him into quotation and into further exposing his weakness by another Shakespeare allusion:

> 'There is, I <u>believe</u>, in <u>every</u> disposition a tendency to some **particular** evil – a **natural defect**, which not even the best education can overcome' (40).

Although Darcy sounds as if he were adducing a proverb, he is echoing Hamlet's description of men that carry 'the stamp of one **defect**' and will 'in the general censure take corruption / From that particular fault'

(*Hamlet* 1.4.34–39). Elizabeth is unimpressed and swiftly brings him back to earth, turning Shakespeare's noun against him: 'And *your* **defect** is a propensity to hate every body' (40). Elizabeth's prejudice against Darcy, not completely unjustified at this juncture, turns on his pride at being clever enough to quote *Hamlet*.

In *Mansfield Park*, so much less 'light & bright & sparkling' (Austen *Letters* 203) than *Pride and Prejudice*, quotation has a more serious moral dimension. Shakespeare quotations are not just silly; they evoke the threatening insincerity and sexual thrill which the novel associates with the stage and performance in general. Tom Bertram and Henry Crawford, both enthusiastic actors and both morally unsound, attempt to make dramatic performance seem harmless by conflating it with the poetic anthology pieces. Henry cleverly says: 'I can conceive no greater harm or danger to any of us in conversing in the elegant written language of some respectable author than in chattering in words of our own' (89). The phrases 'elegant written language' and 'respectable author' are clearly meant to associate drama with recitation from anthologies, those eminently respectable tools of education, but Henry is canvassing for amateur theatricals. Tom Bertram is similarly equivocating when he recalls his father's 'decided taste' 'for any thing of the Acting, Spouting, Reciting kind' to evoke Mark Antony's and Hamlet's great oratorical set pieces: 'How many a time have we mourned <u>over the dead body of **Julius Caesar,** and</u> *to be'd* and not *to be'd*, in this very room, for his amusement!' (90). Tom's brother Edmund is quick to point out that 'acting' (in a play) and 'spouting' (in recitation) are very different things and that their father simply 'wished us, as schoolboys, to speak well' (90), but to no avail. Henry Crawford, the unscrupulous though gentlemanly neighbour, also emphasises the harmlessness of Shakespeare quotations and their undramatic, second-hand character in order to downplay the moral risks of theatre to Fanny Price, who is profoundly suspicious:

> Shakespeare one gets acquainted with without knowing how. It is a part of an Englishman's constitution. His thoughts and beauties are so spread abroad that one touches them everywhere; one is intimate with him by instinct (229).

The word 'beauties', the title of many a contemporary anthology, signals harmlessness to an unworldly girl; to the reader, this speech shows up Henry's topical, fashionable superficiality.

For a more reliable and critical comment on Romantic Routine, we must look to Edmund Bertram's reply:

> 'No doubt one is familiar with Shakespeare in a degree [...] from one's earliest years. His celebrated passages are quoted by everybody;

they are in half the books we open, and we all talk Shakespeare, use his similies, and describe with his descriptions; but this is totally distinct from giving his sense as you gave it. To know him in bits and scraps is common enough; to know him pretty thoroughly is, perhaps, not uncommon' (229).

This critical approach to casual quotation, voiced by a morally superior character, is closer to Austen's own disapproval of facile quotation. However, Edmund is not speaking with the complete moral and emotional clarity that he achieves by the end of the novel. Henry Crawford is working up to suggesting the unfortunate project of having amateur theatricals at Mansfield Park, and Edmund is in collusion with Henry here. The distance which Austen still keeps from Edmund at this juncture is evident in the trendy phrase 'celebrated passages'. Austen's own narratorial voice would never employ such a clichéd phrase, and the fact that Edmund Bertram does so quite seriously betrays an uncertainty that is not yet solved. The finesse with which Austen uses such light hints is masterly.

The resort to clichéd quotation indicates immaturity also in *Emma*. A pompous reference to *A Midsummer Night's Dream* accompanies Emma Woodhouse's wrong-headed insistence that her friend Harriet Smith should aspire to marrying Mr. Elton:

'[...] There does seem to be a something in the air of Hartfield which gives **love** exactly **the right direction**, and sends it into the very channel where it ought to **flow**... A Hartfield edition of Shakespeare would have a long note on that passage.' (48–49).

Such a footnote would be long indeed because the 'course of true love' between Harriet and Mr. Elton is not at all destined to 'run smooth' (*Midsummer Night's Dream* 1.1.136). The silly quotation reflects Emma's inappropriate confidence in her own matchmaking skills at the beginning of the novel. An equally immature and even callous remark in the following chapter is also intensified by the shadow of a quotation: 'If we feel for the wretched, enough to do all we can for them, **the rest is** empty sympathy, only distressing to ourselves' (57). Halfway through the novel, Emma quotes somewhat more pardonably. 'Horror-struck' at the news of Jane Fairfax' long, secret engagement to Frank Churchill, she first lashes out at their 'very abominable sort of proceeding' with its 'hypocrisy and deceit, – espionage, and treachery'. A suggestion from her motherly friend Mrs. Weston that Jane and Frank 'must both have suffered a great deal under such a system of secresy and concealment' (262) does not at first impress Emma; she is too mortified by Frank's engagement, which means that another of her matchmaking plans is destined to fail. She only relents when Mrs. Weston suggests thinking of Jane's feelings:

> '[...] And how much may be said in her situation for even that error!' 'Much indeed!' cried Emma, feelingly. 'If a woman can ever be excused for thinking only of herself, it is in a situation like Jane Fairfax's. Of such, <u>one may almost say</u>, that "**the world is not their's, nor the world's law**"' (263).

With this cliché, Emma manages to integrate the outrageous fact of Jane's secrecy into her own vision of love-in-society; she can make her polite congratulations as she should after returning to conciliatory and socially appropriate discourse with a quotation. It is a casual quotation; Romeo's words to the apothecary, 'The world is not thy friend nor the world's law' (*Romeo* 5.1.76) make no sense in the plot of *Emma*. Isobel Grundy has argued that the choice to quote a Shakespeare play rather than a fashionable novel 'indicates a strong mind', which takes 'sustenance from a canonical text for [Emma's] own independent thinking' and is quite different from a random quotation 'in the style of Catherine Morland' (Grundy 197). However, *Northanger Abbey's* initial list of silly commonplaces includes three Shakespeare passages, which could be said to put Shakespeare quotation firmly in its place. Emma is doing what any conventionally well-educated young lady would do: she uses a banal discursive convention to express – or rather hide – her feelings in a socially appropriate way. Given the context of Romantic Routine, it seems improbable that Austen would have employed an overt quotation to underline Emma's independent thinking.

Austen's own independent mind is evident from the way in which she keeps her own narrative voice completely free of the stylish quotations that were so fashionable in her time. D. A. Miller, describing his adolescent delight on discovering Austen's prose, puts it admirably:

> No extraneous static encumbered the dictation of a grammar that completed, and an art that finished, every crystalline sentence. [Austen's voice was] 'not stylish; it was Style itself' (Miller *Secret of Style* 2).

To be 'stylish' around 1800 would have meant to quote *verbatim* or with minor modifications and with quotation marks. Austen, determined to keep 'to her own style' (*Letters* 312), 'almost without exception quotes [Shakespeare] "slant"' (Grundy 197), and more often in dialogue than in her narrative voice. This control of her own language is evident from the outset. 'Catharine or the Bower', written in 1792 when Austen was seventeen, includes a parody of Tilburnia's mad scene in Sheridan's comedy *The Critic* (itself an Ophelia spoof) as well as a *Hamlet*-echoing platitude. Catharine berates herself for not having seen through an attractive, unworthy man:

> And this, thought she to herself blushing with anger at her own folly, <u>this is</u> the affection for me <u>of which I was so certain</u>. **Oh! What a silly thing is Woman!** How vain, how unreasonable! (174).

This is indeed a well-brought-up young lady applying one of the 'serviceable' quotations mocked in *Northanger Abbey*. On closer inspection, however, her quotation practice does not conform to the style sheet of Romantic Routine. This convention would have dictated the use of the archaizing original form, as in these novels from the same decade:

> Why, oh! why did I consent to quit my native land! – married! – and her residence unknown! – impossible! – **'frailty, thy name is woman!'** (Johnson *Juliana* 2:170)
> <u>How just was Hamlet in exclaiming</u> '*Frailty*, thy name is woman!' <u>How applicable</u> in the present instance! (Bacon *Libertine* 29).

Compared to these trendy sighs, the cool of the teenage Jane Austen is remarkable. Not only does she avoid the coy archaism, her paraphrase **'What a silly thing is Woman!'** transforms Hamlet's misogynist groan into an echo of his admiring exclamation **'What [a] piece of work is a man'** (2.2.327). Even though Catherine's observation is a cliché and clearly meant to come across as such, Austen gives her a phrasing of her own. This may hint at Catherine's emerging mental independence; it is certainly owed to the fact that Jane Austen could not bring herself to reproduce a hackneyed quotation word by word.

Towards the end of Austen's career, in *Persuasion*, the topic of women's frailty is openly referenced as a piece of general received, male, wisdom and contested as such. This time, the young woman is not blaming herself: Anne Elliot, who herself famously wavers just *once*, is defending an absent friend against the accusations of a sentimental young man. He backs up his disappointment with vague literary references:

> 'I could bring you <u>fifty quotations</u> in a moment on my side the argument, and I do not think I ever opened <u>a book</u> in my life which had not something to say upon **woman's inconstancy**. <u>Songs and proverbs</u> all talk of **woman's fickleness**. But perhaps you will say, these were all <u>written</u> by men.' [Anne Eliot:] '[...] Yes, yes, if you please, <u>no reference to examples in books</u>. Men have had every advantage of us in telling their own story. Education has been theirs in so much higher a degree; the pen has been in their hands. I will not allow books to prove any thing' (Persuasion 156).

Here, Austen adds a further layer to her implicit critique of quotation: she refutes it because it rehashes men's words about women. Significantly, it is this spirited refutation that convinces Anne's former fiancé, Captain Wentworth, of her blameless constancy and ensures the happy ending. As with Elizabeth Bennet and Mr. Darcy, seeing through clichés creates complicity in a well-matched couple. Satirical in *Northanger Abbey*, light in *Pride and Prejudice*, ironic in *Emma*, earnest in *Mansfield Park* and passionate in *Persuasion*, Austen's resistance to casual quotation extends through all her work.[4] In all these modes, Austen demonstrates the detachment of a taste that is so completely sure of itself that it only ever mimics others in jest. This continuity confirms how pervasive Romantic Routine was and how deliberately Austen avoided it to safeguard her individual voice. As she wrote to Stanier Clarke: 'I must keep to my own style & go in my own way' (*Letters* 312) – regardless of vicars, fans and fashions.

Austen's insistence on keeping control of her own language even when using that of others is strikingly reminiscent of Ben Jonson's comment that Shakespeare's 'wit was in his own power' ('Discoveries' 539). Shakespeare and Austen, who enjoy 'canonical equivalence' as the 'greatest English dramatist and novelist', are also quite similar as borrowers and lenders of language. Both characterize their protagonists and secondary figures by the quotations that these characters use openly; both keep their 'own power' or 'own style' free from other people's exact words, and both have had a wide and intense afterlife in quotations and a 'matchless prominence in popular culture' (Wells 'Schlockspeare' 447). The same 'forces of transformation' that indicate Shakespeare's popular appeal are evident in Austen's rise to wider fame in the late twentieth century: 'adaptation, travesty and fictionalization of the author' (Troost and Greenfield 'Strange Mutations' 431) are flourishing in prequels, sequels and other fanfiction, games, biopics, merchandise and tourist destinations in Stratford, London, Bath and Chawton. Austen's heroines and her quotable phrases have the same 'rare crossover appeal' as Shakespeare's characters; her novels and his plays both 'insinuat[e themselves] into the way we think and talk – or wish to talk' (Todd 1). Harold Bloom quotes his own, great phrase on Shakespeare in the introduction to a volume of Austen essays: 'Like Shakespeare, Austen invented us' (v). The truth may often be less dramatic: Austen invented many of our phrases for us, as did Shakespeare; but we often use these phrases lightly, even when we remember that they are Shakespeare's or Austen's. The almost complete lack of such random intertextuality in Austen's mature writing can serve as a reminder of how many of our own Shakespeare and Austen quotations have been casual.

Notes

1 In 1838, Thomas de Quincey listed 'patience on a monument' as one of the Shakespearean phrases that 'interweave themselves with our daily conversation, and pass into the currency of the language' (De Quincey 298, note).

De Quincey also includes a phrase from *Romeo and Juliet* and four other *Hamlet* tokens: 'in my mind's eye,' 'o'erstep the modesty of nature,' 'more honor'd in the breach than in the observance' and 'palmy state'.
2 Jane Austen despised fashionable, superficial 'accomplishments' such as piano playing. Like casual quotation, such pointless educational achievements represent both 'a social nuisance and a literary stereotype' (Hohl Trillini *Gaze* 106).
3 Austen's unfinished fragment *Sanditon* features a similar instance of debunking a quotation by taking it literally. After the opening carriage crash, the injured Mr. Parker's rambles on about the merits of a tourist spot: '"Why, in truth Sir, I fancy we may apply to Brinshore, that line of the Poet Cowper in his description of the religious Cottager, as opposed to Voltaire – "*She*, never heard of half a mile from home".'" The answer takes the silly quotation as literally as Elizabeth does Darcy's: '"With all my Heart Sir – Apply any Verses you like to it – but I want to see something applied to your Leg [...]"' (158).
4 As Ina Habermann reminded me, Raymond Williams provides an alternative explanation in *The Country and the City*, where he describes Austen as the product and recorder of a society which is based on acts of enclosure and appropriation, whose memory is continually suppressed. It could be argued that too-obvious acts of linguistic appropriation (such as overt quotation) would draw attention to and thus disturb an analogous process of suppression. The idea is fascinating but problematic because most of Austen's contemporaries – products and recorders of their time as much as she was – mark their quotations so consistently.

Conclusion:
The Lightness of Quotation

This book explores a number of questions about quotation that were inspired by Julia Kristeva's definition of intertextuality, by Roland Barthes' suggested move from 'work' to 'text' and by Michel Foucault's reflections on 'the modes of existence' of discourse. Instead of asking 'Who is the real author?' or 'Have we proof of his authenticity?' (Foucault 138), I have looked at the following issues: What do quotations repeat? How do they modify what they repeat? How do texts draw attention to the fact that something is repeated? What is the effect of juxtaposing quotations from different sources? and What information do texts provide about what is repeated?

The main conclusions are that casual quotation prioritizes the act of quotation and the needs of the quoting text over the original form and meaning of the text that is quoted, and that this form of intertextuality was extensively practiced by Shakespeare himself and by the writers that quoted him in the first two hundred years after his death. These casual quotations are not just indifferent to the original context: even if they often signal the fact that an extraneous element is present, they tend to obscure the origins of that element, so that it becomes 'anonymous' although it is 'already read' (Barthes 'Work to Text' 160). Books that are quoted casually are 'seen as texts' (Kristeva 'Word, Dialogue' 65), not as 'works': they are not fully determined by their authors, but co-written by their readers. In this way, every text can become an 'intersection [...] where at least one other word (text) can be read' (66). Such textual intersections are particularly striking where cross-quotation is present: the use of more than one intertextual element in close proximity can reinforce a sense of detachment, as multiple quotations reduce each other's impact. Quotations that are obviously based on acoustic memory, the sound and rhythm of remembered phrases, are a particularly telling symptom of such distance from original content, and another indicator of casual intertextuality is the use of favourite lines. If a writer quotes a certain phrase again and again in different contexts, it is less probable that this phrase is meant to convey complex associations derived from its earlier context: the fact that one out of every five of Coleridge's

Conclusion: The Lightness of Quotation 155

Hamlet quotations is 'discourse of reason' makes one suspect that the force of habit was at work. The discovery of such patterns of use is a typical result of data-based research, which may work with a complete concordance of one writer's references (my example are John Marston's Shakespeare borrowings, cf. Chapter 4 and Appendix 2) or with a large number of tokens from a certain period such as the 2,400 Romantic *Hamlet* quotations that are explored in Chapter 6. This kind of investigation may also reveal whether the preference for a certain phrase is shared with other writers and may confirm the suspicion that a popular line has become an idiom or the kind of journalistic cliché that was christened 'snowclone' in 2003.

All these features and variants of casual intertextuality are reminders that the word 'quotation' in 'casual quotation' is used without the many connotations that this word has been given. In this book, calling something a 'quotation' does not make any kind of statement about what such a repeated bit of language might or might not mean; it simply points out a recognizable verbal overlap with an earlier text, which may be described in formal detail without attempts at literary exegesis. Stepping back from interpretation in this way has freed up space for research: I can examine text passages that have been considered uninteresting and discover unexpected significance in the patterns of use that they share with many others. Perhaps my favourite instance of this are the snippets of Shakespeare's conversation that can be glimpsed in early anecdotes. Spurious as some of these Shakespeareana may be, they entered the canon of (apocryphal) biographical records because they reflect a widely perceived characteristic of Shakespeare's language: it is saturated with intertextuality. Shakespeare possessed the linked 'twin capacities' of active reading and imaginative writing to a high degree; his 'retentive memory and vigorous powers of association' (Armstrong 32) made him the supreme representative of quotation as reading-into-writing. As seems to have been noticeable even in his conversation, he was an extremely fast reader and attentive listener who remembered thousands of verbal details and used them to make his friends laugh or his characters come alive, with no regard for context. This loss of an authorial core in quotation, the abandonment of the family ties of literary 'paternity', may seem regrettable, but it doubtlessly enhanced the fluency of Shakespeare's writing and widened the subsequent impact of his work. Fractured textual identity is the price at which Shakespeare became 'part and parcel of English-speaking culture' (Belsey 1), since a text

> exerts most influence [...] by giving up its integrity; its moments of greatest agency involve the splitting of what one might call the textual 'self'. (Rothstein 28–29)

156 Conclusion: The Lightness of Quotation

The mass of casual quotations is just as integral to Shakespeare's status of most-quoted-author-of-all-time as are sophisticated literary allusions. If we are to believe Roland Barthes' claim that 'one cannot at one and the same time desire a word and take it to its conclusion' (*Roland Barthes* 74),[1] casual reference is an unavoidable consequence of our love for Shakespeare's phrases.

So much for 'quotation'. The one quibble one might have with the adjective 'casual' is that it is too modern to describe a pre-Victorian literary practice: the *OED's* first entry for 'casual' as 'showing (real or assumed) unconcern or lack of interest' dates from 1916. I take the apparent anachronism to symbolize the fact that we tend to overlook similarities between the past and apparently recent phenomena if these phenomena are described in recently coined words. The casual use of Shakespeare's words has mostly been considered as a modern practice, a symptom of cultural decline that originated in the twentieth century. But casual (Shakespeare) quotation is not a recent phenomenon. It is rife in Shakespeare's own use of older texts and of classical and Biblical motifs, and quotations *from* Shakespeare throughout the two first centuries after his death are casual in many ways that are individually and historically inflected. Comparable differentiations are to be expected from careful scrutiny of materials that have been written since. Future research may well show that the Romantic Routine mode of Shakespeare quotation was followed by things like Victorian Variety or Edwardian Elegance or it may reveal a continuous casual tradition which goes all the way to YouTube. It may also turn out that the period break 'somewhere between us and *Persuasion*' which this book leaves open was indeed 'the greatest of all divisions in the history of the West', as C. S. Lewis puts it in 'De Descriptione Temporum' (7). Lewis' weightiest argument for this periodization is 'the birth of the machines' (10), and this particular gap between us and the early nineteenth century has been further widened since Lewis' 1960 lecture by the birth of electronic computation and the Internet. These developments may threaten the tradition of quotation, but they also strengthen it (quite apart from enabling researchers to trace quotations more efficiently). Quotation does depend on a minimal familiarity with the canon, which may be dwindling, and readers' freedom to determine the length of their reading units is increasingly limited by shrinking attention spans and the habit of communicating in no more than 280 characters. On the other hand, many Elizabethan or eighteenth- and nineteenth-century quotations are not longer than a tweet and were derived from anthologies rather than theatre visits or assiduous reading. Echoing Italo Calvino, we could say that twenty-first century quotation research needs to appreciate 'the lightness of language' just as much as 'language that has some weight to it' (*Six Memos for the Next Millennium* 15). Shakespeare quotations in hypertext, databases, electronic archives, search engines and social media are giving new leases of life to old texts, and 'casual quotation' may be acquiring new meanings and modes of existence which are still to be explored.

Note

1 The original French runs: 'On ne peut en même temps approfondir et désirer un mot' (*Roland Barthes par Roland Barthes*. Paris: Éditions du Seuil 1975. 78).

Appendix I
The *HyperHamlet* database

The following introduction to the *HyperHamlet* database summarizes the analytical categories for the study of quotation which are used in this book and aims to encourage the further use of its data and its search options. New projects can be based on the available data, additional *Hamlet* quotations can be contributed via the wiki facility, and researchers can apply the *HyperHamlet* categories of analysis to other Shakespeare plays or to completely different cases of quotation. The database was designed and built between 2006 and 2010 by a research group at the University of Basel and data continues to be uploaded and edited by volunteers and researchers. *Hamlet* was chosen for this pilot database because its fame promised the most data, but the structure and concept of *HyperHamlet* could be applied to any other text. A reprogramming with relational software as it has been developed since *HyperHamlet's* creation would allow a more flexible representation of intertextual relationships between an open number of primary texts, but the hypertext structure continues to be eminently serviceable.

The structure of the database: Categories for analysis

HyperHamlet is accessible at www.hyperhamlet.unibas.ch. It has the structure of a hypertext of *Hamlet* and its contents can be browsed as well as searched. Every line of the play gives access to text extracts which quote that line or are quoted in Shakespeare's play. In this way, any *Hamlet* phrase can be related 'vertically' to other versions of this phrase that were created at different moments before and after 1600 and up to the present. 'Horizontal' sets of data can be generated by using the search options of the database to filter out *Hamlet* quotations from a given timespan, with particular formal features or with other characteristics that are covered by the annotation of the corpus. The annotation of the *HyperHamlet* corpus that is encoded in its search options covers two main kinds of information: first, bibliographical details about every text passage in which a *Hamlet* quotation occurs and second, the formal characteristics of the intertextual relationship that is evident in such a passage. The first kind of information includes a full bibliographical reference and search fields for AUTHOR and TITLE as well as DATE OF COMPOSITION, DATE OF FIRST PUBLICATION, GENRE and LANGUAGE. Two other parameters, FUNCTION and VOICE, situate the quotation in its new surroundings: is it, for example, an epigraph, a title, a dictionary entry or simply part of the body of a text? If the latter, is it voiced by a narrator or by a fictional character's own utterance in the dialogue of a play, film script or novel?

The second set of analytical parameters represents the central research achievement of the Basel team. It suggests a new model for describing the intertextual relationships by formal characteristics and includes the following kinds of information:

OVERLAP: the grammatical extent of the quotation, from single word through clause to longer passage.
MODIFICATION: the degree and kind of lexical and grammatical modifications which the *Hamlet* phrase undergoes in quotation. This maps the continuum from *verbatim* quote to free paraphrase through settings such as 'substitution' ('to bäh or not to bäh') or omission ('Not to be', an episode title from the TV series *Highlander*).
MARKING FOR QUOTATION: the presence or absence of signals that point to an intertextual insert. This happens in three ways: by TYPOGRAPHY (quotation marks, italics or indentation etc.), by an ANOMALY (language switch, archaism etc.) or verbally by a METALINGUISTIC tag such as 'as they say' or 'in the play'.
MARKING FOR DERIVATION: the presence or absence of pointers to the work that is quoted. In the case of *HyperHamlet* this includes names like 'Rosencrantz', 'Hamlet', 'Elsinore' or 'Shakespeare' but also phrases like 'the Swan of Avon' or 'the greatest English tragedy'.
INTERTEXTUALITY: the overall relationship of the two texts involved. Do *Hamlet* and the later text overlap just in one place, as in an academic citation or one-off quotation? Is the later text an ADAPTATION, which replicates a scene from *Hamlet* in a different style, setting or medium, is it an OFFSHOOT, which expands Shakespeare's storyline, or is it a quotation dictionary which CITES a *Hamlet* phrase under a thematic heading?

These features of intertextuality have all been discussed in many theoretical articles which propose to categorize intertextual relationships. From Gérard Genette's *Palimpsests* onwards, most approach have been taxonomic: terms like 'allusion', 'reference', 'quotation' or 'citation' are newly defined and complemented by new terms to represent a certain outlook on quotation. Genette's suggestions (hypertext, paratext etc.) were extremely successful; other new definitions have not been widely adopted because they complicated rather than clarified matters. The *HyperHamlet* approach is to refrain from *definitions* and instead to provide a *description* of quotations according to the parameters defined above. This method, inspired by the bundles-of-features approach that is familiar from fields such as phonetics, enables researchers to make simple and workable statements about any given token. Daniel Defoe's line 'Wou'd the Great *Be*, and *not to Be* Divide', for example, is annotated as follows:

OVERLAP: double infinitive
MODIFICATION: nominalization, substitution of 'and' for 'or', addition of adjective 'great'
MARKING FOR QUOTATION: italics, nominalization, capitalization
MARKING FOR DERIVATION: none
INTERTEXTUALITY: local overlap

This kind of detailed, unprejudiced description makes comparisons and statistical work possible without enforcing a reductive definition of whether or not this verbal overlap between Defoe and Shakespeare amounts to a true 'quotation'. In this book, the word 'quotation' is a simple shorthand for 'recognized verbal overlap', and such overlaps are described as bundles of features or parameter settings. In this way, taxonomy remains dynamic; it does not mirror a static truth but enables researchers to study quotation 'unencumbered by a need for naming and rigorous definition' (Hohl Trillini and Quaßdorf 3–4). This freedom and flexibility of vision has made it possible to identify unobtrusive phenomena such as Romantic Routine.

The contents of the database: 11,000 Hamlet quotations

At the time of writing, *HyperHamlet* contains almost 11,000 entries, which are owed in roughly equal parts to electronic searches and to the scholarship of philologists who worked in the nineteenth and twentieth centuries. About half the entries were newly identified by the *HyperHamlet* team, who conducted extensive electronic searches in full-text databases. At the same time, quotations that had been pointed out in previously published research were uploaded and annotated on *HyperHamlet* and can now be studied along with the new finds thanks to the flexibility and storage capacity of this electronic research medium.

The historical, geographical and genre range of the contents of the *HyperHamlet* database is wide but unevenly represented. To test the analytical categories of the database as they were developed, as many slots as possible were filled by token entries early in the research period. Thus, the database contains a few hundred quotations in German, a few entries for paintings with captions taken from *Hamlet*, a handful of Russian, Italian and Spanish items, some tweets, blog posts, sermons, opera librettos and an IKEA duvet cover with a floral pattern called

'Ofelia'. Such sample entries can be expanded into larger data sets at any time by interested scholars and students, and specific data of this kind have indeed filled out corners of the *HyperHamlet* collection. Individual writers such as Lord Tennyson and Dorothy L. Sayers, specific *Hamlet* phrases ('sea of troubles'), genres like crime fiction or Gothic novels and verse parodies are more fully represented thanks to such projects. An international community of contributors uploaded several hundred entries via *HyperHamlet's* wiki facility and a concerted research effort focusing on seventeenth- and eighteenth-century English material provided the basis of the research that is set out in Chapters 1 and 4–6 of this book.

Philology the fundamental data for Chapters 2 and 3 of this book, which discuss Shakespeare's use of the Bible and the classical Latin heritage. Integrating this data into *HyperHamlet* made the towering achievements of scholars like Thomas Baldwin, E. K. Chambers, Edward J. Dent, John Munro, C. M. Ingleby and M. P. Tilley newly accessible in the context of more recent results. Shakespeare quotations from the eighteenth century onwards have mostly been researched with a focus on individual authors and are reported in books, articles and the footnotes of annotated editions. These publications provide a solid stock of material from canonical poets and writers, ranging from Robert Burton through James Boswell to Charles Dickens, Joseph Conrad and D. H. Lawrence, whose works have been edited and carefully indexed in massive sets of print volumes. The material mentioned in such print publications was then complemented by the results of electronic searches. Strings corresponding to hundreds of *Hamlet* lines were run through electronic full-text databases such as *Early English Books Online (EEBO)*, *Literature Online (LION)*, *Eighteenth Century Collections Online (ECCO)* or *The Romantic Era Redefined*. Sayre Greenfield describes challenges similar to those encountered by the *HyperHamlet* team in his report on sampling the *ECCO* database for selected Shakespeare quotations ('ECCO-Locating' 7–8). The Internet provided additional material of less consistent quality which took more editing effort but was nevertheless useful: even 'dirty OCR' is 'a remarkable tool' for spotting 'instances of a word or a phrase in its historical moment or in later circulation' (Lavagnino 20). The most significant new result of our electronic research may be the body of quotations by writers who are considered 'minor' and who worked in 'minor' and non-literary genres in the eighteenth and early nineteenth centuries. This material opens the field to new inquiries and exploration of the daily production and consumption of Shakespearean intertextuality.

Appendix II
A Marston-Shakespeare concordance

The following table shows 100 verbal overlaps between the works of William Shakespeare and John Marston. Most of these quotations have been pointed out in scholarly publications, especially the *Shakspere Allusion-Book* and annotated editions of Marston's works; there are probably about twice as many, without counting plot similarities or motifs such as those that link *Hamlet* and *Antonio's Revenge*, for example. The text extracts come from 25 Shakespeare works and from fourteen plays and satires by Marston, including works that are his alone as well as collaborative pieces like *Eastward Ho* and the recently re-attributed *Family of Love*, which used to be considered to be the work of Thomas Middleton. As everywhere in this book, the **quoted text** is set in bold type, while underlined passages highlight words that serve as Marking for Quotation.

The parallels are roughly ordered by formal categories for what is taken up in Marston. Word-by-word repetitions are first, then come quotations that repeat a verbal structure with new lexical content, then paraphrases that are recognizable by repeated key words or fixed expressions and finally passages that repeat a situation or idea in different words. In this latter category, quotation shades into adaptation, which Marston also practiced extensively. Within each category, entries are sorted by the quoted Shakespeare text. Ordering by Marston's texts would have facilitated a different kind of analysis, as would sorting by date or lexical items; this kind of flexible handling would of course be easy with an electronic database.

Repeated verbatim

Coriolanus 4.1.1-2 beast with many heads	*Malcontent* 180 that **beast with many heads**
Hamlet 1.5.124-125 Illo, ho, ho, my lord! / Hillo, ho, ho, boy!	*Dutch* 123 Who goes there **Illo, ho, ho** zounds shall I run mad
	Malcontent 181 **Illo, ho ho ho**, arte there old true peny, / Where hast thou spent thy selfe this morning?
Hamlet 1.5.138 he's an arrant knave	*Malcontent* 181 *Malevole*, thou art an **arrant knave**

Hamlet 1.5.169-170 Art thou there, / truepenny?

Hamlet 1.5. 147 I will go pray.

Hamlet 3.4.65-66 See what a grace was seated on this brow, / Hyperion's curls, the front of Jove himself

Malcontent 181 Illo, ho ho ho, **arte there old true peny,** / Where hast thou spent thy selfe this morning?

Malcontent 146 **Ile go to pray**

Antonio's Revenge 103 Me thinks I pase vpon **the front of** *Jove*

Antonio's Revenge 126 proud pomp shoots mounting tryumph vp, / Borne in lowde accents to **the front of** *Jove*

Insatiate 6-7 **A donative he hath of every God;** / ***Apollo* gave him lockes,** *Jove* **his high front** [...].

What You Will 278 Now by **the front of Ioue** me thinks her eye / Shootes more spirit in me

Love's Labour's Lost 5.1.41-43 I marvel thy master hath not eaten thee for a word, for thou art not so long by the head as honorificabilitudinitatibus.

Love's Labour's Lost 5.2.758-759 Greater than 'Great'! Great, great, great Pompey. Pompey the Huge!

Richard III 1.1.32 Plots have I laid, inductions dangerous

Romeo 1.1.1 we will not carry coals

Dutch 129 his discourse is like the long word, **Honorificabilitudinitatibus:** a great deale Of sound and no sence.

Malcontent 148 Doe the sword daunce [...] even with *Pompey* **the huge.**

Parasitaster 164 **Plots ha you laid? inductions, dangerous.**

Revenge 116 I were as he, **I would beare no coles**

Structure

As You Like It 3.2.88-89 From the east to western Ind, / No jewel is like Rosalind

Hamlet 1.3.124 springes to catch woodcocks

Hamlet 1.4.136 Do not believe his vows, for they are brokers

Hamlet 1.3.124 springes to cach woodcocks

Hamlet 1.4.136 Doe not believe his vowes, for they are brokers

Hamlet 2.2.327-330 What a piece of work is a man, how noble in reason, how infinite in faculties, in form and moving how express and admirable; in action how like an angel, in apprehension how like a god

Mellida 53-54 For wods, trees, sea, or rocky **Apennine,** / Is not so ruthlesse **as my Rossaline.**

Malcontent 213 **On his troth la beleeue him not traps to catch polecats**

Malcontent 213 **On his troth la beleeue him not traps to catch polecats**

Malcontent 154-155 **how** full of rauishing attraction is your prettie, petulant, langushing, laciuiously-composed countenance [...] **in body how delicate, in soule how wittie, in discourse how pregnant, in life how warie, in fauours how iuditious,** in day how sociable, and in night how?

Appendix II 165

Hamlet 2.2.402-403 I am but mad north-north-west. When the wind is southerly, I know a hawk from a handsaw
Richard III 5.4.7 and 5.4.13 A horse, a horse, my kingdom for a horse!

Eastward 142 Do wee not knowe **North-north-east?** North- east and by East? East and by North? nor plaine *Eastward?*
Eastward 133 **A boate, a boate, a boate, a full hunderd Markes for a boate.**
Parasitaster 212 **A foole, a foole, a foole!** my Coxcombe for a foole!
Scourge 202 (Book 2, Satire 7) **A man, a man, a kingdome for a man!**
What You Will 248 Ha he mount[s] *Chirall* on the wings of fame. / **A horse, a horse, my kingdom for a horse,** / Look the I speak play scrapes

---

Salient words and expressions

Hamlet 1.2.133 O, that this too, too **sullied** would melt, / **Thaw, and resolve** itself into a **dew**
Hamlet 1.5.35-36 with wings as **swift** / As meditation or the **thoughts** of love
Hamlet 1.2.154 a **beast** that wants discourse of **reason**

Hamlet 1.2.69 I am too much i'th'sun [son]

Hamlet 1.2.96.-98 But to persever / In obstinate **condolement** is a course / Of impious stubbornness
Hamlet 2.2.190 You are a **fishmonger.**
Hamlet 1.2.210 Armed at point exactly, **cap-à-pie**
Hamlet 2.2.550-551 they are the **abstract** and brief chronicles of the time
Richard III 4.4.2 Brief abstract and record of tedious days

Family sig. A^{3verso} **Oh that this flesh** could like **swift mouing thoughts transfer** it selfe [...] vnseen and vndisolued

Family sig. H^{3recto} What else, sir? I have **reason**. / I know it well, I take you for **no beast**.
Histrio-Mastix 248 What is a man **superior to a beast** / But for his **mind?** nor that ennobles him, / While hee dejects his **reason**; making it / The slave unto his brutish appetite.
Eastward 120 Master me no more **Sonne** if though think's me worthy to by thy father. / **Sunne?** Now good Lord how he shines and you marke him!
Revenge 132 Sing *Mellida* is deade, all hearts will relent / in sad **condolement**
Malcontent 182 Then we agree? / MALEVOLE. As Lent and **fishmongers.** Come a *cape a Pe*, how in forme
Family sig. A^{3verso} This is the **abstract of the spacious world.**

(*Continued*)

166 Appendix II

Hamlet 2.2.83 But look where sadly the poor wretch comes reading

Hamlet 4.2.15-21 *Hamlet* 4.2.15 [a sponge] that soaks up the King's countenance, his rewards, his authorities. But such officers do the King best service in the end. He keeps them like an ape an apple in the corner of his jaw, first mouthed, to be last swallowed. When he needs what you have gleaned, it is but squeezing you, and, sponge, you shall be dry again

Hamlet 4.5.213-224 No, no, he is dead. / Go to thy deathbed. / He never will come again. / His beard was as white as snow, / All flaxen was his poll. / [...] God be wi' you.

Hamlet 4.5.76-78 Come, my coach! Good night, ladies, good night, sweet ladies, good night, good night.

Hamlet 5.2.47 And stand a comma 'tween their amities

Hamlet 5.3.398 And flights of angels sing thee to thy rest

1 Henry IV 1.3.62-63 salt-petre should be digg'd / Out of the bowels of the harmless earth

1 Henry IV 2.4.213-215 the camomile, the more is trodden on, the faster it grows

1 Henry VI 4.7.79-82 the Frenchmen's only scourge, / Your kingdom's terror and black Nemesis

2 Henry IV 2.4.161-162 and 175-176 Have we not Hiren here?

2 Henry IV 2.4.165-168 pack-horses and hollow pampered jades of Asia

2 Henry IV 5.5.86-89 Fear no colours

Twelfth Night 1.5.9 I fear no colours

Julius Caesar 1.2.295 – it was Greek to me

Malcontent 157 Dri'd bisquet! **looke where the base wretch comes**

Scourge 204 (Book 2, Satire 7) He's but a *spunge*, and shortly needes must leese / His wrong got iuice, **when *greatnes fist shal squeeze* / His liquor out**

Eastward 119 His head **as white as mylke**, / **All flaxen was his haire:** / But now **he is dead**, / And laid in his **Bedd**, / **And never will come againe**. / **God be** at your labour

Eastward 117-118 What Coachman? **my Ladyes** coach, **for shame;** her ladiship's ready to come downe; / Sfoote, <u>Hamlet</u>; are you madde? whether run you now? [...] / <u>Gertrude</u>. Thanke you **good people; my coach for the love of Heaven, my coach?** in good truth I shall swoune else

Mellida 49 weele point our speech / With amorous kissing, **kissing commaes**

Insatiate 74 **An host of Angels be thy convey hence**

Insatiate 65 imprison'd gold / **Within the harmlesse bowels of the earth**

Parasitaster 165 For indeed, sir, a repressed fame mounts like a **camomile, the more trod down, the more it grows**

Revenge 116 There is a thing cald **scourging Nemesis**

Eastward 102 Sfoote lend me some money, *hast thou not Hyren here?*

Eastward 101 Holla ye pampered Jades of Asia.

Insatiate 20 one that [...] **fear'd no colours**

Parasitaster 188 *anxoué e ampexou*, (that's **Greeke to you** now.)

Julius Caesar 2.2.34 Cowards die many times before their deaths
Lucrece 876 and 886 O Opportunity [...] thou notorious bawd!

Merry Wives 1.3.51 He hath a legion of angels.
Midsummer Night's Dream 12.1.211-212 O, then, what graces in my love do dwell, / That he hath turn'd a heaven into a hell!

Midsummer Night's Dream 2.3.230-231 Nor doth this wood lack worlds of company, / For you in my respect are all the world
Much Ado 2.1.76-78 and then comes repentance, and with his bad legs falls into the cinquepace faster and faster till he sink into his grave.
Twelfth Night 1.4.26-27 I would not so much as make water but in a sink-a-pace.
Much Ado 2.3.80-83 By my troth, a good song. / [...] And an ill singer, my lord.
Richard III 5.3.160-161 Sleep, Richmond, sleep in peace and wake in joy. / Good angels guard thee from the boar's annoy.
Richard III 5.4.3 Daring an opposite to every danger
Romeo 1.3.136 I do bear a brain

Romeo 1.5.136 We have a trifling foolish Banquet towards
Romeo 1.5.31 A hall! a hall! give room and foot it, girls.

Romeo 2.4.168-170 If ye should lead her into a fool's paradise [...] it were a very gross kind of behavior

Romeo 3.5.245 Ancient damnation, a most wicked fiend
Troilus 3.1.102 Falling in after falling out may make them three

Insatiate 62 **A hundred times in life a coward dies**
Malcontent 179 impudent custome inticed by **that great bawd opportunitie**, thus being prepar'd, clap to her easie eare [...].
Mellida 33 **Legions of Angels** fight vpon her side.
Malcontent 156 Your smiles have bin my **heaven**, your frowns **my hel** / O pitty them; **Grace should with beauty dwell.** [...]<u>Reasonable perfect</u>, bir-lady.
Dutch 82 So could I live in **desart** most vnknowne, / **Your** selfe **to me enough** were Populous

Insatiate 21 Yet you **sinke a pace** sir.

Mellida 34 Tis a **good** boy & **by my troth, well sung**.

Mellida 33 O, a faire cause stands firme, and will abide. / **Legions of Angels fight vpon her side**.

Mellida 33 My selfe, my selfe will **dare all opposits**
Dutch 107 hee knowes nothing of it, 'tis I that beare, tis I that must **beare a braine** for all
Dutch 109 **I bare not a braine**
Insatiate 24 And taste **a homely banquet we entreate**
Scourge 225 (Book 3, Satire 11) **A hall, a hall,** / **Roome** for the Spheres, the Orbes celestiall
Family sig. A² recto If 'a brings thee **to a fool's paradise**, 'a will forsake thee
Malcontent 213 promise of matrimony by a yong gallant, to bring a virgin Lady into a fooles paradise
Malcontent 173 I wil come, friendly **Damnation**, I will come
Dutch 114 Sometimes a **falling out** proves **falling in**

(Continued)

168 *Appendix II*

Troilus 5.1.97-98 I will no more trust him when he leers than I will a serpent when he hisses

Parasitaster 206 **dost thou leere on me?**

Venus and Adonis 199-200 Art thou obdurate, flinty, hard as steel? / Nay, more than flint, for stone at rain relenteth

Pigmalion 136 So *Labeo* did complaine his loue was **stone, / Obdurate, flinty, so relentlesse none.**

Situation, plot element

All's Well 4.3.233-235 a dangerous and lascivious boy, who is a whale to virginity and devours up all the fry it finds.

Jack Drum's Entertainment 186 hee is a quicksand, a Goodwin, a Gulfe, as hungry as the **Jawes of a Jayle**, hee will waste more substance then *Ireland* souldiers: A Die, a Drabbe, and a paunch-swolne Usurer, **deuoure whole Monarchies**

Antony 2.2.264-265 for his ordinary pays his heart / For what his eyes eat only

Parasitaster 190 't is injustice truelie, / For him to judge it fit, that you should starve

Hamlet 1.2.105-106 Fie, 'tis a fault to Heaven

Insatiate 6 Surcease. Beleeve it is a wrong unto the Gods: / They saile against the winde that waile the dead

Hamlet 1.2.187-188 The funeral baked meats / Did coldly furnish forth the marriage tables

Eastward 103 the superfluitie and **colde meate left at their Nuptialls**, will with bountie **furnish ours**

Eastward 119 shee's married by this time to Prentise *Goulding*; your Father, and some one more, stole to church with 'hem, in all the haste, that **the cold meat left at your wedding**, might serve to **furnish their Nuptiall table**

Insatiate 8 Learne of a well composed Epigram [...] The Tapers that stood on her husbands hearse, / *Isabell'* advances to a second bed

Hamlet 1.4.144-146 so loving to my mother / That he might not beteeme the winds of heaven / Visit her face too roughly

Insatiate 73 she had a Lord, / Jealous, **the Aire should ravish her chaste looks**

Hamlet 2.1.88 doublet all unbraced

What You Will 237 [Enter Iacomo **unbraced** and careles drest]

Hamlet 2.2.576 O what a rogue and peasant slave am I!

Insatiate 29-30 Now gins my vengeance mount high in my lust: [...] **yet what a slave am I**, are there not younger Brothers enough, but we must / Branch one another?

Hamlet 2.2.578-584 Is it not monstrous that this player here, / But in a fiction, in a dream of passion, / Could force his soul so to his own conceit / That from her working all his visage wanned, / Tears in his eyes, distraction in his aspect, / A broken voice, and his whole function suiting / With forms to his conceit – and all for nothing!

Insatiate 8 **A Players passion** Ile beleeue hereafter, / And in a Tragicke Sceane weepe for olde Priam, / When fell reuenging Pirrhus with supposde / And artificiall wounds **mangles his breast**

Hamlet 3.1.54-56 I have heard of your paintings too, well enough; God has given you one face and you make yourselves another.

Insatiate 51 **Your painting** will wipe off, which Art did hide.

Hamlet 3.1.87-88 The undiscovered country from whose bourn / No traveller returns

Insatiate 6 **Deaths pangs / From whose sterne Cave none tracks a backward path**

Hamlet 3.2.2-3 but if you mouth it, as many of our players do

Sophonisba 44 speake from all sence / but *loud and full* of players eloquence

Hamlet 3.2.157 What means this, my lord?

Insatiate 20 Good, **my lord, be my expositor**

Hamlet 3.4.207-208 A second time I kill my husband dead / When second husband kisses me in bed

Insatiate 8 The Tapers that stood on her husbands hearse, / *Isabell'* advances to a **second bed**

Hamlet 3.4.94-98 When he is drunk asleep, or in his rage, / Or in th' incestuous pleasure of his bed [...] Then trip him

Insatiate 70 Didst thou not **kill him druncke?** [...] Thou shouldest, or in **the embraces of his lust**

Hamlet 4.3.22 Not where he eats, but where he is eaten

Eastward 112 The old usurer will be here instantly [...] and he (**with a purpose to feed on you**) invites you most solemnly by me to supper

Hamlet 4.7.200-201 Her clothes spread wide, / And mermaid-like awhile they bore her up

Eastward 135 her body is above the water, & **her clothes swim about her** most handsomely. O **they bear her up** most bravely!

1 Henry IV 1.2.110 Why Hal 'tis my vocation, Hal. 'Tis no sin for a man to labor in his vocation.

Family sig. D^{3recto} **Tis my vocation, boy.** We must never be weary of well-doing

1 Henry IV 1.3.35-36 and his chin new reaped / Showed like a stubble-land at harvest-home

Fleire sig. B3^{verso} **his beard was newly cut bare;** marry **it showed** something **like a** Medow newly mowed: stubble, stubble.

2 Henry IV 3.1.5-8 O sleep [...] That thou no more wilt weigh my eyelids down

Malcontent 178 I cannot sleepe, my **eyes ill neighbouring lids / Will holde no fellowship**

(*Continued*)

2 Henry VI 1.4.18-21 Deep night, dark night, the silent of the night, / The time of night when Troy was set on fire, / The time when screech owls cry and bandogs howl, / And spirits walk, and ghosts break up their graves

2 Henry VI 2.2.150-153 And ne'er was Agamemnon's brother [Menelaus] wronged / By that false woman as this king by thee.

2 Henry VI 3.2.240 What stronger breastplate than a breast untainted

Love's Labour's Lost 1.2.70-72 Samson [...] was a man of good carriage, great carriage, for he carried the town gates on his back like a porter

Macbeth 1.2.7 Doubtful it stood

Macbeth 1.3.56-58 From Fife, great king, / Where the Norweyan banners flout the sky / And fan our people cold.

Macbeth 5.2.53-55 Here's the smell of the blood still. All the perfumes of Arabia will not sweeten this little hand.

Merchant 1.1.23-25 My wind cooling my broth / Would blow me to an ague when I thought / What harm a wind too great might do at sea.

Much Ado 2.1.40-41 BEATRICE. [...] lead his apes into Hell

Othello 5.2.406-408 of one whose hand, / Like the base [Indian] threw a pearl away / Richer than all his tribe [The *First Folio* has 'Iudean' for 'Indian']

Richard II 1.1.60-68 Call him a slanderous coward and a villain, / Which to maintain I would allow him odds / And meet him, were I tied to run afoot / Even to the frozen ridges of the Alps

Revenge 104 Now croakes the toad, & **night-crowes screech** aloud, / Fluttering 'bout casements of departed soules. / Now **gapes the graves**, and through their yawnes let loose / Imprison'd **spirits to revisit earth**

Malcontent 165 When *Arthur* first in Court began, – *Agamemnon Menelaus* – was every any Duke a *Cornuto*?

Mellida 33 a faire cause of armes, / Why that's an armie all inuincible. / He who hath that, hath a battalion / Royal, armour of proofe

Family B^{2verso} we sawe **Sampson beare the Towne gates on his necke** [...] with that life and admirable accord, that it shall neuer be equalled (vnlesse the whole new liuery of **Porters** set their shoulders)

Sophonisba 14 yet **doubtful stood** the fight

Sophonisba 13 the Roman eagles stretch'd / Their large spread winges, which fan'd the evening ayre / To us cold breath

Insatiate 69 Although Neptolis cold, the waves of all the northerne sea, / Should flow for ever, through **these guiltie hands**, / Yet the sanguinolent staine would extant be.

Eastward 107 at every shaking of a leafe, hee falles into an agonie, to thinke what daunger his Shippe is in on such a Coast

Eastward 93 Enter Bettrice leading a **Monkey** after her.

Insatiate 59 I was the **Indian**, yet you had the **treasure**.

Insatiate 15 Slave, **I will fight with thee at any oddes**, / Or name an instrument fit for destruction, / That e'er was made to make away a man, / Ile meete thee on the ridges of the Alpes, / Or some inhospitable wildernesse [...].

Appendix II 171

Richard II 1.4.6 none for me, except the northeast wind, / Which then blew bitterly against our faces, / Awaked the sleeping rheum and so by chance / Did grace our hollow parting with a tear.

Mellida 20 **Nothing** sweet *Rossaline*, but **the ayre's sharpe.**

Richard III 5.3.290 Who saw the sun today? / RATCLIFFE. Not I, my lord.

Mellida 33 **I saw no sunne to day.**

Titus Andronicus 3.1.269-270 MARCUS. Why dost thou laugh? It fits not with this hour

Revenge 82 Ha Ha [inapprioprate laughter after a death is announced]

Winter's Tale 4.4.892-894 he is gone abroad a new ship to purge melancholy and air himself

Parasitaster 212 my fooles [...] have launcht out **their ship to purge their stomackes on the water**

Bibliography

Primary texts

Addison, Joseph. *Cato. A tragedy. As it is acted at the Theatre-Royal in Drury-Lane, by Her Majesty's Servants. By Mr. Addison*. London: J. Tonson, 1713.

Aickin, Joseph. *The English grammar: or, the English tongue reduced to grammatical rules containing the four parts of grammar: viz. orthographie, etymology, syntax, prosody or poetry. Being the easiest quickest and most authentick method of teaching it, by rules and pictures: adapted to the capacities of children, youth and those of riper years; in learning whereof the English scholar may now attain the perfection of his mother tongue, without the assistance of Latine; composed for the use of all English schools [...]*. London: M.B. for the author, 1693.

Ainsworth, John. *The trying out of the truth begunn and prosequuted in certayn letters and passages between Iohn Aynsworth and sHenry Aynsworth [...]*. Amsterdam: Giles Thorp, 1615.

Anon. 'The Bachelor's Soliloquy in Imitation of the Celebrated Soliloquy of Hamlet.' *The Poetical Museum*. Hawick: G. Caw, 1784. 307–308.

Anon. 'The Batchelor's Soliloquy, in imitation of a celebrated speech of Hamlet.' *Scots Magazine* 6 (April 1744): 176.

Anon. *The Bible and Holy Scriptvres conteyned in the Olde and Newe Testament [...]*. Geneva: Rouland Hall, 1560 [Geneva Bible].

Anon. 'A Correction of a thought, which by the more sceptical part of mankind has been frequently adopted, to render dubious a principle of the utmost truth and certainty.' *Universal Magazine of Knowledge and Pleasure* 53:370 (November 1773): 283.

Anon. *An essay against too much reading. With The whole Lives and Proceedings of Sancho and Peepo, at Aix la Chapelle in Germany. And a true account and design of the Proceedings this last Year in so many Processions at Bath*. London: A. Moore, 1728.

Anon. *The husband's resentment; or, the history of Lady Manchester. A novel [...]*. London: T. Lowndes, 1776.

Anon. '[Instalment of] *The Sylph; Or, The History of Sophia Merton.*' *Weekly entertainer or, Agreeable and instructive repository* 33 (March 1799): 232–236.

Anon. 'The Maid's Soliloquy. In Imitation of a Speech in Hamlet.' *Edinburgh Weekly Magazine* 57 (September 1783): 338.

Anon. 'The Murder of Abel.' *The Towneley Plays.* Eds. Martin Stevens and A.C. Cawley. Early English Text Society. Oxford: Oxford University Press, 1994. 1: 12–25.

Anon. 'Parody on Hamlet. Recited in a Company of Bachelors.' *Kaleidoscope; or, Literary and Scientific Mirror* 4:196 (March 1824): 325.

Anon. 'Parody on Hamlet's Soliloquy.' *The Culler* 9 (1795): 144–145

Anon. 'A Parody on Hamlet's Soliloquy on Death.' *Hibernia Magazine* (December 1810): 327–328.

Anon. 'A Parody on the Speech of To be, or not to be, in *Hamlet*.' *British Magazine* 2 (March 1747): 128.

Anon. 'A Parody on the Speech of To be, or not to be, in *Hamlet*.' *Newcastle General Magazine* (March 1747): 73.

Anon. 'The Pilgrimage to Parnassus.' *The Three Parnassus Plays (1598–1601).* Ed. J. B. Leishman. London: Ivor Nicholson and Watson, 1949. 25–132.

Anon. 'Singular Suicide of a Lunatic at the Leicester Asylum.' *The Times* 15330 (23 November 1833): 3.

Anon. 'To Marry or not to Marry.' *Cabinet* 6 (June 1809): 537–539.

Anon. *Tom o'Lincoln.* Oxford: Oxford University Press, 1992.

Anon. 'A Touch of the Sublime and Beautiful: Translated from Hamlet's Soliloquy!' *Mirror of Literature, Amusement, and Instruction* 7:195 (May 1826): 300.

Ashley, J., jr. 'The Poet's Soliloquy, a Parody of Cato's celebrated Soliloquy.' *Court Magazine* (June 1763): 303.

Austen, Jane. 'Catharine or the Bower.' *The Juvenilia of Jane Austen and Charlotte Brontë.* Harmondsworth: Penguin, 1986. 136–177.

Austen, Jane. *Emma.* New York: Norton, 2000.

Austen, Jane. *Letters.* Ed. Deirdre Le Faye. Oxford: Oxford University Press, 1995.

Austen, Jane. *Mansfield Park.* New York: Norton, 1998.

Austen, Jane. *Northanger Abbey.* New York: Norton, 2004.

Austen, Jane. *Persuasion.* New York: Norton, 1995.

Austen, Jane. 'Plan of a Novel.' www.janeausten.co.uk//a-plan-of-a-novel. Accessed 15 July 2015.

Austen, Jane. *Pride and Prejudice.* New York: Norton, 2001.

Austen, Jane. *The Watsons and Sanditon.* Harmondsworth: Penguin, 1985.

Ayres, Philip. 'Love's New Philosophy.' *Lyric Poems, Made in Imitation of the Italians.* London: Joseph Knight and F. Saunders, 1687. 63–66.

Bacon, Francis. *Francisci de Verulamio, Summi Angliae Cancellarii, Instauratio magna.* London: Bonham Norton and John Billy, 1620.

Bacon, James. *The Libertine: A Novel in a Series of Letters.* London: W. Miller, 1791.

Baldwin, William. *A treatice of moral philosophy: contaynynge the sayinges of the wise, wherin you may se the woorthy and pithy sayings of philosophers, emperors, kynges, and oratours [...].* London: Richard Tottyll, 1571.

Barbatus. 'A Parody on Hamlet's Soliloquy on Death.' *Walker's Hibernian Magazine, or, Compendium of entertaining knowledge* (April 1797): 367.

Baxter, Richard. 'A sermon preached at the funeral of that holy, painful and fruitful minister of Christ, Mr. Henry Stubbs [...].' *Eleven sermons on special occasions.* artlettRichard Baxter, in four volumes. With a preface;

giving some account of the author, and of this edition of his practical works. London: Thomas Parkhurst, Jonathan Robinson, and John Lawrence, 1707. 881–888.

Beaumont, Francis and John Fletcher. *Comedies and tragedies written by Francis Beaumont and Iohn Fletcher [...].* London: Humphrey Robinson et al., 1647.

Beckford, William Thomas. *Modern Novel Writing, or the Elegant Enthusiast; and Interesting emotions of Arabella Bloomville. A rhapsodical romance; interspersed with Poetry [...]. By the Right Hon. Lady Harriet Marlow.* London: G. G. and J. Robinson, 1796.

Bennett, Agnes Maria. *The beggar girl and her benefactors [...].* London: William Lane, 1797.

Bewick, William. *Life and Letters of William Bewick.* London: Hurst and Blackett, 1871.

Bickerstaff, Isaac. *The Padlock.* London: W. Griffin, 1768.

Boswell, James. *Boswell's Life of Johnson.* Ed. George Birkbeck Hill. Oxford: Clarendon Press, 1964.

Boswell, James. *The Yale Edition of The Private Papers of James Boswell.* Eds. Irma S. Lustig and Frederick A. Pottle. London: Heinemann, 1986.

Bradford, John. 'Conference with the Archbishop of York and the Bishop of Chichester.' *Memoirs of the Life and Martyrdom of John Bradford, M. A. [...].* Ed. William Stevens. London: R. Fenn, 1832. 246–254.

Bright, Timothy. *A treatise of melancholie: Containing the causes thereof, & reasons of the strange effects it worketh in our minds and bodies: with the physicke cure, and spirituall consolation for such as haue thereto adioyned an afflicted conscience [...] By T. Bright doctor of physicke.* London: Thomas Vautrollier, 1586.

Brome, Richard. *The Northern Lass: A comedy, as 'tis Acted at the Theatre-Royal [...].* London: August Matthews, 1632.

Brush. 'To Be or not to Be. A vocal Paraphrase on Hamlet's Soliloquy.' *Town and Country Magazine, or, Universal Repository of Knowledge, Instruction, and Entertainment* 27 (January 1795): 28.

Bull, Henry. *Christian Prayers and Holy Meditations: As well for Private as Public Exercise [...].* [1575]. Cambridge: Cambridge University Press, 1842.

Burghley, William Cecil, Lord of. *Certaine precepts or directions, for the well ordering and carriage of a mans life [...].* London: T. Creede and B. Alsop for Richard Meighen and Thomas Jones, 1617.

Byron, George Gordon Noel, Lord. *Byron's Letters and Journals. The Complete and Unexpurgated Text of all the Letters Available in Manuscript and the Full Printed Version of all Others.* Ed. Leslie A. Marchand. London: John Murray, 1973–1982.

Byron, George Gordon Noel, Lord. 'Don Juan.' *The Major Works.* Ed. Jerome J. McGann. Oxford World's Classics: Oxford: Oxford University Press, 2000. 373–880.

Cartwright, Thomas. *A confutation of the Rhemists translation, glosses and annotations on the Nevv Testament so farre as they contain manifest impieties, heresies, idolatries, superstitions, prophanesse, treasons, slanders, absurdities, falsehoods and other evills. By occasion whereof the true sence, scope, and doctrine of the Scriptures, and humane authors, by them abused,* is now given. VVritten long since by order from the chiefe instruments of the late Queene and state [...]. Leyden: William Brewster, 1618.

Caryll, John. *The English Princess, or, The Death of Richard the III: A Tragedy*. London: Thomas Dring, 1667.

Chapman, George. 'The Conspiracie, and Tragedie of Charles Duke of Byron, Marshall of France.' *The Plays of George Chapman: The Tragedies with Sir Gyles Goosecappe*. Ed. Allan Holaday. Cambridge: D. S. Brewer, 1987. 275–332.

Chesterfield, Earl of (Philip Dormer Stanhope). *Letters Written by the Earl of Chesterfield to His Son*. New York: Derby and Jackson, 1857.

Chesterfield, Earl of (Philip Dormer Stanhope). *Lettres de feu Ph. Dormer Stanhope, comte de Chesterfield, à son fils Ph. Stanhope, écuyer, envoyé exträordinaire à la cour de Dresde [...]*. Amsterdam and Rotterdam: E. van Harrevelt et al., 1776–1777.

Chettle, Henry. *The forrest of fancy Wherein is conteined very prety apothegmes, and pleasaunt histories, both in meeter and prose, songes, sonets, epigrams and epistles, of diuerse matter and in diuerse manner. VVith sundry other deuises, no lesse pithye then pleasaunt and profytable*. London: Thomas Purfoot, 1579.

Chettle, Henry. *Kind-harts dreame Conteining fiue apparitions, vvith their inuectiues against abuses raigning. Deliuered by seuerall ghosts vnto him to be publisht, after Piers Penilesse post had refused the carriage [...]*. London: J. Wolfe and J. Danter for William Wright, 1592.

Cicero, Marcus Tullius. *Tusculanae Quaestiones*. 45 BC. www.thelatinlibrary.com//cic.html. Accessed 19 November 2013.

Clough, Arthur Hugh. 'Lecture on the Development of English Literature from Chaucer to Wordsworth.' *The Poems and Prose Remains [...]*. London: Macmillan, 1869. 1: 337–355.

Coleridge, Samuel Taylor. 'Lectures on Shakespeare and Milton in Illustration of the Principles of Poetry.' *The Collected Works of Samuel Taylor Coleridge*. Ed. Kathleen Coburn. Princeton, NJ: Princeton University Press, 1987. 5:1, 153–414.

Coleridge, Samuel Taylor. 'Logic.' *The Collected Works of Samuel Taylor Coleridge*. Gen. ed. Kathleen Coburn. Princeton, NJ: Princeton University Press, 1981. 13: 247.

Cooper, Thomas. *Thesaurus linguæ Romanæ & Britannicæ tam accurate congestus, vt nihil penè in eo desyderari possit, quod vel Latinè complectatur amplissimus Stephani Thesaurus, vel Anglicè, toties aucta Eliotæ Bibliotheca: opera & industria Thomæ Cooperi Magdalenensis [...]. Accessit dictionarium historicum et poëticum propria vocabula virorum, mulierum, sectarum, populorum, vrbium, montium, & cæterorum locorum complectens, & in his iucundissimas & omnium cognitione dignissimas historias*. London: Henry Denham, 1578.

Cotgrave, John. *The English treasury of wit and language collected out of the most, and best of our English drammatick poems; methodically digested into common places for generall use*. London: Humphrey Moseley, 1655.

Covell, William. *Polimanteia*. Cambridge: John Leggatt, 1595.

Cowley, Abraham. 'Life.' *Pindarique Odes. The Works of Mr. Abraham Cowley. Consisting of Those which were formerly Printed: And Those which* he Design'd for the Press, Now Published out of the Authors Original Copies. Ed. A. R. Waller. Cambridge: Cambridge University Press, 1905. 209.

Cowley, Hannah. *More Ways Than One: A Comedy*. London: J. Davies for T. Evans, 1784.

Cudworth, Ralph. *The true intellectual system of the universe: the first part [...]*. London: Richard Royston, 1678.

Culmann, Leonhard. *Sentences for children, English and Latine collected out of sundry authors long since / by Leonard Culman; and now translated into English by Charles Hoole, for the first enterers into Latin*. London: Printed for the Company of Stationers, 1658.

Cumberland, Richard. *The Box-Lobby Challenge: A Comedy*. London: J. Debrett, 1794.

Daborne, Robert. *A Christian turn'd Turke: or, The tragicall liues and deaths of the two famous pyrates, Ward and Dansiker As it hath beene publickly acted. VVritten by Robert Daborn, Gentleman*. London: Nicholas Okes, 1612.

Daborne, Robert. *The poor-mans comfort a tragi-comedy: as it was divers times acted at the Cock-pit in Drury Lane with great applause*. London: Robert Pollard et al., 1655.

Davies of Hereford, Sir John. *Mirum in Modum: A Glimpse of Gods Glorie, and the Soules Shape*. London: William Aspley, 1602.

Davies of Hereford, Sir John. *The Muses Sacrifice*. London: George Norton, 1612.

Davies of Hereford, Sir John. *The Scourge of Folly, consisting of Satyricall Epigramms and others [...]*. London: E. A. for Richard Redmer, 1611.

Davies of Hereford, Sir John. *Yehovah summa totalis or, All in all, and, the same for euer: or, an addition to Mirum in modum [...]*. London: William Jaggard, 1607.

Defoe, Daniel. *The Fortunes and Misfortunes of the Famous Moll Flanders, &c*. The Shakespeare Head Edition of the Novels and Selected Writings. Oxford: Blackwell, 1974.

Defoe, Daniel. *The fortunate mistress: or, A history of the life and vast variety of fortunes of Mademoiselle [...]. Being the person known by the name of the Lady Roxana, in the time of King Charles II*. Ed. Jane Jack. Oxford: Oxford University Press, 1969.

Defoe, Daniel. *A Hymn to Peace. Occasion'D, by the Two Houses Joining in One Address to the Queen*. London: J. Nutt, 1706.

Defoe, Daniel. *The life and strange surprizing adventures of Robinson Crusoe, of York, mariner [...]*. The Shakespeare Head Edition of the Novels and Selected Writings. Oxford: Blackwell, 1974.

Defoe, Daniel. *The Political History of the Devil, as well ancient as modern*. London: T. Warner, 1726.

De Quincey, Thomas. 'Charles Lamb.' *The Works of Thomas De Quincey*. London: Pickering and Chatto, 2003. 16: 365–397.

De Quincey, Thomas. 'Shakespeare.' *The Works of Thomas De Quincey*. Eds. Grevel Lindop and John Whale. London: Pickering and Chatto, 2001. 13: 286–333.

Digges, Leonard. 'Vpon Master William Shakespeare, the Deceased Authour, and his Poems.' *Poems Written By Wil. Shakespeare, Gent*. London: Thomas Coates, 1640. Unpaginated opening section.

Dolman, John, trans. Marcus Tullius Cicero. *Those fyue questions, which Marke Tullye Cicero, disputed in his manor of Tusculanum: written afterwardes by him, in as manye bookes, to his frende, and familiar Brutus, in the Latine tounge. And nowe, oute of the same translated, & englished, by Iohn Dolman, studente and felowe of the Inner Temple. 1561.* London: Thomas Marsh, 1561.

Donne, John. 'Upon Mr Thomas Coryat's Crudities.' *The Complete English Poems*. Ed. A. J. Smith. Harmondsworth: Penguin, 1980. 173–175.

Downame, John. *The Christian warfare against the devill world and flesh [...]*. London: William Stansby, 1634.

Dryden, John and Nathaniel Lee. 'The Duke of Guise: A Tragedy.' *The Works of John Dryden*. Ed. Alan Roper. Berkeley: University of California Press, 1996. 14: 205–230.

Edgeworth, Maria. *The Absentee*. The Novels and Selected Works of Maria Edgeworth. Eds. Heidi Van de Veire et al. London: Pickering and Chatto, 1999. 5: 1–203.

Edgeworth, Maria. *Manœuvring*. The Novels and Selected Works of Maria Edgeworth. Eds. Claire Connolly and Marilyn Butler. London: Pickering and Chatto, 1999. 4: 1–127.

Edgeworth, Maria. 'Thoughts on Bores.' *Tales and Novels*. London: Baldwin and Cradock, 1833. 17: 305–328.

Erasmus, Desiderius. *On Copia of Words and Ideas*. Trans. Donald B. King and David H. Rix. Milwaukee, WI: Marquette University Press 1963.

Fenner, Dudley. *The Artes of Logicke and Rethorike*. Middleburgh, NY: R. Schilders, 1584.

Ferrier, Susan Edmonstone. *Marriage: A Novel*. Ed. Herbert Foltinek. London: Oxford University Press, 1971.

Fielding, Henry. *The History of Tom Jones, a Foundling*. Eds. Thomas Keymer and Alice Wakely. Harmondsworth: Penguin, 2005.

Fielding, Sarah. *The Countess of Dellwyn*. London: A. Millar, 1759.

Fielding, Sarah. *The cry: a new dramatic fable*. London: R. and J. Dodsley, 1754.

Fletcher, John and Philip Massinger. 'The Little French laywer.' *Comedies and Tragedies Written by Francis Beaumont and Iohn Fletcher [...]*. London: Humphrey Robinson et al., 1647. 51–75.

Florio, John. *Florio his firste fruites which yeelde familiar speech, merie prouerbes, wittie sentences, and golden sayings. Also a perfect induction to the Italian, and English tongues, as in the table appeareth [...]*. London: Thomas Dawson for Thomas Woodcocke, 1578.

Florio, John. *Florios second frutes to be gathered of twelue trees, of diuers but delightsome tastes to the tongues of Italians and Englishmen [...]*. London: T. Orwin for Thomas Woodcock, 1591.

Fowler, H. W. 'Longman's Magazine.' *Longman's Magazine, Review of Reviews* (January 1901): 67.

Freeman, Thomas. *Rubbe, and a Great Cast. Epigrams [...]*. London: N. p., 1614.

Garrick, David. *The Irish Widow*. London: T. Becket, 1772.

Garrick, David. *The Letters of David Garrick*. Eds. David M. Little and George M. Kahrl. Cambridge, MA: The Belknap Press of Harvard University Press, 1963.

Gibbes, Phoebe. *The woman of fashion: or, the history of Lady Diana Dormer [...]*. London: J. Wilkie, 1767.
Godwin, William. Deloraine. The Collected Novels and Memoirs of William Godwin. Ed. Maurice Hindle. 8 vols. London: Pickering and Chatto, 1992.
Golding, Arthur, trans. *The XV. Bookes of P. Ovidius Naso, entytuled Metamorphosis, translated out of Latin into English meter, by Arthur Golding. Gentleman, A worke very pleasaunt and delectable*. London: William Seres, 1567.
Greene, Robert. *Greenes, groats-vvorth of witte, bought with a million of repentance Describing the follie of youth, the falshoode of makeshifte flatterers, the miserie of the negligent, and mischiefes of deceiuing courtezans. Written before his death, and published at his dyeing request*. London: Imprinted J. Wolfe and J. Danter for William Wright, 1592.
Guazzo, Stefano, trans. George Pettie. *The ciuile conuersation of M. Steeuen Guazzo written first in Italian, and nowe translated out of French by George Pettie [...]*. London: Richard Watkins, 1581.
Hawkins, Joseph. 'The Bachelor's Soliloquy: A Parody on Hamlet's.' *Monthly Mirror Reflecting Men and Manners, with Strictures on Their Epitome, the Stage*. London: Vernor et al., 1808. 4: 114–115.
Hazlitt, William. *The Collected Works of William Hazlitt*. Eds. A. R. Waller and Arnold Glover. London: Dent, 1904.
Hazlitt, William. 'Life of Sir Joshua Reynolds.' *The Edinburgh Review* 34. Edinburgh: Constable; London: Longman et al., 1820. 79–108.
Hazlitt, William. *The Selected Writings of William Hazlitt*. Ed. Duncan Wu. London: Pickering and Chatto, 1998.
Hazlitt, William. 'Travelling Abroad.' *New Monthly Magazine and Literary Journal: Original Papers Volume 22*. London: Henry Colburn, 1828. 529–535.
Heminges, William. *The Jewes tragedy, or, Their fatal and final overthrow by Vespatian and Titus [...]*. London: Matthew Inman, 1662.
Heywood, Thomas. *The hierarchie of the blessed angells Their names, orders and offices the fall of Lucifer with his angells [...]*. London: Adam Islip, 1635.
Hooker, Richard. *The Laws of Ecclesiastical Polity. The Works of [...] Mr. Richard Hooker: with an account of his life and death by Isaak Walton*. Ed. John Keble. New York: D. Appleton, 1857.
Horatius Flaccus, Quintus. *Oden und Epoden Lateinisch/Deutsch*. Ed. Bernhard Kytzler. Stuttgart: Reclam, 1995.
Hubert, Sir Francis. *The deplorable life and death of Edward the Second, King of England Together with the downefall of the two vnfortunate fauorits, Gaueston and Spencer. Storied in an excellent poëm*. London: Nicholas Okes for Roger Michell, 1628.
Hutchinson. A. A. *Exhibitions of the heart: a novel*. London: For the Author, 1799.
Jackson, J. 'The Soliloquy of a Bachelor, on the Anniversary of his Birthday.' *Gentleman's Magazine* (March 1812): 263.
Johnson, Mrs. *Juliana: A novel [...]*. London: William Lane, 1786.
Johnson, Samuel. *The Letters of Samuel Johnson*. The Hyde Edition. Ed. Bruce Redford. Oxford: Clarendon Press, 1992.
Johnson, Samuel. 'Preface to Shakespeare.' *The Norton Anthology of English Literature*. Ed. M. H. Abrams. 6th ed. New York and London: Norton, 1993. 1: 2393–2404.

Jones, Mary. 'Of Patience: An Epistle to the Right Honourable Samuel Lord Masham.' *Miscellanies in Prose and Verse. By Mary Jones*. Oxford: Dodsley, 1750. 10–25.

Jonson, Ben. 'Cynthia's Revels.' *The Workes of Beniamin Jonson*. London: Will Stansby, 1616. 177–269.

Jonson, Ben. 'Discoveries.' *The Oxford Jonson*. Ed. Ian Donaldson. Oxford and New York: Oxford University Press, 1985.

Jonson, Ben. 'Poetaster.' *Complete Critical Edition*. Oxford: Oxford University Press, 1986. 4: 185–321.

Joyce, James. *Ulysses*. London: Penguin, 1986.

Kean, Philo. 'Dramatic Parodies No. 4. Hamlet's Soliloquy.' *The Drama; or Theatrical Magazine* 6:4 (June 1824): 169.

Knowles, James Sheridan. *The Love-Chase: A Comedy in Five Acts [...]*. London: Edward Moxon, 1837. 51–52.

Lamb, Charles. 'On the Tragedies of Shakspeare.' *The Life, Letters, and Writings of Charles Lamb*. Ed. Percy Fitzgerald. London: Moxon, 1876. 4: 188–213.

Lichtenberg, Georg Christoph. 'Über Hrn. Vossens Verteidigung gegen mich im März des Deutschen Museums 1782.' *Gesammelte Werke*. Ed. Wilhelm Grenzmann. Frankfurt Main: Holle, 1949. 2: 139–190.

Lloyd, Charles. *Edmund Oliver*. Eds. Philip Cox and W. M. Verhoeven. *Anti-Jacobin Novels*. Gen. ed. Wil M. Verhoeven. London: Pickering and Chatto, 2005.

Locke, John. *An Essay Concerning Human Understanding*. Ed. Alexander Campbell Fraser. Oxford. Oxford University Press, 1894. Reprint: New York: Dover Publications, 1959.

Lyly, John. *Euphues and His England*. London: Gabriell Cawood, 1580.

Lyly, John. *Euphues: The Anatomy of Wit*. Eds. Morris William Croll and Harry Clemons. London: George Routledge, 1916.

Marlowe, Christopher. 'Dido, Queen of Carthage.' *The Complete Plays*. Eds. Frank Romany and Robert Lindsey. London: Penguin, 2003. 1–67.

Marlowe, Christopher. 'Tamburlaine the Great.' *The Complete Plays*. Ed. J. B. Steane. London: Penguin 1986. 101–258.

Marston, John. 'Antonio and Mellida.' *The Plays of John Marston in Three Volumes*. Ed. H. Harvey Wood. Edinburgh and London: Oliver and Boyd, 1934–1939. 1: 1–64.

Marston, John. 'Antonios Revenge.' *The Plays of John Marston in Three Volumes*. Ed. H. Harvey Wood. Edinburgh and London: Oliver and Boyd, 1934–1939. 1: 65–134.

Marston, John. 'The Dutch Curtezan.' *The Plays of John Marston in Three Volumes*. Ed. H. Harvey Wood. Edinburgh and London: Oliver and Boyd, 1934–1939. 2: 65–138.

Marston, John. *The familie of loue Acted by the children of his Maiesties Reuells*. London: Richard Braddock for John Helmes, 1608.

Marston, John. 'Histrio-Mastix.' *The Plays of John Marston in Three Volumes*. Ed. H. Harvey Wood. Edinburgh and London: Oliver and Boyd, 1934–1939. 3: 243–302.

Marston, John. 'The Insatiate Countesse.' *The Plays of John Marston in Three Volumes*. Ed. H. Harvey Wood. Edinburgh and London: Oliver and Boyd, 1934–1939. 3: 1–82.

Marston, John. 'Jacke Drums Entertainment: Or the Comedie of Pasquill and Katherine.' *The Plays of John Marston in Three Volumes*. Ed. H. Harvey Wood. Edinburgh and London: Oliver and Boyd, 1934–1939. 3: 175–241.

Marston, John. 'The Malcontent.' *The Plays of John Marston in Three Volumes*. Ed. H. Harvey Wood. Edinburgh and London: Oliver and Boyd, 1934–1939. 1: 135–218.

Marston, John. '[Parasitaster, or] The Fawne.' *The Plays of John Marston in Three Volumes*. Ed. H. Harvey Wood. Edinburgh and London: Oliver and Boyd, 1934–1939. 2: 139–226.

Marston, John. 'Pigmalion.' *Miscellaneous pieces of antient English poesie. Viz. The troublesome raigne of King John, written by Shakespeare, extant in no edition of his writings. The metamorphosis of Pigmalion's image, and certain satyres. By John Marston. The scourge of villanie. By the same. All printed before the year 1600*. London: Robert Horsefield, 1764. 123–136.

Marston, John. 'Satyres.' *Miscellaneous pieces of antient English poesie. Viz. The troublesome raigne of King John, written by Shakespeare, extant in no edition of his writings. The metamorphosis of Pigmalion's image, and certain satyres. By John Marston. The scourge of villanie. By the same. All printed before the year 1600*. London: Robert Horsefield, 1764. 137–162.

Marston, John. 'The Scourge of Villanie: Three Books of Satyres.' *Miscellaneous pieces of antient English poesie. Viz. The troublesome raigne of King John, written by Shakespeare, extant in no edition of his writings. The metamorphosis of Pigmalion's image, and certain satyres. By John Marston. The scourge of villanie. By the same. All printed before the year 1600*. London: Robert Horsefield, 1764. 163–237.

Marston, John. 'Sophonisba.' *The Plays of John Marston in Three Volumes*. Ed. H. Harvey Wood. Edinburgh and London: Oliver and Boyd, 1934–1939. 2: 1–64.

Marston, John. 'What You Will.' *The Plays of John Marston in Three Volumes*. Ed. H. Harvey Wood. Edinburgh and London: Oliver and Boyd, 1934–1939. 2: 227–295.

Marston, John and Edward Sharpham. *The Fleire. As it hath beene often played in the Blacke-Fryers by the Children of the Reuells*. London: Edward Allde, 1607.

Marston, John, George Chapman and Ben Jonson. 'Eastward Ho.' *The Plays of John Marston in Three Volumes*. Ed. H. Harvey Wood. Edinburgh and London: Oliver and Boyd, 1934–1939. 3: 83–174.

Marx, Karl. 'Die Kontrerevolution in Berlin.' Karl Marx, Friedrich Engels. *Werke*. Berlin: Dietz Verlag, 1959. 6: 7–12.

Marx, Karl. 'Kritik des Hegelschen Staatsrechts.' Karl Marx, Friedrich Engels. *Werke*. Berlin: Dietz Verlag, 1957. 1: 201–333.

Marx, Karl. 'Zur Kritik der Hegelschen Rechtsphilosophie. Einleitung.' Karl Marx, Friedrich Engels. *Werke*. Berlin: Dietz Verlag, 1957. 1: 378–391.

Mason, John. 'Dives and Lazarus.' *Spiritual songs, or, Songs of praise to Almighty God upon several occasions [...]*. London: Thomas Parkhurst, 1699. 1–20.

McLeish, Archibald. 'Ars Poetica.' *The Broadview Anthology of Poetry*. Eds. Amanda Goldrick-Jones and Herbert Rosengarten. Peterborough, ON: Broadview Press, 2009. 426.

Melbancke, Brian. *Philotimus: The Warre betwixt Nature and Fortune.* London: Roger Warde, 1583.

Menander. 'Imitations of Shakespeare No. 2: Coelebs' Soliloquy.' *Universal Magazine* 11:64 (March 1809): 239–240.

Meres, Francis. *Palladis Tamia. Wits Treasury being the Second Part of Wits Common Wealth.* London: P. Short for Cuthbert Burbie, 1598.

Mey, J. L. 'To Grice or Not to Grice.' *Journal of Pragmatics* 34 (August 2002): 911.

Milton, John. *Paradise Lost.* New York: Norton, 2005.

Minshull, John. *He Stoops to Conquer, or The Virgin Wife Triumphant.* New York: G. and R. Waite, 1804.

Mulcaster, Richard. *The first part of the elementarie: vvhich entreateth chefelie of the right writing of our English tung [...].* London: Thomas Vautrollier, 1582.

Nashe, Thomas. *Christs teares over Ierusalem. Wherevnto is annexed, a comparatiue admonition to London.* London: Andrew Wise, 1594. N. p.

Nashe, Thomas. *Pierce Pennilesse His SUPPLICATION to the Diuell.* London: Abell Jeffres for John Busby, 1592.

Nashe, Thomas. 'To the Gentlemen Students of both Uniuersities.' *Menaphon. Camillas alarum to slumbering Euphues, in his melancholie Cell at Silexedra [...].* London: T. O. for Sampson Clarke, 1589. 6–18.

Nashe, Thomas. *The vnfortunate traueller. Or, The life of Iacke Wilton.* London: T. Scarlet for C. Burby, 1594.

Norris, John. *An idea of happiness, in a letter to a friend enquiring wherein the greatest happiness attainable by man in this life does consist [...].* London: For James Norris, 1683.

Osborne, F. 'The Conclusion of the Defence of the Revolution.' *Daily Gazetteer* 312 (26 June 1736): 798.

Painter, William. *The second Tome of the Palace of Pleasure, conteyning store of goodly Histories, Tragicall matters, and other Morall argument [...].* London: Henry Bynneman, 1567.

Payne, Henry Neville. *The Fatal Jealousie. A Tragedy [...].* London: Thomas Dring et al., 1673.

Pepys, Samuel. *Diary.* www.pepysdiary.com. Accessed December 2014.

Perkins, William. *A christian and plaine treatise of the manner and order of predestination, and of the largeness of Gods grace.* Cambridge: John Legatt, 1617.

Perkins, William. *An exposition of the Symbole or Creed of the Apostles [...].* Cambridge: John Legatt, 1616.

Perkins, William. *A reformed catholike, or, a declaration shewing how neere we may come to the present church of Rome.* London: Waterson, 1611.

Perkins, William. *A Treatise of Gods free grace and mans free-will.* Cambridge: John Legatt, 1616.

Philips, Ambrose. *Humfrey, Duke of Gloucester. A Tragedy [...].* London: J. Roberts, 1723.

Phillips, Teresia Constantia. *An Apology for the Conduct of Mrs. Teresia Constantia Phillips.* London: For the author, 1748–1749.

Philomeides. 'A Parody on Hamlet.' *Gentleman's Magazine* 62:3 (March 1792): 263.

P-o. 'The Bachelor's Soliloquy.' *Scots Magazine* 20 (June 1758): 306.

Pye, Henry James. 'The Aristocrat. A Novel.' *Anti-Jacobin Novels*. Gen. ed. W. M. Verhoeven. London: Pickering and Chatto, 2005. 1: 107–274.

Richardson, Samuel. *Pamela: Or, Virtue Rewarded. In a Series of Familiar Letters from a Beautiful Young Damsel, to her Parents: Now first Published In order to cultivate the Principles of Virtue and Religion in the Minds of the Youth of Both Sexes [...]*. London: C. Rivington et al., 1742.

Rider. 'Socrates on Death. Translated from Plato's Apology in Shakespeare's Manner.' *Newcastle General Magazine* 12 (December 1751): 648.

Robertson, Hannah. *The life of Mrs. Robertson, grand-daughter of Charles II written by herself: A Tale of Truth as Well as of Sorrow*. Edinburgh: J. Robertson, 1792.

Scoloker, Anthony. *Daiphantus, or the passions of loue Comicall to reade, but tragicall to act: as full of wit, as experience. By An. Sc. gentleman. Wherevnto is added, The passionate mans pilgrimage*. London: T. Creede for William Cotton, 1604.

Scott, Sir Walter. *The Abbot*. The Edinburgh Edition of the Waverley Novels. Gen. ed. David Hewitt. Edinburgh: Edinburgh University Press, 2000.

Scott, Sir Walter. *The Antiquary*. The Edinburgh Edition of the Waverley Novels. Gen. ed. David Hewitt. Edinburgh: Edinburgh University Press, 1995.

Scott, Sir Walter. *Ivanhoe: A Romance*. The Edinburgh Edition of the Waverley Novels. Gen. ed. David Hewitt. Edinburgh: Edinburgh University Press, 1998.

Scott, Sir Walter. *Journal*. www.online-literature.com/walter_scott/journal-of-scott/. Accessed 4 October 2014.

Scott, Sir Walter. *Kenilworth: A Romance*. The Edinburgh Edition of the Waverley Novels. Gen. ed. David Hewitt. Edinburgh: Edinburgh University Press, 1993.

Scott, Sir Walter. *The Letters of Sir Walter Scott*. Ed. Sir Herbert Grierson. London: Constable, 1932.

Scott, Sir Walter. *Rob Roy*. The Edinburgh Edition of the Waverley Novels. Gen. ed. David Hewitt. Edinburgh: Robert Cadell; London: Whittaker and Co. 1830.

Scott, Sir Walter. *Saint Ronan's Well*. The Edinburgh Edition of the Waverley Novels. Gen. ed. David Hewitt. Edinburgh: Edinburgh University Press, 1995.

Scott, Sir Walter. *Woodstock: Chronicles of the Canongate*. Philadelphia, PA: J. B. Lippincott & Co., 1856.

Shaftesbury, Anthony Ashley Cooper, Earl of. *Soliloquy: or, advice to an author*. London: John Morphew, 1710.

Shakespeare, William. *Shakespeare's Plays from Folger Digital Texts*. Ed. Barbara Mowat, Paul Werstine, Michael Poston, and Rebecca Niles. Folger Shakespeare Library, 30 June, 2017. www.folgerdigitaltexts.org.

Shakespeare, William. *The tragicall historie of Hamlet Prince of Denmarke by William Shake-speare. As it hath beene diuerse times acted by his Highnesse seruants in the cittie of London: as also in the two vniuersities of Cambridge and Oxford, and else-where [First Quarto]*. London: Valentine Simmes for Nicholas Ling and John Trundell, 1603.

Shelley, Mary Wollstonecraft. *The Last Man*. Ed. Nora Crook. London: William Pickering, 1996.
Sidney, Sir Henry. 'The Learner, Part II.' *Oxford & Cambridge Magazine* 3 (March 1856): 129–135.
Sidney, Sir Philip. 'Sonnet 74 [from *Astrophil and Stella*].' *The Norton Anthology of English Literature*. Ed. M. H. Abrams. 6th ed. New York and London: Norton, 1993. 1: 469.
Single, John. *The Batchelor's Recantation; or this estimate of the expences of a Married Life. Reconsidered Paragraph by Paragraph, and retracted [...]*. London: M. Payne, 1748.
Smollett, Tobias. *Peregrine Pickle*. London: For the Author, 1751.
Smollett, Tobias. *The Works of Tobias Smollett*. Ed. William Ernest Henley. Westminster: Constable; New York: Scribner's, 1899.
Spenser, Edmund. *The Faerie Queene*. Eds. Thomas P. Roche and C. Patrick O'Donnell. Harmondsworth: Penguin, 1978.
Spenser, Edmund. 'Teares of the Muses.' *Works of Edmund Spenser: A Variorum Edition*. Ed. Edwin Greenlaw et al. Baltimore: The Johns Hopkins Press, 1932–1949. 2: 61–79.
Stanyhurst, Richard, trans. *Thee first foure bookes of Virgil his Aeneis translated intoo English heroical verse by Richard Stanyhurst, wyth oother poëtical diuises theretoo annexed*. Leyden: John Pates, 1582.
Stevens, George Alexander. 'Song the Last, or Epilogue.' *Songs, Comic and Satyrical*. Oxford: For the Author, 1772. 246–247.
T. G. *The tragedy of Selimus Emperour of the Turkes. Written T. G.* London: Thomas Creede et al., 1638.
Theobald, Lewis. '[Untitled article].' *The Censor* 3:90 (18 May 1717): 198–205 (201–202).
Tomkis, Thomas. *Lingua: or the combat of the tongue and the fiue senses for superiority*. London: G. Eld for Simon Waterson, 1607.
Tousey, George Philip. 'The Batchelor's Deliberation. A Parody of the Soliloquy of Hamlet, (To be or not to be) versified.' *Flights to Helicon: or, Petites Pieces, in Verse*. London: T. W. Gisborne, 1768. 153–154.
Twiss, Horace. 'A Bachelor's Soliloquy, Being a Paraphrase of a Passage in the Play of Hamlet, by William Shakespeare.' Ed. Walter Hamilton. *Parodies of the Works of English and American Authors, Collected and Edited by Walter Hamilton*. London: Reeves and Turner, 1885. 2:80.
Twisse, William. Amsterdam: *A discovery of D. Iacksons vanitie [...]*. Amsterdam: N. p., 1631.
Usk, Thomas. 'The Testament of Love.' *The workes of Geffray Chaucer newlye printed, [...]*. London: Richard Grafton for William Bonham, 1542. N. p.
Vergilius Maro, Publius. *Aeneis Libri I–VI*. Zurich: Orell Füssli, 1979.
Walkington, Thomas. *The optick glasse of humors. Or The touchstone of a golden temperature, or the Philosophers stone to make a golden temper wherein the foure complections sanguine, cholericke, phlegmaticke, melancholicke are succinctly painted forth [...]*. London: John Windet for Martin Clerke, 1607.
Weever, John. *Epigrammes in the oldest cut, and newest fashion [...]*. London: Thomas Bushell, 1599.
Whitgift, John. *An ansvvere to a certen Libel intituled, An Admonition to the Parliament*. London: Henrie Bynneman for Humfrey Toy, 1573.

Wilson, Harriette. *Memoirs of Harriette Wilson, vol. II*. Eds. Julie Peakman and Alexander Pettis. London: Pickering and Chatto, 2007.
Wither, George. 'Wither's Motto.' *Juvenilia, or A Collection of Poems*. London: T. S. for John Budge, 1622. 359–453.
Wolcot, John. 'Peter Pindar's Soliloquy.' *The Times* (30 December 1786):2; column D.
Wollstonecraft, Mary. *The Collected Letters of Mary Wollstonecraft*. Ed. Ralph M. Warlde. Ithaca, NY and London: Cornell University Press, 1979.
Wollstonecraft, Mary. 'The Wrongs of Woman, or Maria, a Fragment.' *Mary, a Fiction and The Wrongs of Woman*. Ed. Gary Kelly. London et al.: Oxford University Press, 1976. 69–199.

Secondary texts

Allen, Graham. *Intertextuality*. London: Routledge, 1999.
Altman, Rick. *Film/Genre*. London: British Film Institute, 1999.
Anders, H. R. D. *Shakespeare's Books*. Berlin: Georg Reimer, 1904.
Anon. 'The word: Snowclone.' *The New Scientist* (18 November 2006): 80.
Armstrong, Edward A. *Shakespeare's Imagination: A Study of the Psychology of Association and Inspiration*. London: Lindsay Drummond, 1946.
Baldwin, Thomas Whitfield. *William Shakspere's Small Latine and Lesse Greeke*. Urbana: University of Illinois Press, 1944.
Barthes, Roland. 'The Death of the Author.' *Modern Criticism and Theory: A Reader*. Ed. David Lodge. London and New York: Longman, 1993. 167–172.
Barthes, Roland. 'From Work to Text.' *Image, Music, Text: Essays*. London: Fontana, 1984. 155–164.
Barthes, Roland. *Roland Barthes by Roland Barthes*. Berkeley: University of California Press, 1994.
Barthes, Roland. 'Textual Analysis of Poe's "Valdemar".' *Modern Criticism and Theory: A Reader*. Ed. David Lodge. London and New York: Longman, 1993. 172–195.
Barthes, Roland. 'Theory of the Text.' *Untying the Text: A Post-Structuralist Reader*. Ed. Robert J. C. Young. Boston, MA: Routledge and Kegan Paul, 1981. 31–47.
Bate, Jonathan. 'Hazlitt's Shakespearean Quotations.' *Prose Studies* 7:1 (1984): 26–37.
Bate, Jonathan. 'Parodies of Shakespeare.' *Journal of Popular Culture* 19:1 (1985): 75–89.
Belsey, Catherine. *Why Shakespeare?* Basingstoke: Palgrave Macmillan, 2007.
Bennett, Josephine Waters. 'Characterization in Polonius' Advice to Laertes.' *Shakespeare Quarterly* 4:1 (January 1953): 3–9.
Ben-Porat, Ziva. 'The Poetics of Literary Allusion.' *Poetics and Theory of Literature* 1 (1976): 105–128.
Bentley, Gerald Eades. *Shakespeare and Jonson: Their Reputations in the Seventeenth Century Compared*. Chicago, IL: University of Chicago Press, 1945.
Best, Stephen and Sharon Marcus. 'Surface Reading: An Introduction.' *Representations* 108:1 (Fall 2009): 1–21.
Bezzola Lambert, Ladina. *Shakespeare's Authorial Fictions: Venus and Adonis, Lucrece and the Sonnets*. Work in progress.

Blades, William. *Shakspere and Typography: Being an Attempt to Show Shakspere's Personal Connection with, and Technical Knowledge of, the Art of Printing.* New York: Burt Franklin 1969 (reprint of 1872 New York edition).

Bloom, Harold. 'Foreword.' *A Truth Universally Acknowledged: 33 Great Writers on Why We Read Jane Austen.* Ed. Susannah Carson. New York: Random House, 2009. v–vi.

Bowring, Sir John. 'Latin Aphorisms and Proverbs.' *Transactions of the Royal Historical Society* (1872): 82–103.

Braden, Gordon. 'Ovid, Plutarch and Shakespeare's Sonnets.' *Shakespeare's Ovid: The Metamorphoses in the Plays and Poems.* Ed. Anthony Brian Taylor. Cambridge: Cambridge University Press, 2000. 96–112.

Bruster, Douglas. *Quoting Shakespeare: Form and Culture in Early Modern Drama.* Lincoln: University of Nebraska Press, 2000.

Bruster, Douglas. *To Be or Not to Be.* London and New York: Continuum 2007.

Buck, H. Michael. 'A Message in her Madness: Socio-Political Bias in Scott's Portrayal of Mad Clara Mowbray of St. Ronan's Well.' *Studies in Scottish Literature* 24:1:16 (January 1989): 181–193.

Burrow, Colin. *Shakespeare and Classical Antiquity.* Oxford: Oxford University Press, 2013.

Calvino, Italo. *Six Memos for the Next Millennium.* Cambridge, MA: Harvard University Press, 1988.

Caselli, Daniela. *Beckett's Dantes: Intertextuality in the Fictions and Criticism.* Manchester: Manchester University Press, 2005.

Chambers, Edmund K. *Shakespeare: A Study of Facts and Problems.* Oxford: Clarendon Press, 1930.

Chambers, Edmund K. *Sources for a Biography of Shakespeare.* Oxford: Clarendon Press, 1946.

Chaudhuri, Pramit. 'Classical Quotation in *Titus Andronicus*.' *English Literary History* 81:3 (Fall 2014): 787–810.

Clare, Janet. *Shakespeare's Stage Traffic: Imitation, Borrowing and competition in Renaissance Theatre.* Cambridge: Cambridge University Press, 2014.

Coffman, George R. 'A Note on Shakespeare and Nash.' *Modern Language Notes* 42:5 (May 1927): 317–319.

Collinson, Patrick. 'The Coherence of the Text: How it Hangeth Together: The Bible in Reformation England.' *The Bible, the Reformation and the Church: Essays in Honour of James Atkinson.* Ed. W. P. Stephens. Sheffield: Sheffield Academic Press, 1995. 84–108.

Compagnon, Antoine. 'The Resistance to Interpretation.' *New Literary History* (Spring 2014): 271–280.

Connaughton, Michael E. 'Richardson's Familiar Quotations: *Clarissa* and Bysshe's *Art of English Poetry*.' *Philological Quarterly* 60:2 (Spring 1981): 183–195.

Cook, Trevor James Neilson. *Plagiarism and Proprietary Authorship in Early Modern England, 1590–1640.* PhD University of Toronto, 2011.

Corti, Maria. 'Il binomio intertestualità e fonti: funzioni della storia nel sistema letterario.' *La scrittura e la storia: Problemi di storiografia letteraria.* Ed. Alberto Asor Rosa. Florence: La Nuova Italia, 1995. 115–130.

Culler, Jonathan. 'Presupposition and Intertextuality.' *MLN* 91:6 (December 1976): 1380–1396.

Culler, Jonathan. *The Pursuit of Signs: Semiotics, Literature, Deconstruction.* New York: Cornell University Press, 1981.
Currell, David. '"Away with him! He speaks Latin": 2 Henry IV and the Uses of Roman Antiquity.' *Shakespeare Survey* 69 (2016): 30–45.
Davenport, A. 'Shakespeare and Nashe's "Pierce Pennilesse".' *Notes and Queries* 198 (September 1953): 371–374.
Dávidházi, Péter. '"O Jephthah, Judge of Israel": From Original to Accreted Meanings in Hamlet's Allusion.' *Shakespeare Survey* 58 (2015): 48–61.
De Grazia, Margreta. 'Shakespeare in Quotation Marks.' *The Appropriation of Shakespeare.* Ed. Jean Marsden. New York: Harvester Wheatsheaf, 1991. 57–71.
Dent, R. W. *Shakespeare's Proverbial Language.* Berkeley: University of California Press, 1981.
Dentith, Simon. *Parody.* London and New York: Routledge, 2000.
Derrida, Jacques. *Margins of Philosophy.* Trans. Alan Bass. Chicago, IL: University of Chicago Press, 1982.
Dobson, Michael. *The Making of the National Poet: Shakespeare, Adaptation and Authorship, 1660–1769.* Oxford: Clarendon Press, 1992.
Dobson, Richard B. *The Peasants' Revolt of 1381.* Bath: Pitman, 1970.
Dowden, Edward. *Shakspere: A Critical Study of His Mind and Art.* London: H. S. King, 1875.
Duncan-Jones, Katherine. *Ungentle Shakespeare: Scenes from His Life.* London: Arden Shakespeare, 2001.
Engler, Balz. *Poetry and Community.* Tübingen: Stauffenburg, 1990.
Fischer, Kuno. *Francis Bacon of Verulam: Realistic Philosophy and Its Age.* Trans. John Oxenford. London: Longman, Brown, Green, Longmans and Roberts, 1857.
Foucault, Michel. 'What is an Author?' *Language, Counter-Memory, Practice: Selected Essays and Interviews.* Ed. Donald F. Bouchard. Ithaca, NY: Cornell University Press, 1977. 113–138.
Fowler, Alastair. *Kinds of Literature.* Oxford: Clarendon Press, 1987.
Fox, Charles O. 'Early Echoes of Shakespeare's "Sonnets", and "Passionate Pilgrim".' *Notes and Queries* 198 (September 1953): 370.
Frow, John. *Genre.* London: Routledge, 2006.
Frye, Northrop. *The Great Code.* Toronto, ON: University of Toronto Press, 2006.
Furness, Horace Howard, ed. William Shakespeare. *The Tragedie of Ivlivs Caesar.* New Variorum Edition. Philadelphia, PA and London: J. B. Lippincott, 1913.
Garber, Marjorie B. *Shakespeare after All.* New York: Pantheon Books, 2004.
Gardiner, Michael. *The Constitution of English Literature: The State, the Nation and the Canon.* London: Bloomsbury, 2013.
Gay, Penny. 'Women and Eloquence in Shakespeare and Austen.' *Shakespeare* 6:4 (December 2010): 463–477.
Geckle, George L. *John Marston, Drama: Themes, Images, Sources.* Rutherford et al.: Associated University Presses, 1980.
Genette, Gérard. *Palimpsests: Literature in the Second Degree.* Trans. Channa Newman and Claude Doubinsky. Lincoln: University of Nebraska Press, 1997.

Greenblatt, Stephen, ed. *Cultural Mobility: A Manifesto*. Cambridge: Cambridge University Press, 2009.
Greenfield, Sayre. 'ECCO-Locating the Eighteenth Century.' *The Eighteenth-Century Intelligencer* 21:1 (2007): 1–9.
Greenfield, Sayre. 'Quoting *Hamlet* in the Early Seventeenth Century.' *Modern Philology* 105:3 (2008): 510–534.
Greenfield, Sayre. 'Quoting *Hamlet* outside Britain in the Eighteenth Century.' *Shakespeare's World – World Shakespeares*. Newark: University of Delaware Press, 2008. 237–246 (241).
Grundy, Isobel. 'Jane Austen and Literary Traditions.' *The Cambridge Companion to Jane Austen*. Eds. Edward Copeland and Juliet McMaster. Cambridge: Cambridge University Press, 1997. 170–188.
Hadfield, Andrew. 'Richard Barnfield, John Weever, William Basse and Other Encomiasts.' *The Shakespeare Circle: An Alternative Biography*. Eds. Paul Edmondson and Stanley Wells. Cambridge: Cambridge University Press, 2015. 199–212.
Hamilton, Walter, ed. *Parodies of the Works of English and American Authors, Collected and Edited by Walter Hamilton*. London: Reeves and Turner, 1885.
Hamilton, William. 'A Soliloquy in Imitation of Hamlet.' *Poems on Several Occasions*. Glasgow: Robert and Andrew Foulis, 1749. 110–111.
Hamlin, Hannibal. *The Bible in Shakespeare*. Oxford: Oxford University Press, 2013.
Harding, D. W. 'Regulated Hatred: An Aspect of the Work of Jane Austen.' *Scrutiny* (March 1940): 346–362.
Harries, Martin. 'Homo Alludens: Marx's "Eighteenth Brumaire".' *New German Critique* 66 (Autumn 1995): 35–64.
Hibbard, George R., ed. William Shakespeare. *Hamlet*. The Oxford Shakespeare. Oxford and New York: Oxford University Press, 1994.
Hohl Trillini, Regula. *The Gaze of the Listener: English Representations of Domestic Music-Making*. Amsterdam: Rodopi, 2008.
Hohl Trillini, Regula and Andreas Langlotz. 'The Grammar of "To Be or not to Be".' *Phraseologie disziplinär und interdisziplinär*. Ed. Csaba Földes. Tübingen: Günter Narr, 2009. 155–166.
Hohl Trillini, Regula and Sixta Quaßdorf. 'A "Key to all Quotations"? A Corpus-Based Parameter Model of Intertextuality.' *Literary and Linguistic Computing* 25:3 (2010): 269–286; doi: 10.1093/llc/fqq003.
Hollander, John. *The Figure of Echo: A Mode of Allusion in Milton and After*. Berkeley: University of California, 1981.
Hunter, G. K. 'The Marking of *Sententiae* in Elizabethan Printed Plays, Poems and Romances.' *Library* 5:6 (1951–1952): 171–188.
Hurd, Richard, ed. *Q. Horatii Flacci epistola ad Augustum. With an English commentary and notes. To which is added, a discourse concerning poetical imitation [...]*. London: W. Thurlbourn and R. Dodsley, 1751.
Hutcheon, Linda. *A Theory of Parody: The Teachings of Twentieth-Century Art Forms*. New York: Methuen, 1985.
Jenkins, Harold, ed. *Hamlet*. The Arden Shakespeare. London: Methuen 1986.
Jost, Jacob Sider. '*Hamlet*'s Horatio as an Allusion to Horace's *Odes*.' *Notes and Queries* 59:1 (2012): 76–77.

Kermode, Frank. *Shakespeare's Language*. New York: Farar, Straus and Grioux, 2000.
Keymer, Thomas. 'Shakespeare in the Novel.' *Shakespeare in the Eighteenth Century*. Eds. Fiona Ritchie and Peter Sabor. Cambridge: Cambridge University Press, 2012. 118–141.
King, Edmund G. C. '"Small-Scale Copyrights"? Quotation Marks in Theory and in Practice.' *The Papers of the Bibliographical Society of America* 98 (March 2004): 39–53.
Knowles, Richard. 'Shakespeare and Shorthand Once Again.' *Papers of the Bibliographical Society of America* 104 (2010): 141–180.
Kristeva, Julia. 'Pour une sémiologie des paragrammes.' *Σημειοτικη: Recherches pour une sémanalyse*. Paris: Éditions du Seuil, 1983. 113–146.
Kristeva, Julia. 'Word, Dialogue and the Novel.' Trans. Alice Jardine, Thomas Gora and Léon S. Roudiez. *The Kristeva Reader*. Ed. Toril Moi. New York: Columbia University Press, 1986. 34–61.
Landow, George P. *Hypertext 3.0: Critical Theory and New Media in an Era of Globalization*. 3rd ed. Baltimore, MD: Johns Hopkins University Press, 2006.
Langlotz, Andreas. *Idiomatic Creativity: A Cognitive-Linguistic Model of Idiom-Representation and Idiom-Variation in English*. Amsterdam and Philadelphia, PA: John Benjamins, 2006.
Lavagnino, John. 'Shakespeare in the Digital Humanities.' *Shakespeare and the Digital World: Redefining Scholarship and Practice*. Eds. Christie Carson and Peter Kirwan. Cambridge: Cambridge University Press, 2014. 14–23.
Lawrence, Jason. *Who the Devil Taught Thee So Much Italian? Italian Language Learning and Literary Imitation in Early Modern England*. Manchester: Manchester University Press, 2005.
Lee, Sir Sidney. *Great Englishmen of the Sixteenth Century*. New York: Charles Scribner's Sons, 1904.
Lewis, C. S. 'De Descriptione Temporum.' *Selected Literary Essays*. Ed. Walter Hooper. Cambridge: Cambridge University Press, 1979. 1–14.
Lynch, Stephen J. *Shakespearean Intertextuality: Studies in Selected Sources and Plays*. Westport, CT: Greenwood Press, 1998.
Marti, Markus, ed. and trans. William Shakespeare. *Timon of Athens – Timon von Athen*. Tübingen and Basel: Francke Verlag, 1995.
Maxwell, Julie. 'How the Renaissance (Mis)Used Sources: The Art of Misquotation.' *How to Do Things with Shakespeare*. Ed. Laurie Maguire. Oxford: Blackwell, 2008. 54–76.
McCombie, Frank. 'Scott, *Hamlet*, and *The Bride of Lammermoor*.' *Essays in Criticism* 25:4 (January 1975): 419–436.
Miller, D. A. *Jane Austen, or the Secret of Style*. Princeton, NJ: Princeton University Press, 2003.
Moore, John Robert. 'Defoe and Shakespeare.' *Shakespeare Quarterly* 19:1 (Winter 1968): 71–80.
Moretti, Franco. *Distant Reading*. London: Verso, 2013.
Mowat, Barbara. 'Shakespeare Reads the Geneva Bible.' *Shakespeare, the Bible, and the Form of the Book: Contested Scriptures*. Ed. Travis De Cook and Alan Galey. London: Routledge, 2012. 25–39.

Müller, Beate. 'Hamlet at the Dentist's: Parodies of Shakespeare.' *Parody: Dimensions and Perspectives*. Ed. Beate Müller. Amsterdam: Rodopi, 1997. 127–154.

Munro, John, Clement Mansfield Ingleby et al., eds. *The Shakspere Allusion-Book: A Collection of Allusions to Shakspere from 1591 to 1700 [...]*. London: Chatto and Windus; New York: Duffield and Co., 1909.

Natarajan, Uttara. 'William Hazlitt.' *Great Shakespeareans*. Gen. eds. Peter Holland and Adrian Poole. London: Continuum, 2010. 4: 64–108.

Olive, W. J. 'Imitation of Shakespeare in Middleton's *The Family of Love*.' *Philological Quarterly* 29 (1 January 1950): 75–78.

O'Neill, Stephen. *Shakespeare and YouTube: New Media Forms of the Bard*. London: Bloomsbury, 2014.

Pigman, G. W. 'Versions of Imitation in the Renaissance.' *Renaissance Quarterly* 33:1 (1980): 1–32.

Potter, Lois. *The Life of William Shakespeare: A Critical Biography*. Oxford: Wiley-Blackwell, 2012.

Potts, Abbie Findlay. 'Hamlet and Gloriana's Knights.' *Shakespeare Quarterly* 6:1 (Winter 1955): 31–43.

Price, Leah. *The Anthology and the Rise of the Novel*. Cambridge: Cambridge University Press, 2000.

Price, Leah. 'The Poetics of Pedantry from Thomas Bowdler to Susan Ferrier.' *Women's Writing* 7:1 (March 2000): 75–88.

Quaßdorf, Sixta. *'A little more than kin': Quotations as a linguistic phenomenon: a study based on quotations from Shakespeare's Hamlet*. Freiburg: Albert-Ludwigs-Universität, Universitätsbibliothek, 2016.

Riffaterre, Michael. 'Contraintes intertextuelles.' *Texte (s) et intertexte (s)*. Eds. Eric Le Calvez and Marie-Claude Canova-Green. Amsterdam: Rodopi, 1997. 35–53.

Rogers, Pat. '"Caro Sposo": Mrs Elton, Burneys, Thrales, and Noels.' *The Review of English Studies* 45:177 (February 1994): 70–75.

Rothstein, Eric. 'Diversity and Change in Literary Histories.' *Influence and Intertextuality in Literary History*. Eds. Jay Clayton and Eric Rothstein. Madison: University of Wisconsin Press, 1991. 114–145.

Rumbold, Kate. *Shakespeare and the Eighteenth-Century Novel: Cultures of Quotation from Samuel Richardson to Jane Austen*. Cambridge: Cambridge University Press, 2016.

Rumbold, Kate. '"So Common-Hackneyed in the Eyes of Men": Banal Shakespeare and the Eighteenth-Century Novel.' *Literature Compass* 4:3 (2007): 610–621.

Schleiner, Louise. 'Latinized Greek Drama in Shakespeare's Writing of *Hamlet*.' *Shakespeare Quarterly* 41:1 (Spring 1990): 29–48.

Scouten, Arthur H. 'The Increase in Popularity of Shakespeare's Plays in the Eighteenth Century: A Caveat for Interpretors of Stage History.' *Shakespeare Quarterly* 7:2 (1956): 189–202.

Shaheen, Naseeb. *Biblical References in Shakespeare's Plays*. Newark: University of Delaware Press, 1999.

Silk, Michael. 'Puns and Prose: Reflections on Shakespeare's Usage.' *Shakespeare Survey* 69 (2016): 7–29.

Smith, Charles G. *Shakespeare's Proverb Lore: His Use of the Sententiae of Leonard Culman and Publilius Syrus*. Cambridge, MA: Harvard University Press, 1963.

Stallybrass, Peter. '"Well grubbed, old mole": Marx, Hamlet and the (Un-) Fixing of Representation.' *Cultural Studies* 12:1 (1998): 3–14. doi:10.1080/095023898335582.

Stallybrass, Peter and Roger Chartier. 'Reading and Authorship: The Circulation of Shakespeare 1590–1619.' *A Concise Companion to Shakespeare and the Text*. Ed. Andrew Murphy. Oxford: Blackwell, 2007. 35–56.

Stevenson, Ruth. '*Hamlet's* Mice, Motes, Moles, and Minching Malecho.' *New Literary History* 33:3 (2002): 435–459.

Sträuli, Barbara. 'Word and Image Clusters in Shakespeare.' *Swiss Papers in English Language and Literature (SPELL)* 3 *The Structure of Texts* (1987): 133–157.

Taylor, Anthony Brian, ed. *Shakespeare's Ovid: The Metamorphoses in the Plays and Poems*. Cambridge: Cambridge University Press, 2000.

Taylor, Gary. 'The Incredible Shrinking Bard.' *Shakespeare and Appropriation*. Eds. Christy Desmet and Robert Sawyer. London: Routledge, 1999. 197–205.

Taylor, Gary. 'Thomas Middleton: Lives and Afterlives.' *Thomas Middleton: The Collected Works*. Eds. Gary Taylor and John Lavagnino. Oxford: Oxford University Press, 2007. 29–58.

Taylor, Megan. 'Jane Austen and "Banal Shakespeare".' *Eighteenth-Century Fiction* 27:1 (Fall 2014): 105–125.

Thompson, Ann and Neil Taylor, eds. William Shakespeare. *Hamlet: The Texts of 1603 and 1623*. The New Arden Shakespeare. London: Thomson Learning, 2006.

Tilley, Morris Palmer. *A Dictionary of the Proverbs in England in the Sixteenth and Seventeenth Centuries [...]*. Ann Arbor: University of Michigan Press, 1950.

Todd, Janet. *The Cambridge Introduction to Jane Austen*. Cambridge: Cambridge University Press, 2006.

Troost, Linda and Sayre Greenfield. '"Strange mutations": Shakespeare, Austen and Cultural Success.' *Shakespeare* 6:4 (December 2010): 431–445.

Vickers, Brian. *Shakespeare, 'A Lover's Complaint', and John Davies of Hereford*. Cambridge: Cambridge University Press, 2007.

Wahl, Moritz Callman. 'Das parömiologische Sprachgut bei Shakespeare.' *Jahrbuch der Deutschen Shakespeare-Gesellschaft* 22 (1887): 45–130.

Walker, Eric. *Marriage, Writing, and Romanticism: Wordsworth and Austen after War*. Stanford, CA: Stanford University Press, 2009.

Wechsler, Max and Barbara Sträuli, eds. *William Shakespeare: Henry V. Studienausgabe*. Tübingen: Stauffenburg, 1999.

Wells, Juliette. 'From Schlockspeare to Austenpop.' *Shakespeare* 6:4 (December 2010): 446–462.

Welsh, Alexander. *Hamlet in His Modern Guises*. Princeton, NJ: Princeton University Press, 2001.

Wentersdorf, Karl P. 'The Authenticity of *The Taming of the Shrew.*' *Shakespeare Quarterly* 5:1 (January 1954): 11–32.

Wentersdorf, Karl P. 'Imagery as a Criterion of Authenticity: A Reconsideration of the Problem.' *Shakespeare Quarterly* 23:3 (Summer 1972): 231–259.

White, Laura Mooneyham. 'Another Response to "Across the pale parabola of Joy: Wodehouse Parodist".' *Connotations* 14:1–3 (2004/2005): 177–182.

White, R. S. *Keats as a Reader of Shakespeare.* London: The Athlone Press, 1987.

Whiter, Walter. 'An attempt to explain and illustrate various passages, on a New Principle of Criticism, Derived from Mr. Locke's Doctrine of the Association of Ideas.' *A specimen of a commentary on Shakspeare [...].* London: T. Cadell, 1794. 61–258.

Wiggins, Martin. *Shakespeare and the Drama of His Time.* Oxford: Oxford University Press, 2000.

Wilson, F. P. 'Shakespeare's Reading.' *Shakespeare Survey* 3 (1950): 15–21.

York, Ernest C. 'Shakespeare and Nashe.' *Notes and Queries* 198 (September 1953): 370–371.

Index

Abbot, The (Scott) 136
active reading 5, 155
Adagia (Erasmus) 61
Ad Demonicum (Erasmus, Isocrates) 97
Addison, Joseph (*Cato*) 112–13
Aeschylus 9
Aickin, Joseph (*English Grammar*) 95
Aleman, Mateo (*Guzman*) 115
All's Well That Ends Well (Shakespeare) 38, 168
Altman, Rick 115
Antiquary, The (Scott) 138
Antonio and Mellida (Marston) 93, 164, 166, 170, 171
Antonio's Revenge (Marston) 76, 87, 163, 164
Antony, Mark 38, 148
Antony and Cleopatra (Shakespeare) 52n6, 67, 69, 168
Ariosto, Ludovico 144
Aristotle 59
Armstrong, Edward 66, 70
Astrophil and Stella (Sidney) 89
As You Like It (Shakespeare) 39, 40, 54, 59, 117n8, 164
Austen, Jane 10, 14, 105, 110, 138, 141–52, 153n2. See also *specific works*
Authorized Version (Bible) 48
Ayres, Philip 27, 29

Bachelor's Recantation, The 110, 113
Bachelor's Soliloquies 104–10, 114, 117n6
Bacon, Francis 65
Baldwin, Thomas 22
Baldwin, William (*Treatise of moral philosophy* 61
Ball, John 45

ballads 44, 46–47
Bandello, Matteo 12
Barthes, Roland 4–9, 32–35, 69, 101, 156
Bate, Jonathan 99–100, 117n5, 130, 141n1
Battle of Culloden 108
Beaumont, Francis (Shakespeare's *First Folio*) 42
Beauties 114
Beckford, William (*Modern Novel Writing*) 126, 144
Bedingfield Thomas (*Cardan's Comfort*) 22
bee metaphor 53, 59, 65, 77
Best, Stephen 6
Betterton, Thomas 63
Bewick, William 125
Bible, the 4, 42–54, 61, 78–80, 124, 129–30, 156. See also *specific versions*
Biblical References in Shakespeare's Plays (Shaheen) 48, 52n5
Bickerstaff, Isaac (*The Padlock*) 29
Bishop's Bible 48
Blades, William 86
Bloom, Harold 152
Borderers, The (Wordsworth) 119
Boswell, James 122
Bradford, William (*Of Plymouth Plantation*) 9
Bride of Lammermoor, The (Scott) 119, 139
Bright, Timothy (*Treatise of Melancholy*) 80–86
Brutus, Marcus Junius 37–38, 54–55
Burbage, Richard 41
Burghley, William Cecil, Lord of 96–97
Burke, Edmund 127

194 *Index*

Burney, Frances 105, 110
Burrow, Colin 37, 84
Byron, George Gordon (Lord) 14, 113, 139

Caesar, Julius 36–41, 52n2, 54–56, 59. See also *Julius Caesar* (Shakespeare)
Caesar and Pompey (anonymous) 38
Cain and Abel 47–49
Calderón, Pedro (*El alcalde de Zalamea*) 97
Calvino, Italo 156
Canterbury Tales, The (Chaucer) 129
Caryll, John (*The English Princess*) 25
casual quotation: of the Bible and folk materials 35–52; Classical borrowings and 13, 53–75, 156; Jane Austen and 142–52, 153nn2–3; Romantic Routine and 118–41; Shakespeare as borrower and lender of 1–9, 76–98, 154–57; 'To be or not to be' and 13–14, 16–34; verse parody and 99–116
'Catharine or the Bower' (Austen) 150
Cecil, William (Lord Burghley) 96–97
Chambers, E.K. 41
Chapman, George 19, 87, 94
Chaucer, Geoffrey 71, 98n1, 129
Christian Turned Turk (Daborne) 19
Cicero, Marcus Tullius 22–23, 54, 58
classical borrowings in Shakespeare 40, 47, 51, 53–75, 77–78, 98. See also *specific references*
Clough, Arthur Hugh ('Lecture on the Development of English Literature') 19
Coleridge, Samuel Taylor 7, 21, 100, 124, 139, 154–55
Conspiracy and Tragedy of Charles, Duke of Byron, The 19
Cooper, Thomas 75n3
Coriolanus (Shakespeare) 73, 163
Cotgrave, John 77
Countess of Dellwyn, The (Fielding) 121
courtship novel 105–9
Cowley, Abraham 26
Cowley, Hannah 31
Critic, The (Sheridan) 150
Critique of Hegel's Constitutional Law (Marx) 2–3
cross-quotation 1, 8, 45–49, 60–62, 76–92, 110–14, 118, 123–29, 154

The Cry (Fielding) 140
Cudworth, Ralph 20
Culman, Leonard (*Sententiae pueriles*) 61
Cultural Mobility (Greenblatt) 6
Cymbeline (Shakespeare) 39, 45, 51, 67, 71

Daborne, Robert 19, 91
data-based research 6, 9–14, 15n8, 31, 35, 51, 75n3, 112–13, 119–20, 124, 137, 155
Davies of Hereford, Sir John 24–25, 34n8, 98
'The Death of the Author' (Barthes) 4–5, 8, 61, 77
De Bello Gallico (Caesar) 56
Defoe, Daniel 2, 28, 39, 161
Dekker, Thomas 87
Deplorable Life and Death of Edward the Second, The (Hubert) 76
de Quincey, Thomas 125, 152n1
Dido, Queen of Carthage (Marlowe) 72
Digges, Leonard 60
digital quotation research 6, 9–14, 15n8, 31, 35, 51, 75n3, 112–13, 119–20, 124, 137, 155
Display of Heraldry, A (Guillim) 34n8
distant reading 6, 9, 119. See also data-based research; surface reading
'Dives and Lazarus' (Mason) 27–28
Dolman, John 22
Don Juan (Byron) 113
Duke of Wellington 128
Dutch Courtesan, The (Marston) 163, 164, 167

Earl of Chesterfield 2, 29
Early English Books Online (EEBO) 51, 75n3, 162
Eastward Ho (Chapman, Jonson, Marston) 89–95, 165–66, 168–70
Ecclesiastical Politie (Hooker) 17
ECCO 11, 14, 15n8, 112–13, 124, 137, 162
echo chamber 8–9, 69, 81, 109, 113 See also intertextuality
Eclogues (Mantuanus) 56
Edgeworth, Maria 32, 133–35, 139–40
EEBO 51, 75n3, 162

Eighteenth-Century Collections Online (ECCO) 11, 14, 15n8, 112–13, 124, 137, 162
Emma (Austen) 144–46, 149–50, 152
English treasury of wit and language (Cotgrave) 77
'Epigramme 92' (Freeman) 75, 98
epigraphs 144–45
Epistulae Morales (Seneca) 61
Erasmus, Desiderius 35, 61, 65, 97
Essay Concerning Human Understanding, An (Locke) 19–20, 68
Euphues and His England (Lyly) 96–97
Euphues: The Anatomy of Wit (Lyly) 96
Euripides (*Electra*) 64

Faerie Queene, The (Spenser) 83–86, 94
Familiares (Petrarch) 60
Family of Love, The (Marston) 91, 92, 163, 165, 169, 170
Ferrier, Susan 125, 131, 135, 138
Field, Richard 86
Fielding, Henry 30
Fielding, Sarah 121, 140
First Folio (Beaumont, Fletcher) 42, 87, 124
first-person narration 132–35
Fleire, The (Marston) 169
Fletcher, John 42, 91
Florio, John (*First Fruits* and *Second Fruits*) 56, 78–80, 98n4
folk borrowings 35–52, 54–55, 63, 136
Ford, Thomas 117n8
Foucault, Michel 5, 7, 154
Fowler, Alastair 114
Fox, Charles O. 34n8
Freeman, Thomas 75, 98

Garber, Marjorie 3
Gardiner, Michael 123
Garrick, David 63
Gay, Penny 147
gender. See textual patriarchy
Genesis 17, 44–45, 49–50. See also Bible, the
Geneva Bible 48–49
Genevan Psalter (Calvin) 52n4
Gentleman's Magazine 114, 117n8
Gesta Danorum (Grammaticus) 12
Godwin, William (*Deloraine*) 124, 133
Golding, Arthur (*Metamorphoses* translation) 64, 75n7

Great Bible 48
Great Train Robbery, The 115
Greenblatt, Stephen 6
Greene, Robert 43, 62, 86, 88–89, 96
Greenfield, Sayre 16, 99, 162
Guardian, The 7, 27
Guillim, John 34n8

Habermann, Ina 98n5, 153n4
Haden, Charles Thomas 146
Hadfield, Andrew 75n4
Hamilton, Walter 99
Hamilton, William 108, 111
Hamlet (Shakespeare): Bible and folk materials in 35–52; casual quotation and 7–8, 12–14, 76, 79–97, 141n1, 152n1, 166; classical borrowings in 54–55, 60–64, 69–73; Jane Austen and 148, 150–51; parody and 100–116, 117n4, 117nn6–8; Romantic Routine and 118–21, 124–30, 134–39; 'To be or not to be' quotation and 2–5, 16–34. See also *HyperHamlet*; 'To be or not to be' quotation
Hamlin, Hannibal 4
Harsnett, Samuel (*Declaration of egregious Popish Impostures* 85–86
Hazlitt, William 92, 125–30, 135, 139, 141n1
Heminges, William 19
1 Henry IV (Shakespeare) 45, 84, 85, 166, 169
2 Henry IV (Shakespeare) 39, 50, 94, 166, 169
Henry V (Shakespeare) 52n2, 129
1 Henry VI (Shakespeare) 49, 52n2, 166
2 Henry VI (Shakespeare) 43, 44, 54, 55, 70, 170
3 Henry VI (Shakespeare) 71, 74
'Herod of Jewry', 47, 52n6
Herod the Great 52n6
Herod the Tetrarch 52n6
Heroides (Ovid) 71
Hesiod 96
Heywood, Thomas 26
Hibernia Magazine 113
Hierarchy of the Blessed Angels (Heywood) 26
Histrio-Mastix (Marston) 91, 165
Homer 115

homographs 69, 74
homophones 69–70
Hooker, Richard 17
Horace (*Carmina*) 56–58, 62, 65, 144
horizontal browsing 9, 114
Hubert, Francis 76
Hurd, Richard 62–63
Hutchinson, A.A. *Exhibitions of the Heart*) 134–35
'Hymn to Peace' (Defoe) 2
HyperHamlet 9–14, 35, 119–20, 124, 159–62

Icarus 70–71
image clusters 54, 65–75
'Imitations of Shakespeare No. 2: Coeleb's Soliloquy' (Menander) 114
Insatiate Countess, The (Marston) 92, 94, 164, 166–70
intertextuality: Bible and folks materials and 35–52; casual quotation and 1–9, 13, 154–57; Classical borrowings and 53–75; data-based approach to 9–11, 14; Jane Austen and 14, 142–52; Marking for Quotation Only and 8; Romantic Routine and 118–41; Shakespeare as a borrower and lender and 76–98; 'To be or not to be' quotation and 16–34; verse parody and 99–116. See also cross-quotation
Isocrates 97
Ivanhoe (Scott) 136

Jack Drum's Entertainment (Marston) 168
Jackson, J. 110
Jephthah 37, 46, 52n5
Jews' Tragedy, The (Heminges) 19
Johnson, Samuel 63
John the Baptist 52n6
Jonson, Ben 36–37, 40–42, 52n1, 87–89, 94, 133, 152
Jost, Sider 65
Joyce, James 7
Julius Caesar (Shakespeare) 37–40, 166–67
Justice Shallow (in *2 Henry IV* (Shakespeare)) 50, 117n8
Juvenal 55, 80

Keats, John 139
Kenilworth (Scott) 136
Keymer, Thomas 52
Kinds of Literature (Fowler) 114
King Lear (Shakespeare) 67, 69
Kristeva, Julia 4–5, 11, 12, 61, 154
Kyd, Thomas 64

Lamb, Charles 116
Last Man, The (Shelley) 118, 124
Lawrence, Jason 98n4
Lazarillo (anonymous) 115
Lee, Sir Sidney 80–81
Legend of Dido (Chaucer) 71
Leininger, Carol 116n1
Lewis, C.S. 156
lexia (Barthes) 3–6
Licensing Act 100
Lichtenberg, Georg Friedrich 3
'Life and Fame' (Cowley) 26
Life and Opinions of Tristram Shandy, Gentleman, The (Sterne) 129–30
Life of Caesar (Plutarch) 38
Life of Samuel Johnson (Boswell) 52n1
Lily, William 75n2
linguistic anomalies 2, 7, 39, 79
LION 11, 14, 31, 124, 137
Literature Online (LION) 11, 14, 31, 124, 137
Little French Lawyer, The (Fletcher, Massinger) 91
Locke, John 20, 68
Longman's Magazine 32
Lover's Complaint, A (Shakespeare) 24
Love's Labour's Lost (Shakespeare) 12, 45–47, 56, 78, 89, 164, 170
'Love's New Philosophy' (Ayres) 27
Lyly, John 96

Macbeth (Shakespeare) 13, 31, 38, 60, 67, 68, 71–73, 93, 98, 129, 170
MacLeish, Archibald 3
Madrigal and Trulletta (Reed) 99
Malcontent, The (Marston) 90, 92, 163–70
Manningham, John 41
Manœuvering (Edgeworth) 134
Mansfield Park (Austen) 146, 148–49, 152
Mantuanus, Baptista 56–57, 78
Marcus, Sharon 6
marking for derivation 7–9, 23, 28–30, 39–40, 50, 90, 94, 113, 120–37, 144

marking for quotation: Bible and folk materials and 39–51; casual 2–9; Classical materials and 53–60; *Hamlet* and 23–32, 83; Jane Austen and 14; parody and 103–4, 113–14, 116n3; Romantic Routine and 118–36, 144; of and by Shakespeare 90–96
marking for quotation only 8–9, 90–92, 120–25, 131–33
Marlowe, Christopher 72, 85, 94–95
Marriage (Ferrier) 131
marriage question 104–9, 115
Marston, John 13, 43, 76, 87–94, 124, 138, 163–72. See also *specific works*
Marx, Karl 2–3, 8, 23
Mason, John 27–28
Massacre of the Innocents 52n6
Massinger, Philip 91, 96
Matrimonial Causes Act 104
Maxwell, Julie 45
McGann, Jerome J. 124
Measure for Measure (Shakespeare) 38, 143
Merchant of Venice, The (Shakespeare) 45, 140, 146, 170
Meres, Francis 59, 77, 97
Merry Wives of Windsor, The (Shakespeare) 39, 43, 45, 47, 167
metalinguistic tags 3, 7, 24, 43–46, 49
Metamorphoses (Ovid) 58–59, 64, 70
Middlemarch (Eliot) 11
Midsummer Night's Dream, A (Shakespeare) 90, 149, 167
Miller, D.A. 150
Milton, John 18, 34n1, 113, 140
Minshull, John (*He Stoops to Conquer*) 31
mobile lexias (Barthes) 3–6
Moll Flanders (Defoe) 28
More, Hannah (*Coelebs in Search of a Wife*) 110–11, 144
Moretti, Franco 6, 123
More Ways (Cowley) 31
Much Ado About Nothing (Shakespeare) 43, 89, 167, 170
Müller, Beate 100
Murder of Abel, The (anonymous) 47

narrative voice 130–35
Nashe, Thomas 12, 32, 81–85
New Scientist 33

nominalization 23–28, 39, 46, 161
Norris, John (*An Idea of Happiness*) 21
Northanger Abbey (Austen) 142–46, 150–52

Old Hundredth, The 52n4
O'Neill, Stephen 100, 113
Othello (Shakespeare) 38, 45, 67, 98n4, 127, 143–44, 170
Ovid 11, 58–59, 64, 71, 84, 97
Oxford English Dictionary (*OED*) 41, 43, 88, 93, 156

Palladis Tamia (Meres) 59
Pamela (Richardson) 105
Paradise Lost (Milton) 18, 34n1, 113, 129, 140
Parasitaster (Marston) 90, 164–66, 167, 168, 171
parody 99–116
Peasant's Revolt 45
Pepys, Samuel 117n7
Peregrine Pickle (Smollett) 75n5
Pericles (Shakespeare) 43, 67
perpetual copyright 122
Persuasion (Austen) 151–52, 156
Petrarch 60, 66, 85
Phillips, Edward 42
Pierce Penniless (Nashe) 81–83
Pigmalion (Marston) 88, 168
pillow cluster 66–69, 71, 84
'Plan of a Novel' (Austen) 145
Plato (*Apologia*) 22, 61, 111–13
Plautus 98
Plume, Thomas 37
Plume Manuscript 36
Plutarch 38
Poetaster (Jonson) 40
'Poet's Soliloquy, The' (Ashley) 103, 111–12
Political History (Defoe) 28
Poor Man's Comfort (Daborne) 91
poststructuralism 4, 11–12
Potts, Abbie Findlay 86
Price, Leah 125
Pride and Prejudice (Austen) 146–48, 152
Procter, Bryan (*The Broken Heart* 118
proverbs 30, 35, 42–44, 46–51, 61, 78–79, 147, 151
puns 36–42
Pye, Henry James (*The Aristocrat*) 139

198 Index

quantitative historiography. See data-based research
quotation. See casual quotation

Rape of Lucrece, The (Shakespeare) 67, 68, 71, 74, 76, 86, 167
Rehearsal, The (Viller) 130
Richard II (Shakespeare) 38, 51, 92–93, 170–71
Richard III (Shakespeare) 38, 41, 45, 48, 90–92, 138, 164, 165, 167, 171
Richardson, Samuel 29–30, 105, 133
Riffaterre, Michael 7
Robertson, Hannah 122
Rob Roy (Scott) 135
Robinson Crusoe (Defoe) 28
Romantic era 13–14, 118–41
Romantic Era 15n8
Romantic Era Redefined, The 11, 14, 124
Romantic Routine 14, 118–52, 156
Romantic Routine Corpus (RR Corpus) 119–23, 125, 139, 141n2
Romeo and Juliet (Shakespeare) 12, 43, 76, 89, 117n8, 150, 152n1, 164, 167
Roxana (Defoe) 28
RR Corpus 119–23, 125, 139, 141n2
Rumbold, Kate 125

Saint Ronan's Well (Scott) 138
Sanditon (Austen) 153n3
Satire III (Juvenal) 80
Satires (Marston) 43, 55, 87–88
Schlegel-Tieck translation of Shakespeare's works 34n5
Scoloker, Anthony (*Daiphantus*) 35
Scott, Walter 14, 119, 124, 135–39, 141n2, 144
Scourge of Villainie, The (Marston) 88, 90, 165–67
Segar, William (*Book of Honour and Arms*) 86
Selimus (anonymous) 72
Seneca, Lucius Annaeus 61, 65
'Seven Ages of Man' 117n8
Shaheen, Naseeb 48
Shakespeare, William: as borrower and lender of quotations 1–9, 76–98, 154–57; Classical borrowings and 13, 53–75, 156; Jane Austen and 142–52; Marston's concordance with 163–72; Romantic Routine and 118–41; 'To be or not to be' quotation and 2–5, 13–14, 16–34, 39, 100–16, 117n4, 117nn7–8, 126–27; use of the Bible and folk materials by 35–52; verse parody and 99–116. See also *specific works*
Shakespearean Negotiations (Greenblatt) 6
Shakespeare Circle, The (Edmonson, Wells) 87
Shakespeare in Love 12
Shakespere Allusion-Book (Munro) 87, 89–90, 162
Shelley, Mary 118, 124–25, 133, 139
Shelley, Percy Bysshe 14, 118
Sheridan, Richard Brinsley 150
Sidney, Sir Henry 96–97
Sidney, Sir Philip 43
Silver Fork novelists 105, 125
Sleath, Eleanor (*The Nocturnal Minstrel*) 144
Smollett, Tobias 75n5, 99
snowclones 33
Socrates 22, 37, 111–12
Sophocles 62–63
Sophonisba (Marston) 169, 170
Southey, Robert 129
Spanish Tragedy (Kyd) 64
Spenser, Edmund 75n4, 83–85, 94–95
Stanhope, Philip 2, 29
Stanier-Clarke, James 145–46, 152
Stanyhurst, Richard 51, 71
Sträuli, Barbara 66–71
surface reading 6, 9. See also distant reading
Sylph, The 2–3, 104
symptomatic reading 6

Tamburlaine (Marlowe) 94–95
Taming of the Shrew, The (Shakespeare) 37, 59, 67, 70
Taylor, Arthur Brian 75n7
Terence 54, 98
Testament of Love, The (Usk) 20
textual patriarchy 4–5, 32
Theobald, Lewis 63
Theobald, W.M. 61, 80
Thesaurus linguæ Romanæ (Cooper) 75n3
third-person narration 132–35
tiger cluster 66–74
Times, The 122
Timon of Athens (Shakespeare) 13, 70, 81

Titus Andronicus (Shakespeare) 49, 57–58, 66–67, 73, 84–85, 171
'To be or not to be' quotation 2–5, 13–14, 16–34, 39, 100–116, 117n4, 117nn7–8, 126–27. See also *Hamlet* (Shakespeare)
Tom Jones (Fielding) 30
Tom o' Lincoln (anonymous) 17
Tottel's Miscellany (Tottel) 136
Tousey, George ('The Bachelor's Deliberation') 108
Towneley Mystery Plays 47, 52n6
Treatise of Melancholy (Bright) 80–82, 86
Troilus and Cressida (Shakespeare) 167, 168
True Intellectual System of the Universe (Cudworth) 20
Tusculanae Quæstiones (Cicero) 22–23, 61
Twelfth Night (Shakespeare) 45, 143, 144, 147, 166–167
Twisse, William (*A discovery of D. Iacksons vanitie*) 20, 34n4
Twitter 9–10, 156, 161
Two Noble Kinsmen (Fletcher, Shakespeare) 98n1

Ulysses (Joyce) 7, 39
Unfortunate Traveller, The 84–85
Universal Magazine 114
Urban Dictionary 33
Ur-Hamlet (anonymous) 87

Varus, Quintilius 62
Vautrollier, Thomas 86
Vaux, Thomas ('The Aged Lover Renounceth Love') 136
Venus and Adonis (Shakespeare) 76, 86, 88, 168

verse parody 99–116
vertical browsing 9
Vickers, Brian 24
Villier, George (*The Rehearsal*) 130
Virgil (*Aeneid*) 51, 54, 61, 66, 67, 71–73, 84–85, 115, 124–25
Vulgate (Bible) 48

Wahl, Moritz 43
Wakefield Mystery Plays (anonymous) 47, 52n6
Walker's Hibernian Magazine 114
Walkington, Thomas (*The optick glasse of humors*) 77
War of the Theatres 87
Waverly novels 124
'What is an Author' (Foucault) 5–6
What You Will (Marston) 90, 140, 164, 168
Whiter, Walter 68
Whitgift, John (*Admonition to the Parliament*) 23
Wieland, Christoph 34n5
Williams, Raymond 153n4
Wilson, F.P. 85
Wilson, Harriette (*Memoirs*) 128
Wither, George ('Wither's Motto') 18–19
Wolcot, John ('Peter Pindar's Soliloquy') 116n2
Wollstonecraft, Mary 128, 134
Woodstock (Scott) 137
'Word, Dialogue and the Novel' (Kristeva) 4, 11, 12, 61, 154
Wordsworth, William 119, 124, 139
Wrongs of Woman (Wollstonecraft) 134

York, Ernest C. 81
YouTube 100, 113, 156